POSTCARD HISTORY SERIES

Around Fitzgerald, Georgia in Vintage Postcards

POSTCARD HISTORY SERIES

Around Fitzgerald, Georgia

IN VINTAGE POSTCARDS

Milton N. Hopkins Jr.

ARCADIA PUBLISHING

ISBN 978-0-7385-1406-2

Published by Arcadia Publishing
Charleston, South Carolina

Printed in the United States of America

Library of Congress Catalog Card Number: 2001094993

For all general information contact Arcadia Publishing at:
Telephone 843-853-2070
Fax 843-853-0044
E-mail sales@arcadiapublishing.com
For customer service and orders:
Toll-Free 1-888-313-2665

Visit us on the Internet at www.arcadiapublishing.com

Contents

Acknowledgments

Without the good and generous help of people with kindred interests, the scope of this book would be narrow. I am especially grateful to the following people who have shared postcards, pictures, and other historic documents with me: Wilson Baker, Mildred D. Cook, Jim Cottingham, C.M. Copeland, Beth Davis, Gary Doster, Louis Harper, Tobie Hingson, Jack Paulk, Roger Reeb, Frankie Snow, C.T. Trowell, and Carol Weeks. Additional thanks go to Katie White, editor with Arcadia Publishing of Charleston, for being most helpful in keeping me in line with her many valuable suggestions.

Introduction

Fitzgerald, the Colony City, was the dream of Philander H. Fitzgerald, a publisher of the ***The American Tribune***, in Indianapolis, Indiana, then a weekly newspaper with the largest circulation in our country.

He brought forth the idea of a colony in the South where aging Union veterans and their families could settle and engage in farming, turpentining, and various businesses. As he began to espouse his dream and plans the idea caught hold like wildfire and he was deluged with correspondence urging him forward to make it become a reality.

Mr. Fitzgerald, thinking that South Georgia might be the Garden of Eden of his dreams, wrote to Georgia's governor William J. Northern and told him of his plans. Governor Northern, liking the sound of what he heard, invited Fitzgerald to come to Georgia, and together they traveled over most of the state looking at possible sites.

After inspecting several sites they determined that the present location of Swan in the center of South Georgia's wiregrass region and almost equal distance from the Atlantic Ocean and the Gulf of Mexico was the ideal spot. Almost all of the area was then virgin longleaf pine, stretching for miles in all directions. Fitzgerald organized the American Tribune Soldiers Colony Company. From the sale of stock his company purchased 50,000 acres in Irwin and Wilcox Counties. This area was enlarged at a later date to almost double the original acreage. The first purchase was made in 1895 and before the ink was dry on the paper and the land not yet surveyed, people began to emigrate toward the spot.

Stock sold for $10 per share and no family could purchase over 10 shares. Fitzgerald selected a square mile in almost the middle of the original purchase for his town. The square mile encompassed 640 acres in the midst of the primeval pine forest. The square mile tract was divided into four wards. Four city blocks were designated for schools, twelve for parks, thirty-six for businesses, and the balance for residential lots. The four drives around the proposed city were named after Civil War Union and Confederate warships. The planned city was quartered by Main Street and Central Avenue, each 120 feet wide with parks in the middle for their entire length. Streets east of Main Street were named after generals of the Union armies and streets west of Main Street after Confederate generals. In retrospect it is almost inconceivable that the early settlers came to this harmonious solution of equal representation.

Outside the town limits were five-acre tracts, then ten-, twenty-, and forty-acre tracts as one got into the surrounding country. In 1895 Swan, originally a turpentine village, had a tax value of $100 and a population of 40. By December of that year 2,500 people had arrived. In less than one year the colony had 2 railroads, 25 miles of open streets, 250 business houses, and 11 churches, plus an opera house seating 1,200 people.

The city of Fitzgerald was incorporated in December 1896 and its charter provided $23,000 for clearing the land and building schools. Ben Hill County was formed by constitutional amendment in 1906, effective January 1, 1907.

For many years, Fitzgerald observed two Memorial Days, April 26 being Georgia's Confederate Day and May 30, a national holiday in honor of Union dead. Within a few years, the former enemies marched together in all parades.

The young city, wanting a railroad, bought most of the right of way for the Waycross Air Line Railroad, later the Atlanta, Birmingham, and Atlantic. When the A. B. & A. wanted land for construction of its yards the city borrowed $20,000 to purchase land for its "Westwood" shops.

Fitzgerald has always been a progressive city, partly as a result of the cooperation of people from nearly every state in the Union. Much of this information comes from Col. Harvey L. Jay's eloquent rendition of "The Unique Story of a Unique City." Beth Davis, curator of the Blue & Gray Museum, longtime local historian, and lover of things gone by, probably has a better knowledge of the early days than any other living person in Fitzgerald.

With a hint of nepotism I must include a few photographs of family members. Taking black-and-white photographs of friends and kinfolks and then having them reproduced on Kodak paper as postcards was very popular in earlier times; these cards are are special and unique. Very few people bought duplicates. Around 1906–1910, the majority of the really attractive cards were produced in Germany and hand colored, with many others coming from Great Britain. Some of these cards are included in this collection.

One

Businesses and Banks

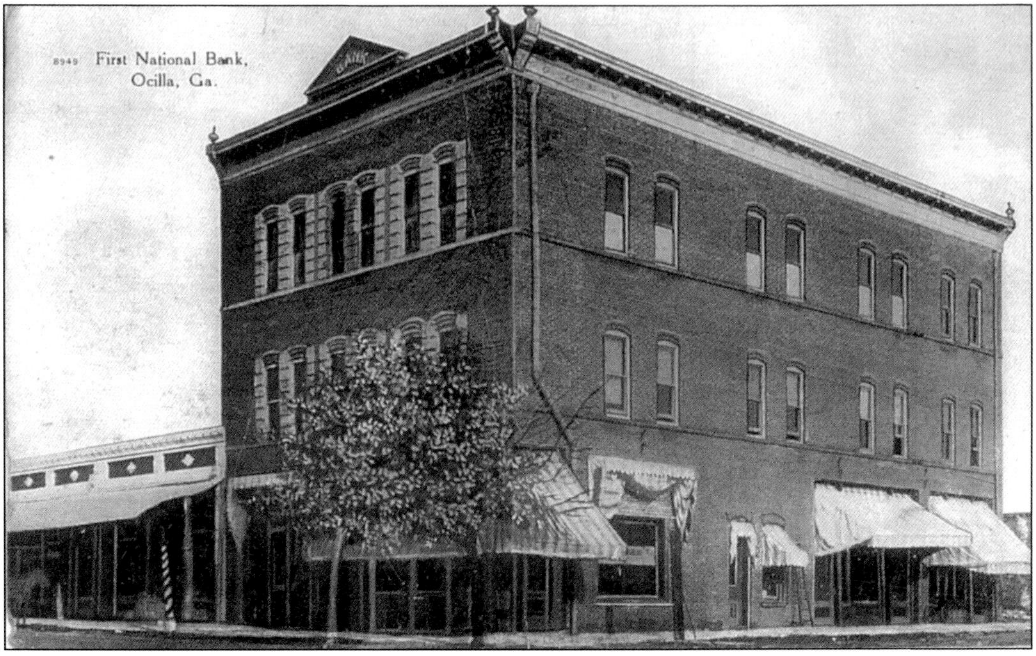

First National Bank, Ocilla, Early 1900s. This building is still located on Fourth Street but the top floor has been removed. (Courtesy of Mildred D. Cook.)

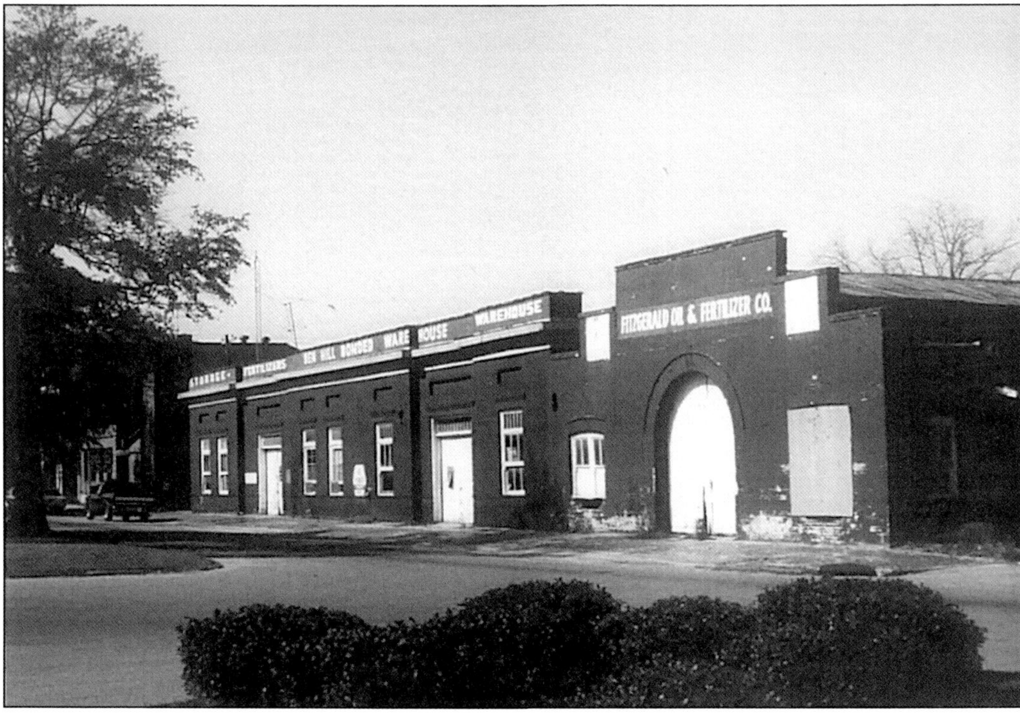

Ben Hill Bonded Warehouse and Fitzgerald Oil & Fertilizer Company. Located on East Central Avenue, this building was torn down in the 1980s.

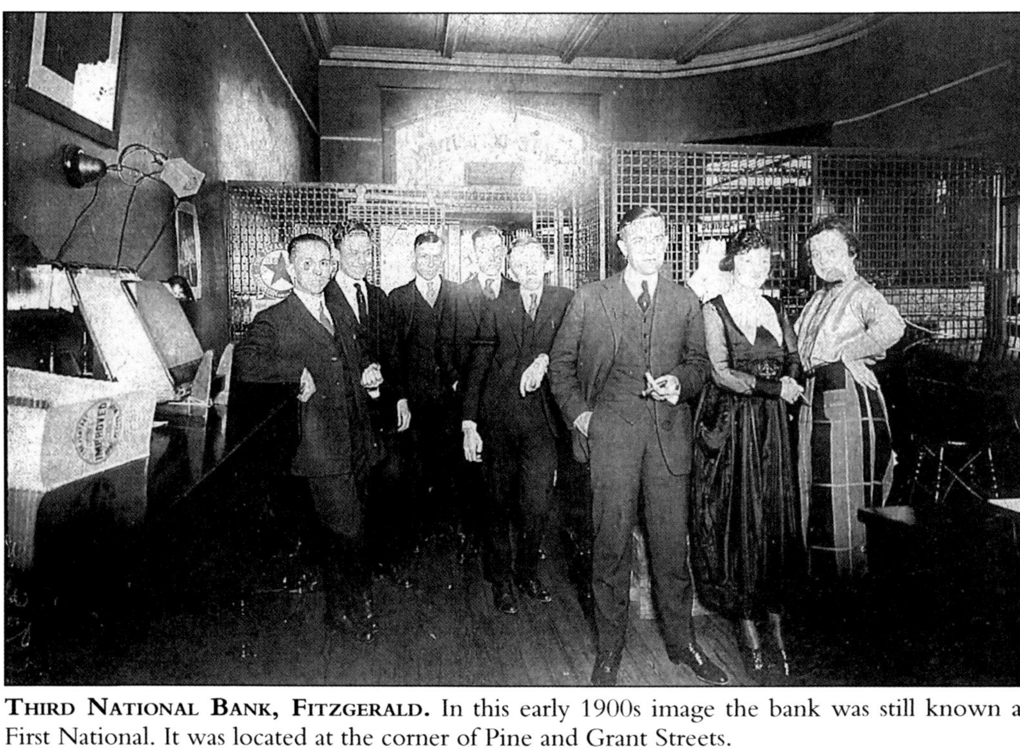

Third National Bank, Fitzgerald. In this early 1900s image the bank was still known as First National. It was located at the corner of Pine and Grant Streets.

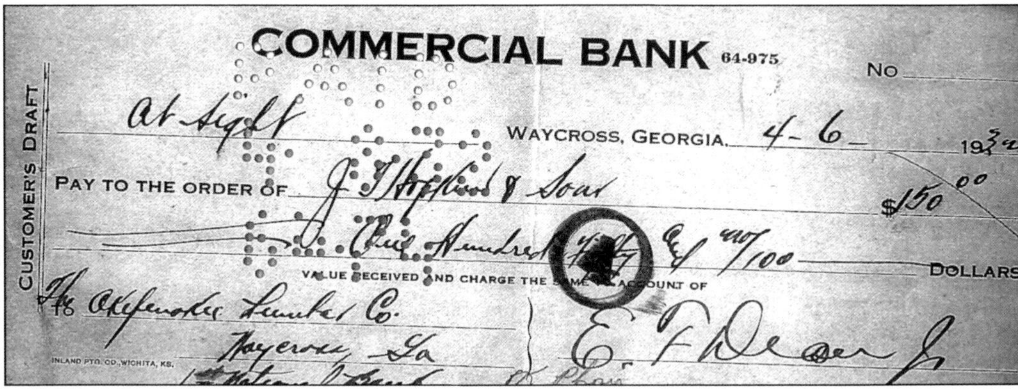

COMMERCIAL BANK, WAYCROSS, C. 1932. This payment was made to John M. Hopkins, surveyor and timber cruiser, by The Okefenokee Lumber Company for services rendered.

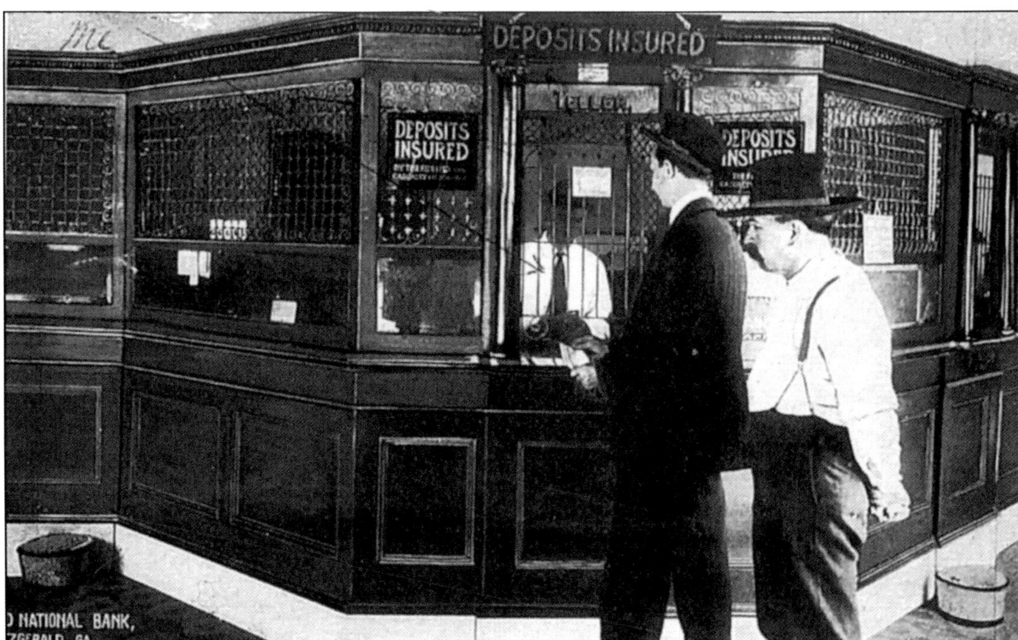

THIRD NATIONAL BANK, FITZGERALD, C. 1908. The young teller counts out cash for a customer; he was also the sender of the card as he drew an arrow and wrote "this is me" in the upper left corner. The man behind the customer is the first sheriff of Ben Hill County (1907–1921), W.H. Fountain. Note the spittoons on the floor to the left and right. This building is extant but now houses an insurance office.

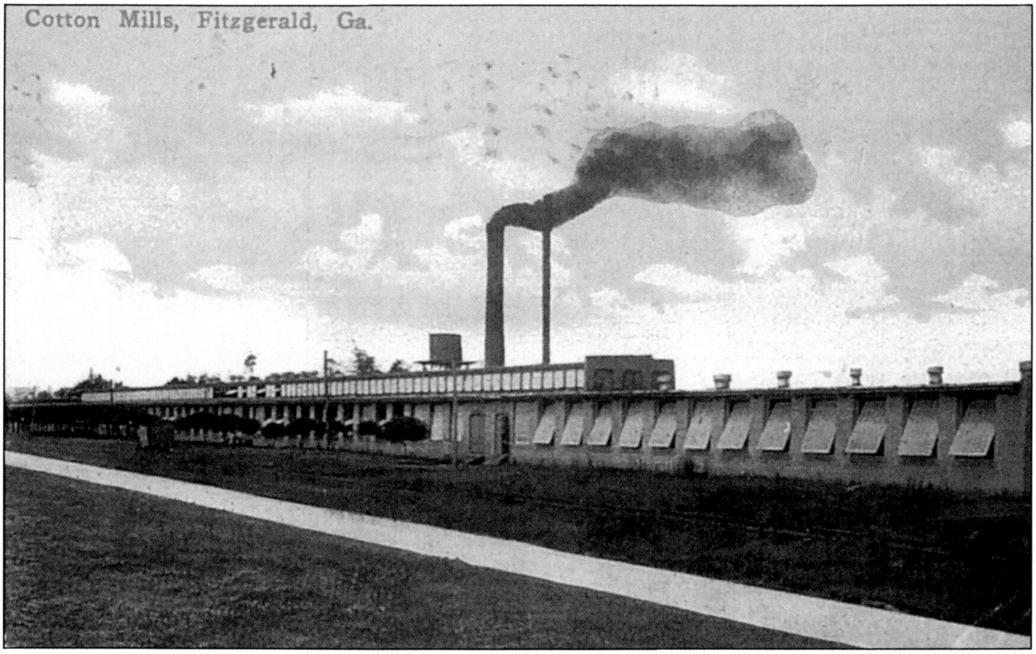

COTTON MILLS, FITZGERALD. Located about two miles northeast of Fitzgerald, the mills employed hundreds of workers. All that remains is the boiler smoke stack.

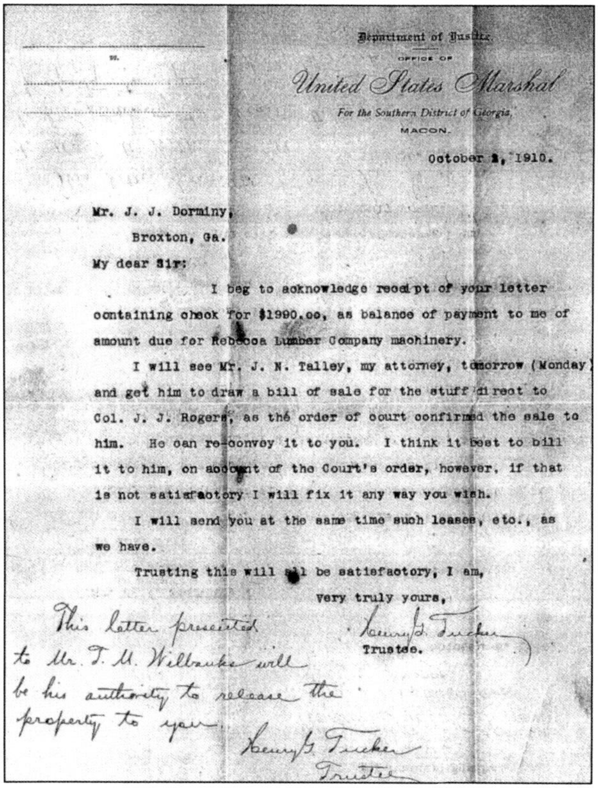

Department of Justice.
OFFICE OF
United States Marshal
For the Southern District of Georgia,
MACON.

October 2, 1910.

Mr. J. J. Dorminy,
Broxton, Ga.

My dear Sir:

I beg to acknowledge receipt of your letter containing check for $1990.00, as balance of payment to me of amount due for Rebecca Lumber Company machinery.

I will see Mr. J. N. Talley, my attorney, tomorrow (Monday) and get him to draw a bill of sale for the stuff direct to Col. J. J. Rogers, as the order of court confirmed the sale to him. He can re-convey it to you. I think it best to bill it to him, on account of the Court's order, however, if that is not satisfactory I will fix it any way you wish.

I will send you at the same time such leases, etc., as we have.

Trusting this will all be satisfactory, I am,

Very truly yours,

Henry G. Tucker
Trustee.

This letter presented to Mr. T. M. Wilbanks will be his authority to release the property to you.

Henry G. Tucker
Trustee

BILL OF SALE, REBECCA LUMBER COMPANY. This letter, dated October 2, 1910, acknowledged receipt of sawmill machinery from the Rebecca Lumber Company in Osierfield.

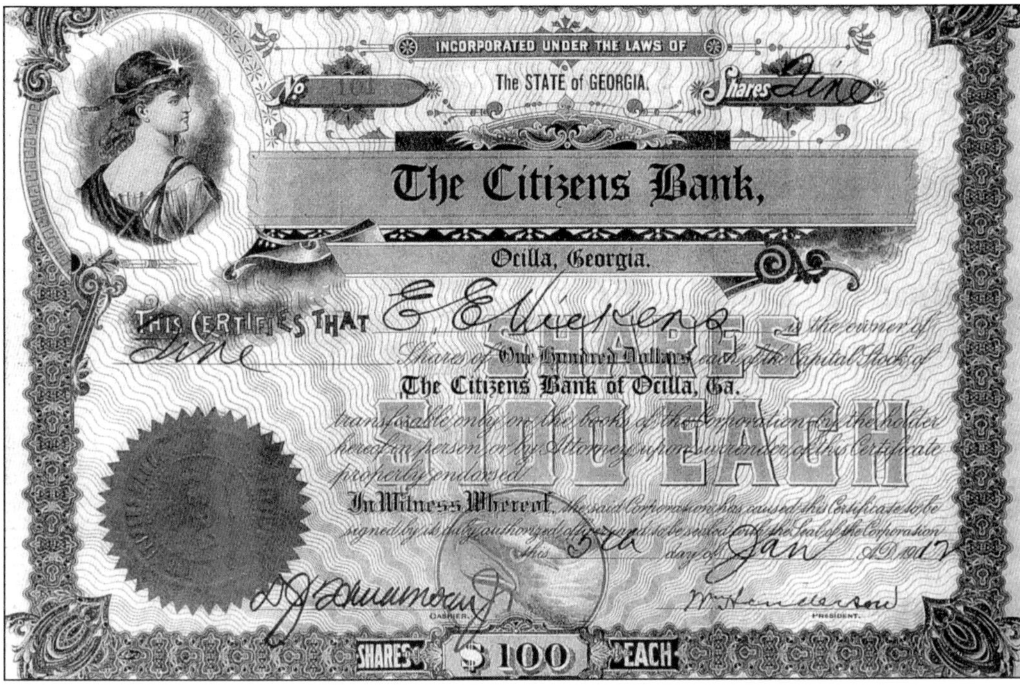

The Citizens Bank, Ocilla. This stock certificate from the Citizens Bank is dated January 5, 1912.

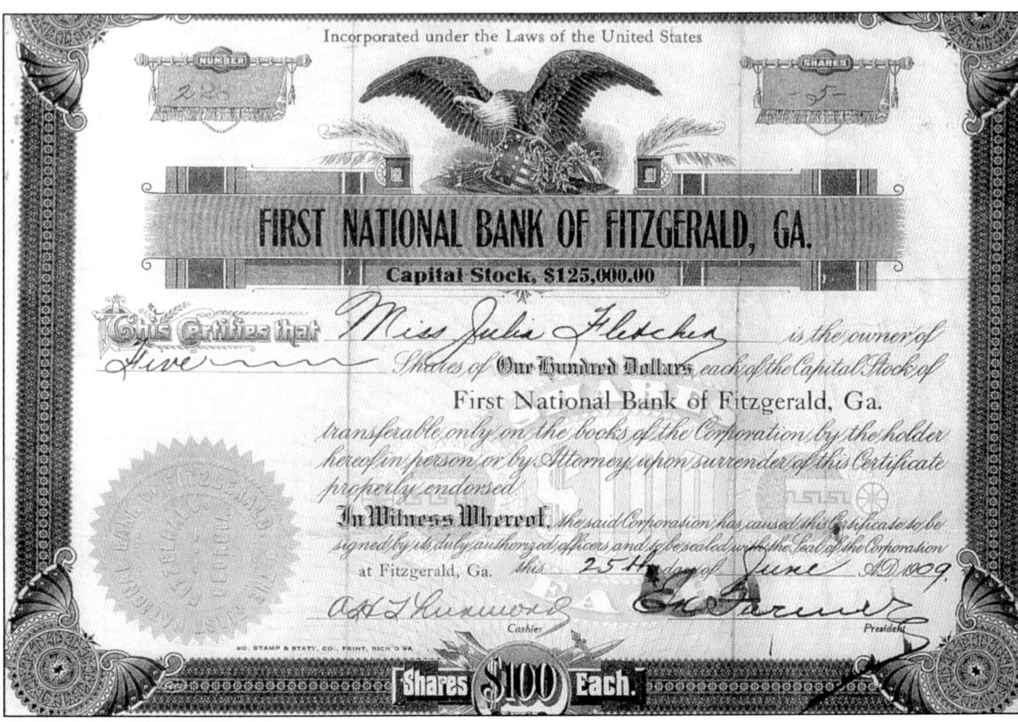

First National Bank, Fitzgerald. A June 1909 certificate proclaims Miss Julia Fletcher to own five shares of stock, at $100 each, in the First National Bank.

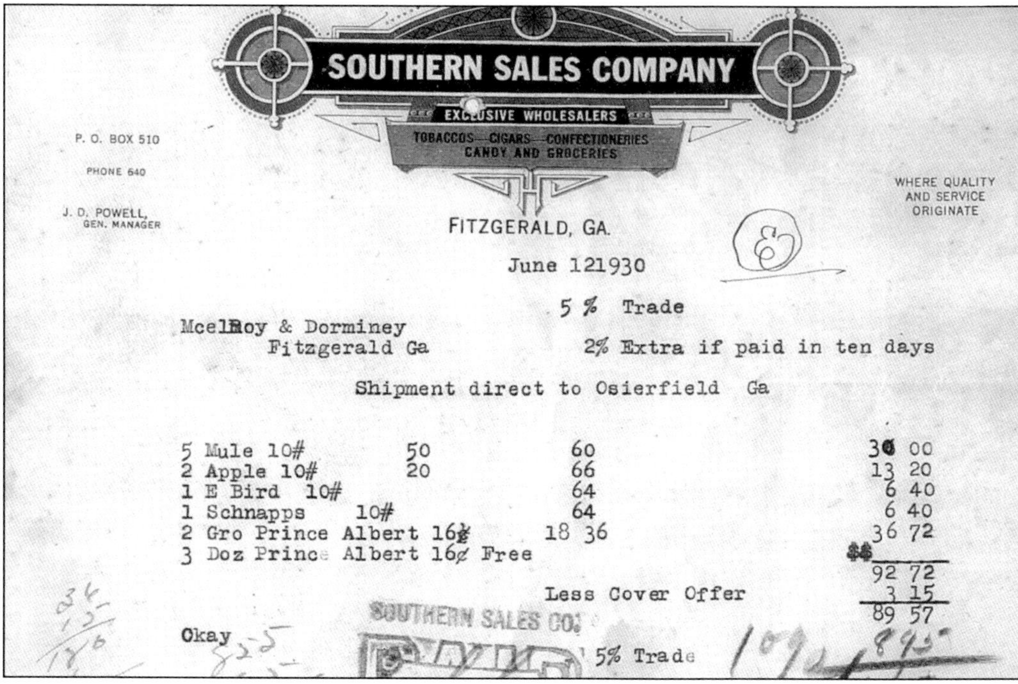

SOUTHERN SALES COMPANY
EXCLUSIVE WHOLESALERS
TOBACCOS—CIGARS—CONFECTIONERIES
CANDY AND GROCERIES

P. O. BOX 510
PHONE 640
J. D. POWELL,
GEN. MANAGER

WHERE QUALITY
AND SERVICE
ORIGINATE

FITZGERALD, GA.

June 121930

5 % Trade

McelRoy & Dorminey
Fitzgerald Ga
2% Extra if paid in ten days

Shipment direct to Osierfield Ga

5 Mule 10#	50	60	30 00
2 Apple 10#	20	66	13 20
1 E Bird 10#		64	6 40
1 Schnapps 10#		64	6 40
2 Gro Prince Albert 16¢		18 36	36 72
3 Doz Prince Albert 16¢ Free			
			92 72
Less Cover Offer			3 15
			89 57

SOUTHERN SALES CO.

Okay

5% Trade

SOUTHERN SALES COMPANY, FITZGERALD. This invoice for tobacco and tobacco products was probably written for a supply that replenished the Turpentine Commissary at Osierfield. General Manager J.D. Powell of the Southern Sales Company taught the author's Sunday School class in the 1930s.

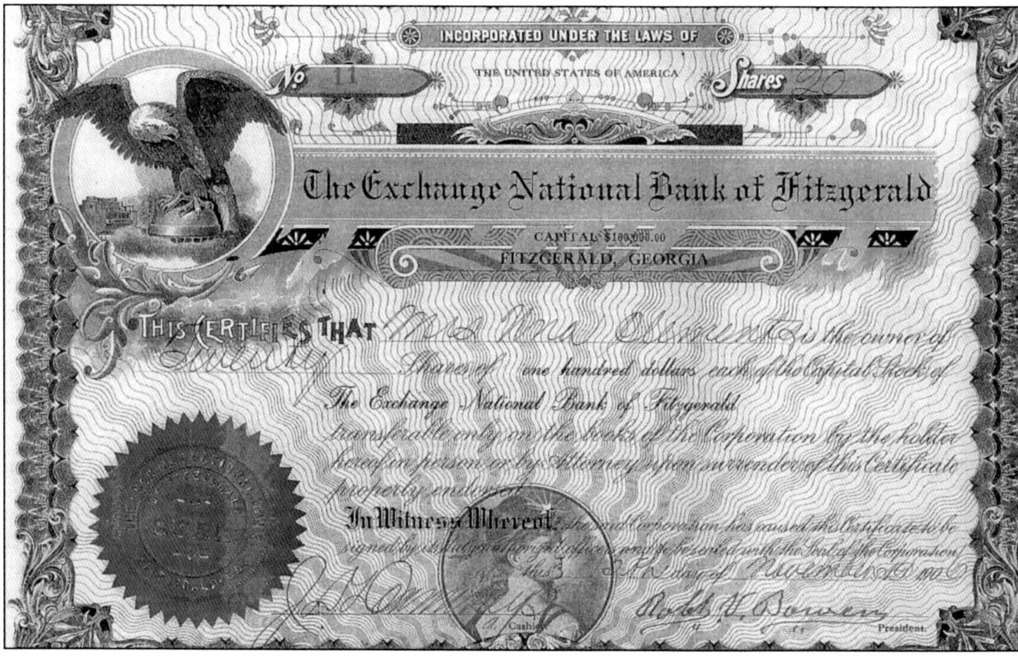

INCORPORATED UNDER THE LAWS OF
THE UNITED STATES OF AMERICA
No. 11 Shares 20

The Exchange National Bank of Fitzgerald

CAPITAL $100,000.00
FITZGERALD, GEORGIA

This Certifies that Mrs Nora Osburn is the owner of Twenty Shares of one hundred dollars each of the Capital Stock of The Exchange National Bank of Fitzgerald transferable only on the books of the Corporation by the holder hereof in person or by Attorney upon surrender of this Certificate properly endorsed.

In Witness Whereof, the said Corporation has caused this Certificate to be signed by its duly authorized officers and to be sealed with the Seal of the Corporation this 2nd day of November A.D. 1906

Cashier. President.

THE EXCHANGE NATIONAL BANK, FITZGERALD. A November 1906 certificate entitled the bearer to 20 shares of stock.

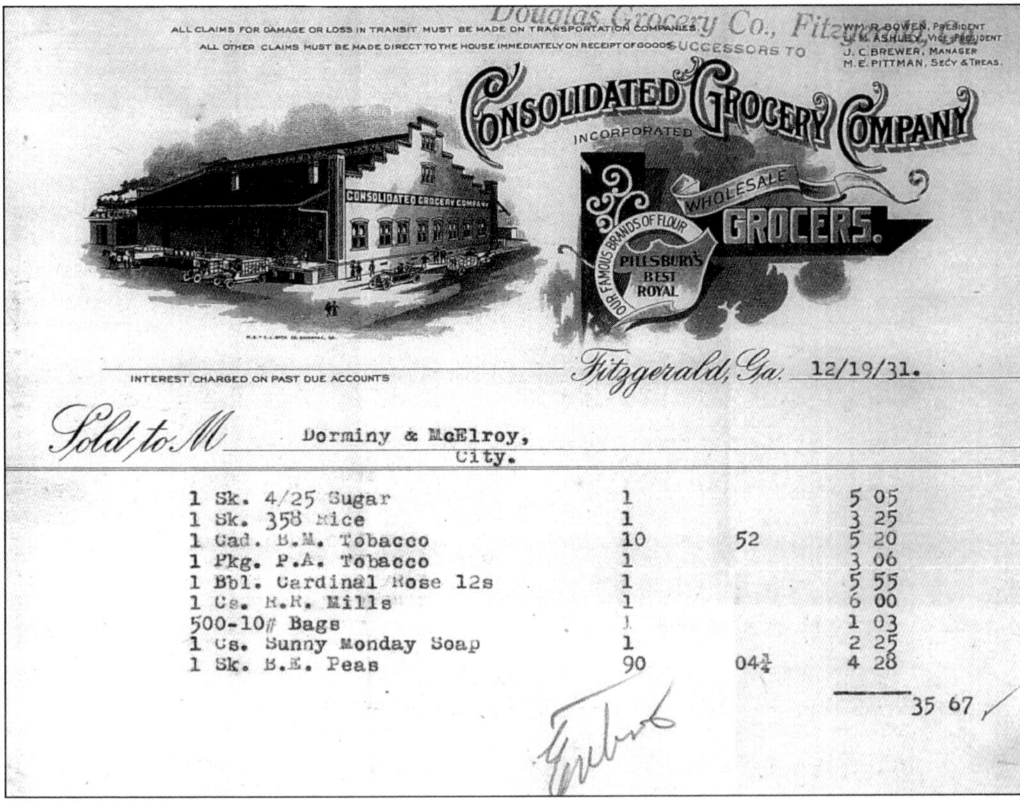

ALL CLAIMS FOR DAMAGE OR LOSS IN TRANSIT MUST BE MADE ON TRANSPORTATION COMPANIES.
ALL OTHER CLAIMS MUST BE MADE DIRECT TO THE HOUSE IMMEDIATELY ON RECEIPT OF GOODS.

Douglas Grocery Co., Fitzgerald, Ga. SUCCESSORS TO

WM. R. BOWEN, PRESIDENT
J. M. ASHLEY, VICE-PRESIDENT
J. C. BREWER, MANAGER
M. E. PITTMAN, SEC'Y & TREAS.

CONSOLIDATED GROCERY COMPANY
INCORPORATED
WHOLESALE GROCERS.
OUR FAMOUS BRANDS OF FLOUR PILLSBURY'S BEST ROYAL

INTEREST CHARGED ON PAST DUE ACCOUNTS

Fitzgerald, Ga. 12/19/31.

Sold to M Dorminy & McElroy,
City.

1 Sk. 4/25 Sugar	1		5 05
1 Sk. 358 Rice	1		3 25
1 Cad. B.M. Tobacco	10	52	5 20
1 Pkg. P.A. Tobacco	1		3 06
1 Bbl. Cardinal Rose 12s	1		5 55
1 Cs. R.R. Mills	1		6 00
500-10# Bags	1		1 03
1 Cs. Sunny Monday Soap	1		2 25
1 Sk. B.E. Peas	90	04¾	4 28
			35 67

Enbst

CONSOLIDATED GROCERY COMPANY, FITZGERALD. Consolidated was an early wholesale grocery in Fitzgerald. This invoice to Dorminy and McElroy probably helped stock their Turpentine Commissary at Osierfield. Compare the prices to those of the present-day—500 ten-pound bags of flour sure would make a lot of biscuits.

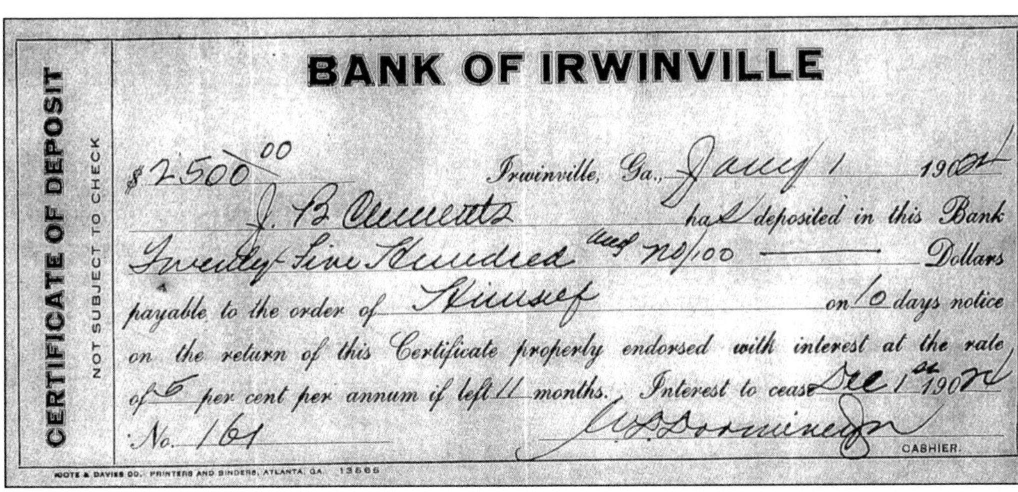

CERTIFICATE OF DEPOSIT
NOT SUBJECT TO CHECK

BANK OF IRWINVILLE

$2500 00 Irwinville, Ga., Jany 1 1902
J. B. Clements has deposited in this Bank
Twenty-Five Hundred and no/100 Dollars
payable to the order of Himself on 10 days notice
on the return of this Certificate properly endorsed with interest at the rate
of 6 per cent per annum if left 11 months. Interest to cease Dec 1st 1902
No. 161 W.B. Dorminey CASHIER.

FOOTE & DAVIES CO. PRINTERS AND BINDERS, ATLANTA, GA. 13566

BANK OF IRWINVILLE. Judge J.B. Clements, author of ***History of Irwin County,*** placed this sum on deposit with the Bank of Irwinville.

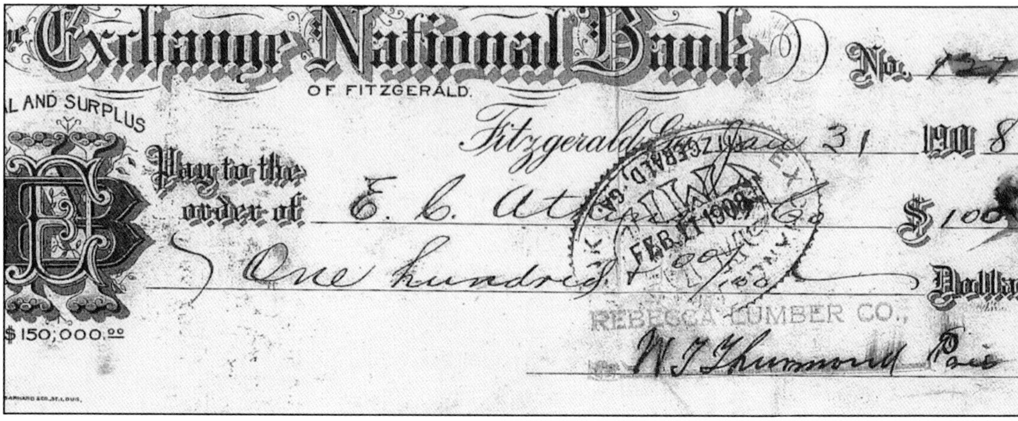

The Exchange National Bank of Fitzgerald, 1908. The check is signed by W.T. Thurmond, who was president of Rebecca Lumber Company in Osierfield.

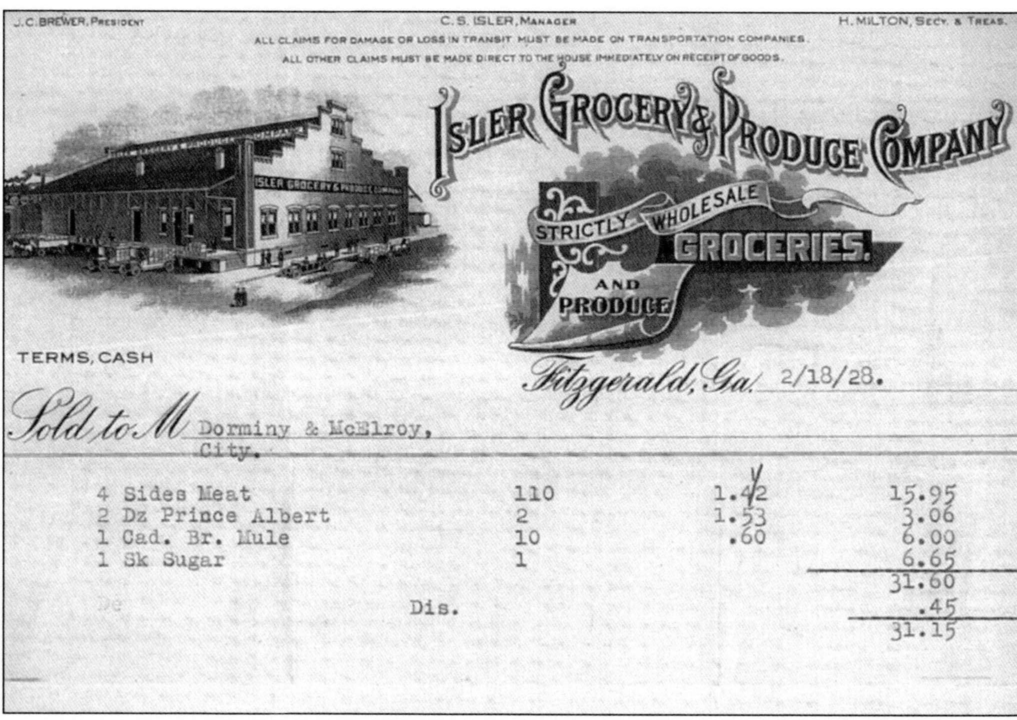

Isler Grocery and Produce Company, Fitzgerald. This receipt, made out to Dorminy and McElroy, shows that they purchased four sides of meat. Pork side meat was kept in a box of salt and cut to the customers' request on a chop block in the Osierfield Commissary.

The National Bank of Fitzgerald. Cashier Battle Sparks sent this notice to J.J. Dorminy, president of the Okefenokee Lumber Company, on December 19, 1936.

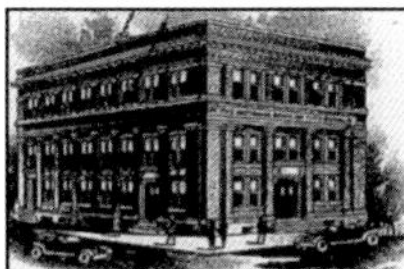

NO. 13550

THE NATIONAL BANK OF FITZGERALD

CAPITAL $ 100,000 SURPLUS $ 20,000

J. H. DORMINY, President
J. L. PERRY, Vice-President
N. N. LITTLEFIELD, Vice-President
BATTLE SPARKS, Cashier
C. A. NEWCOMER, JR., Assistant Cashier

FITZGERALD, GA. Dec. 19th 1936

Mr. J. J. Dorminy, President,
Okefenokee Lumber Co.,
City.
Dear Sir;

We are enclosing herewith a renewal of Okefenokee Lumber Company note dated April 17th, 1936 balance due $4392.75, interest to date $252.78, the rate is 6% interest.

Please sign the new note and the old note is endorsed by you, and we will send you the old note.

Under the National Banking law, we are not permitted to carry a demand note longer than six months.

New note for $4645.53, interest from date, Dec. 19th, at 6%.

Yours very truly,

Battle Sparks
Battle Sparks, Cashier.

Shipment to J.B. Dorminy and Son, Wilcox County, Georgia, 1873. The goods were probably shipped from Savannah to Darien then up the Ocmulgee River by steamboat to Camp Brooklyn.

Messrs J B Dorminy & Son

BOUGHT OF **GEORGE W. ALLEN,**

IMPORTER OF AND DEALER IN

China, Glass and Crockery, Tin & Willow-Ware,

HOUSE FURNISHING GOODS OF EVERY DESCRIPTION, KEROSENE OIL, LAMPS, CHIMNEYS, &C.

No. 192 BROUGHTON STREET.

2	Doz Yellow Bowls 85 + 100	1	85
1/2	" CC "		53
2	" " Cups & Saucers @ 75	1	50
4	" Assorted Handled Teas 175	7	00
2	" unhandled " 1 25	2	50
4	" W.G Plates assorted 7 inch 1 15	4	60
3	" Tea " 1	3	00
3	" Assorted Tumblers 75 85 100	2	60
1	" Goblets	1	10
4	" Table Spoons 1 50 100 110	3	60
2000	Water Proof Caps	2	00
1	Cask 50 Drayage 25		75
2	W.G Bowls 175 + 225	4	00
		35	03

Rec'd Payment
Geo W Allen

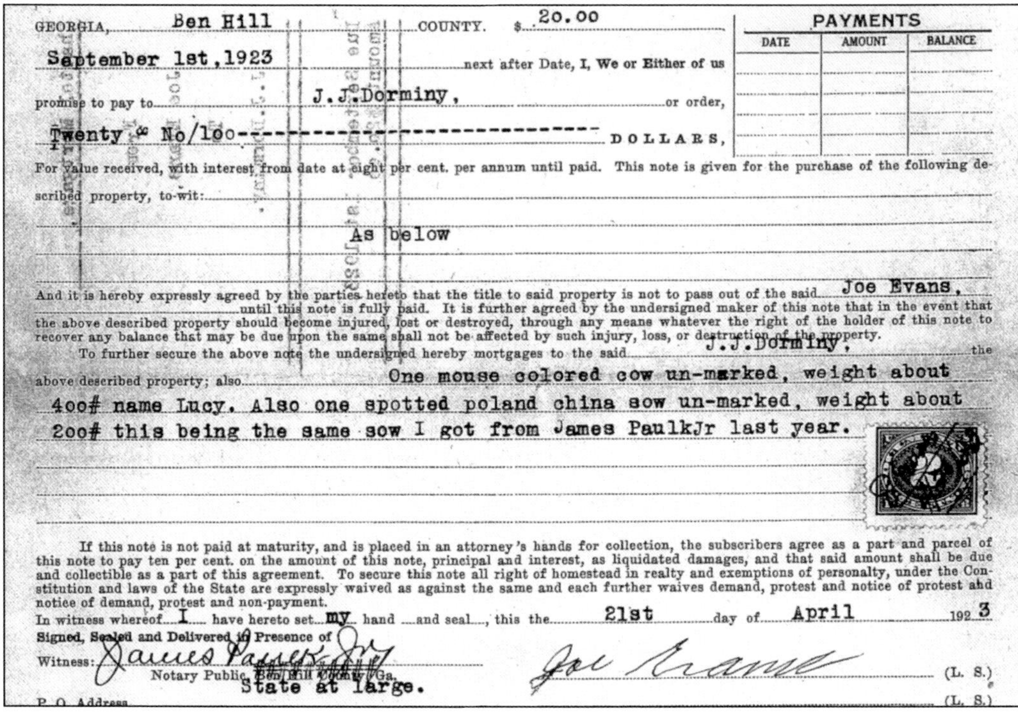

GEORGIA, Ben Hill COUNTY. $ 20.00

September 1st, 1923 next after Date, I, We or Either of us promise to pay to J. J. Dorminy, or order, Twenty & No/100 DOLLARS,

For value received, with interest from date at eight per cent. per annum until paid. This note is given for the purchase of the following described property, to-wit:

As below

And it is hereby expressly agreed by the parties hereto that the title to said property is not to pass out of the said Joe Evans, until this note is fully paid. It is further agreed by the undersigned maker of this note that in the event that the above described property should become injured, lost or destroyed, through any means whatever the right of the holder of this note to recover any balance that may be due upon the same shall not be affected by such injury, loss, or destruction of the property.

To further secure the above note the undersigned hereby mortgages to the said J. J. Dorminy, the above described property; also One mouse colored cow un-marked, weight about 400# name Lucy. Also one spotted poland china sow un-marked, weight about 200# this being the same sow I got from James PaulkJr last year.

If this note is not paid at maturity, and is placed in an attorney's hands for collection, the subscribers agree as a part and parcel of this note to pay ten per cent. on the amount of this note, principal and interest, as liquidated damages, and that said amount shall be due and collectible as a part of this agreement. To secure this note all right of homestead in realty and exemptions of personalty, under the Constitution and laws of the State are expressly waived as against the same and each further waives demand, protest and notice of protest and notice of demand, protest and non-payment.

In witness whereof I have hereto set my hand and seal, this the 21st day of April 1923

Signed, Sealed and Delivered in Presence of

Witness: James Paulk Jr

Notary Public, Ben Hill County, Ga. State at large.

Joe Evans (L. S.)

P. O. Address (L. S.)

PAYMENTS		
DATE	AMOUNT	BALANCE

Cow Note and Hog Note, 1923. Payment was made to J.J. Dorminy in the amount of $20 for a 400-pound cow and a 200-pound hog in September of 1923.

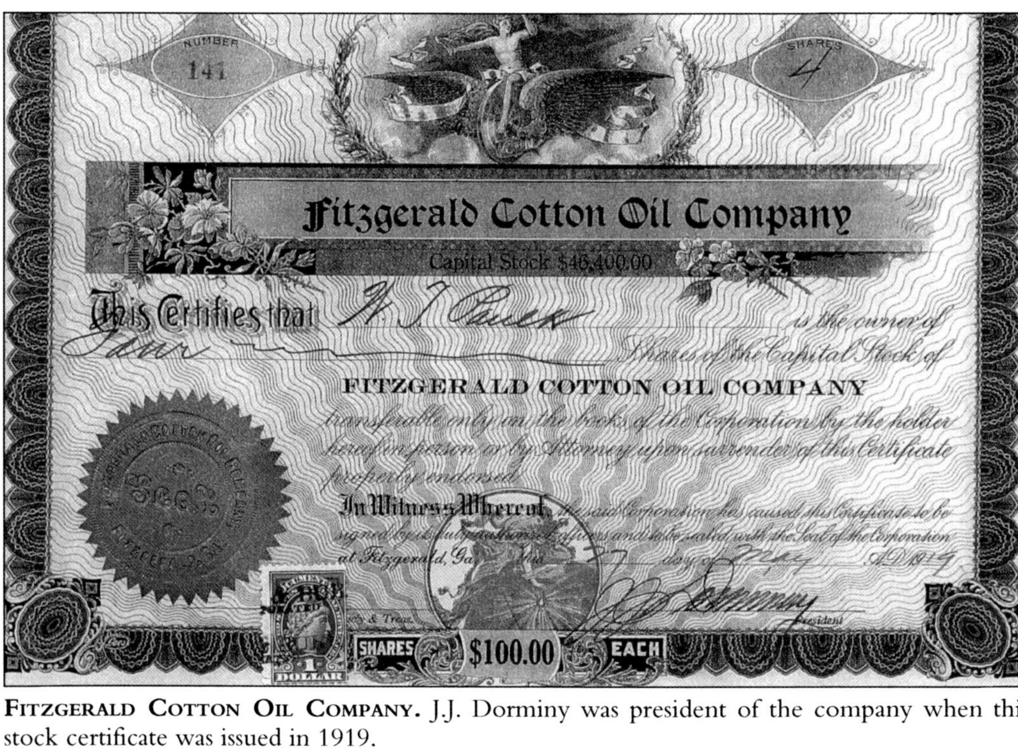

Fitzgerald Cotton Oil Company. J.J. Dorminy was president of the company when this stock certificate was issued in 1919.

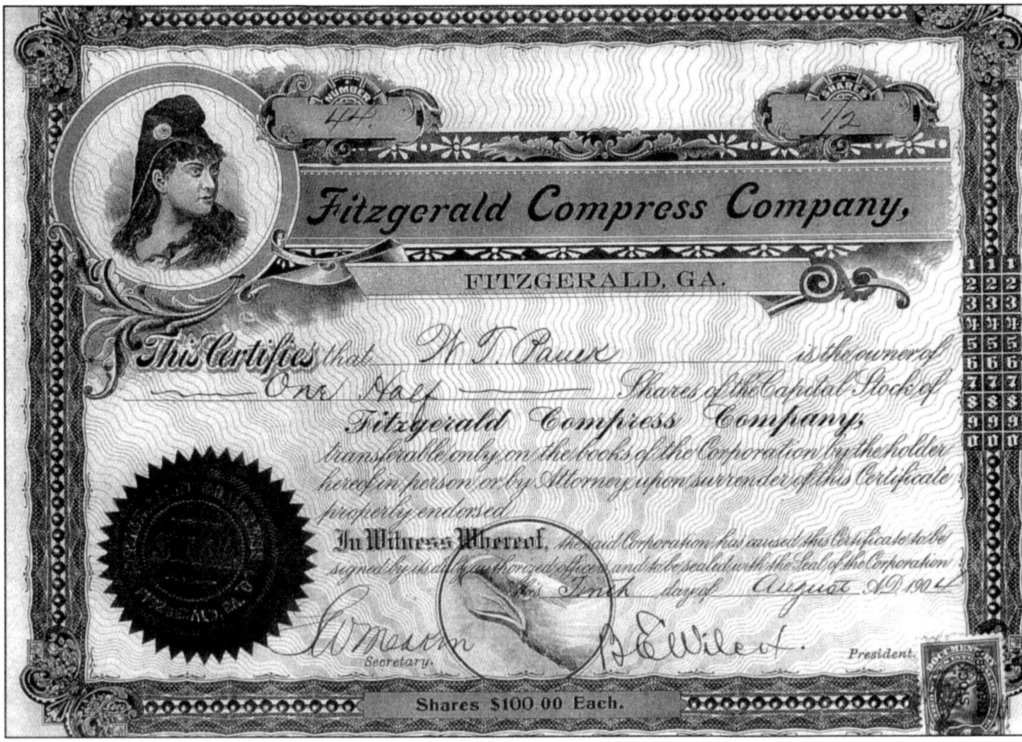

Number 44.

Shares 1/2

Fitzgerald Compress Company,

FITZGERALD, GA.

This Certifies that W. T. Paulk is the owner of One Half Shares of the Capital Stock of Fitzgerald Compress Company, transferable only on the books of the Corporation by the holder hereof in person or by Attorney, upon surrender of this Certificate properly endorsed.

In Witness Whereof, the said Corporation has caused this Certificate to be signed by its duly authorized officers and to be sealed with the Seal of the Corporation this Tenth day of August A.D. 1904

Secretary. President.

Shares $100.00 Each.

FITZGERALD COMPRESS COMPANY. This one-half share was sold to W.T. Paulk in 1904.

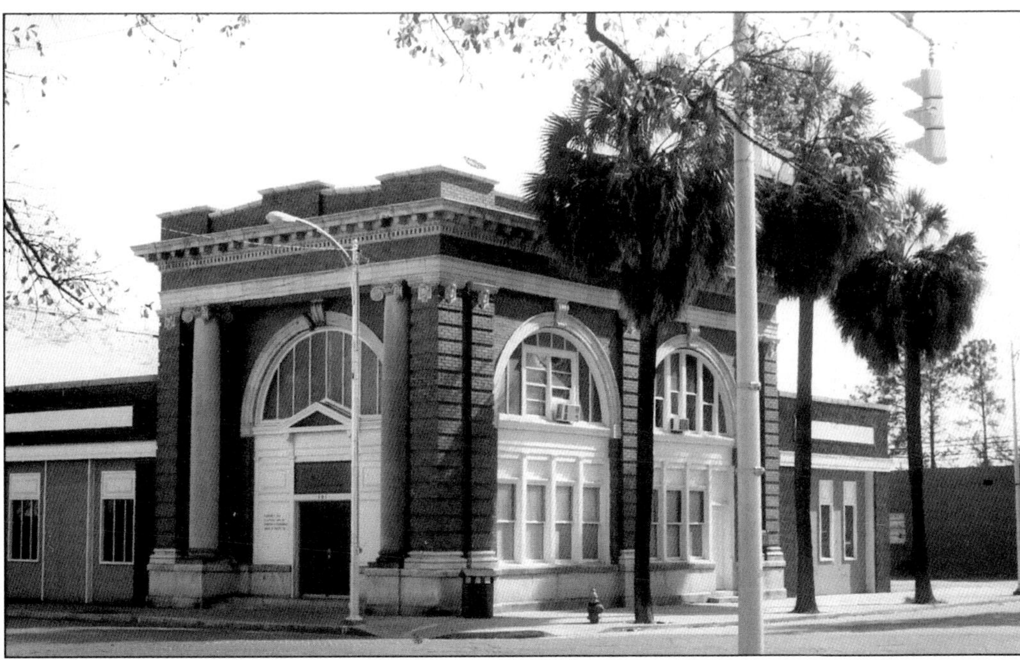

JAY, GARDEN, AND JAY LAW OFFICES. The law offices are located at the corner of Pine and Main Streets. The building is pictured on many early 1900s postcards; the palm trees are nearly the same size in 2001.

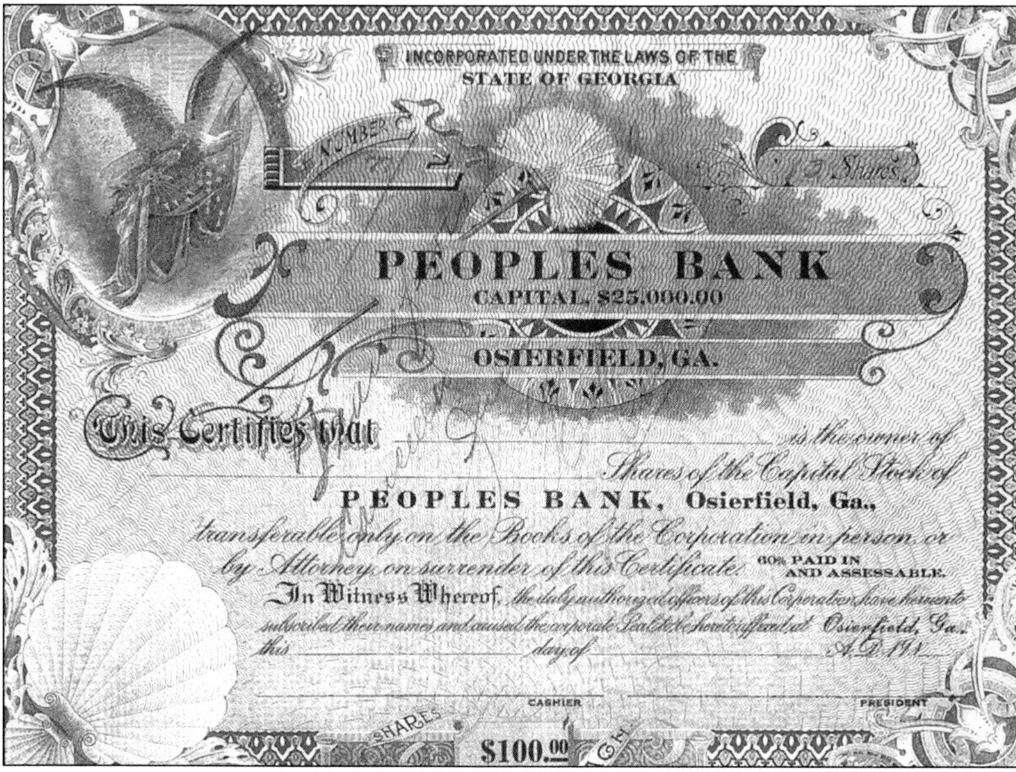
INCORPORATED UNDER THE LAWS OF THE
STATE OF GEORGIA

NUMBER

Shares

PEOPLES BANK
CAPITAL, $25,000.00
OSIERFIELD, GA.

This Certifies that ______ is the owner of ______ Shares of the Capital Stock of PEOPLES BANK, Osierfield, Ga., transferable only on the Books of the Corporation in person or by Attorney on surrender of this Certificate. 60% PAID IN AND ASSESSABLE.

In Witness Whereof, the duly authorized officers of this Corporation have hereunto subscribed their names and caused the corporate Seal to be hereto affixed at Osierfield, Ga. this ______ day of ______ A.D. 191

CASHIER

PRESIDENT

SHARES

$100.00

PEOPLES BANK OF OSIERFIELD, 1917. J.E. Pittman served as cashier and Aubrey Harper as president. This certificate notes that 13 shares were transferred from J.H. Holley to J.D. Walker.

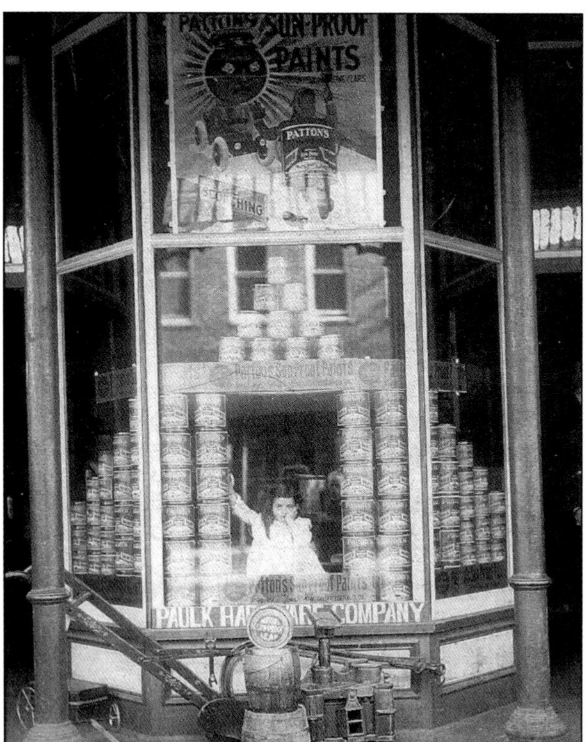

PAULK HARDWARE COMPANY, FITZGERALD. A little girl stares out the window and the sidewalk boasts two hoss-turning plows, a keg of nails, a sugar cane grinder, and a toy wagon.|

Two

Farming, Logging, and Turpentining

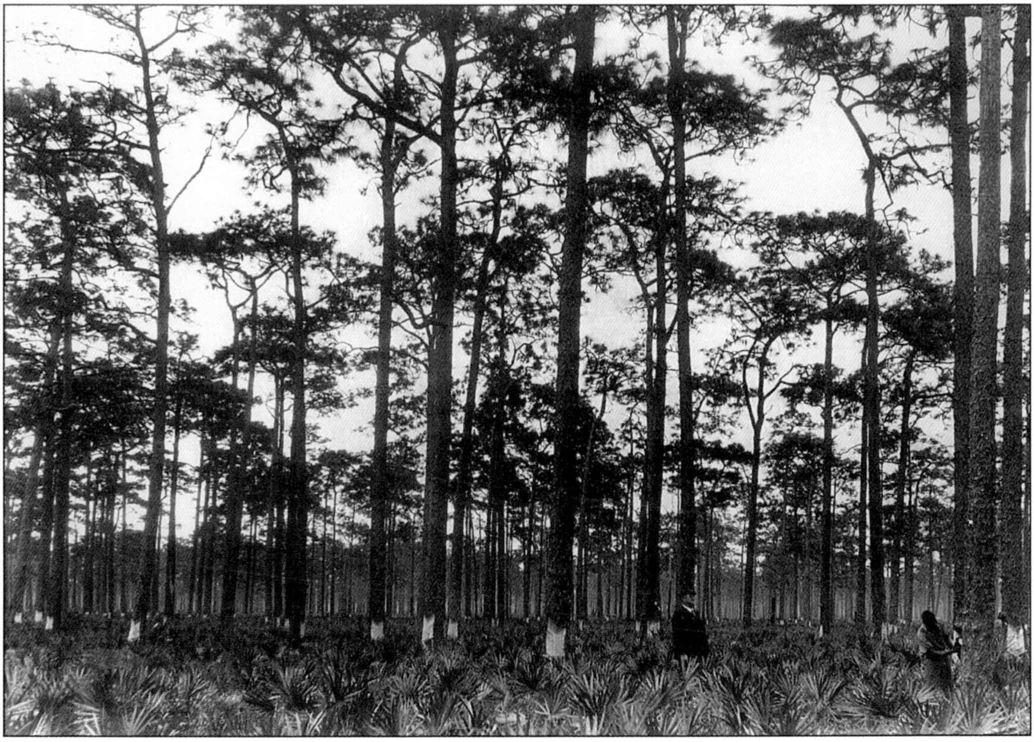

Virgin Longleaf Pine Timber. Most of the trees pictured are over 100 years old. A Red Cockaded Woodpecker cavity can be seen in the upper right.

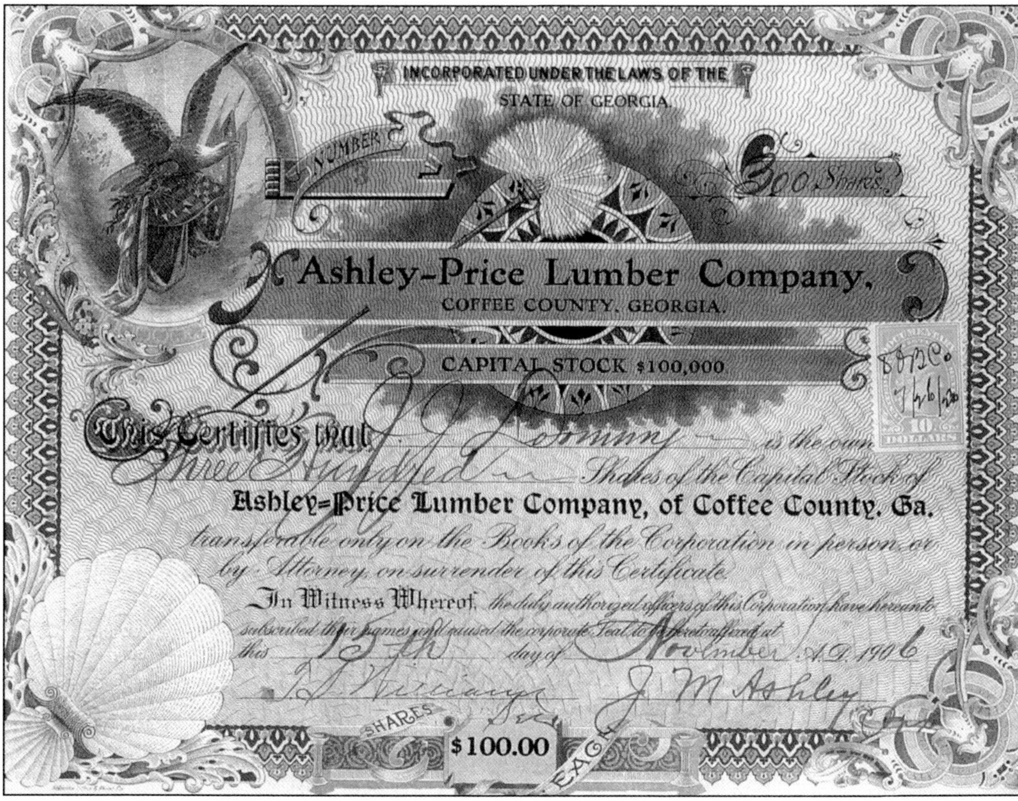

INCORPORATED UNDER THE LAWS OF THE STATE OF GEORGIA.

NUMBER

300 Shares

Ashley-Price Lumber Company,
COFFEE COUNTY, GEORGIA.

CAPITAL STOCK $100,000

This Certifies that J. J. Dorminy is the own[er of] Three Hundred Shares of the Capital Stock of
Ashley-Price Lumber Company, of Coffee County, Ga.
transferable only on the Books of the Corporation in person or by Attorney on surrender of this Certificate.

In Witness Whereof, the duly authorized officers of this Corporation have hereunto subscribed their names and caused the corporate Seal to be hereto affixed at this 15th day of November A.D. 1906

J. M. Ashley

SHARES $100.00

Ashley-Price Lumber Company, Coffee County. This 1906 certificate entitled J.J. Dorminy to 300 shares of stock in the company.

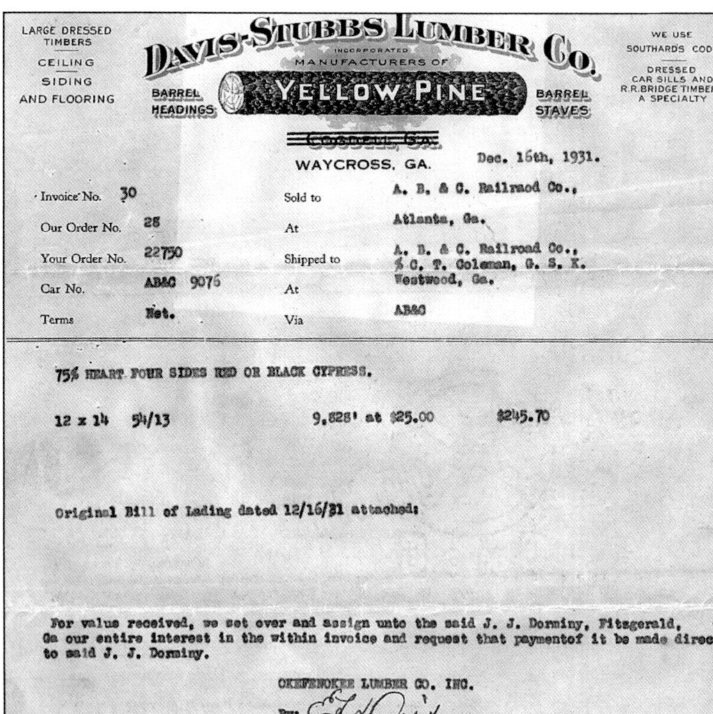

LARGE DRESSED TIMBERS
CEILING
SIDING
AND FLOORING

DAVIS-STUBBS LUMBER CO.
INCORPORATED
MANUFACTURERS OF
BARREL HEADINGS YELLOW PINE BARREL STAVES

WE USE SOUTHARDS CODE
DRESSED CAR SILLS AND R.R.BRIDGE TIMBERS A SPECIALTY

WAYCROSS, GA. Dec. 16th, 1931.

Invoice No.	30	Sold to	A. B. & C. Railroad Co.,
Our Order No.	28	At	Atlanta, Ga.
Your Order No.	22750	Shipped to	A. B. & C. Railroad Co., % C. T. Coleman, G. S. K.
Car No.	AB&C 9076	At	Westwood, Ga.
Terms	Net.	Via	AB&C

75% HEART FOUR SIDES RED OR BLACK CYPRESS.

12 x 14 54/13 9,828' at $25.00 $245.70

Original Bill of Lading dated 12/16/31 attached:

For value received, we set over and assign unto the said J. J. Dorminy, Fitzgerald, Ga our entire interest in the within invoice and request that paymentof it be made direct to said J. J. Dorminy.

OKEFENOKEE LUMBER CO. INC.

By:

Davis-Stubbs Lumber Company, Waycross. The huge, 12-by-14-foot timbers on this invoice were used to build a railroad bridge and shipped from Waycross to Westwood (Fitzgerald).

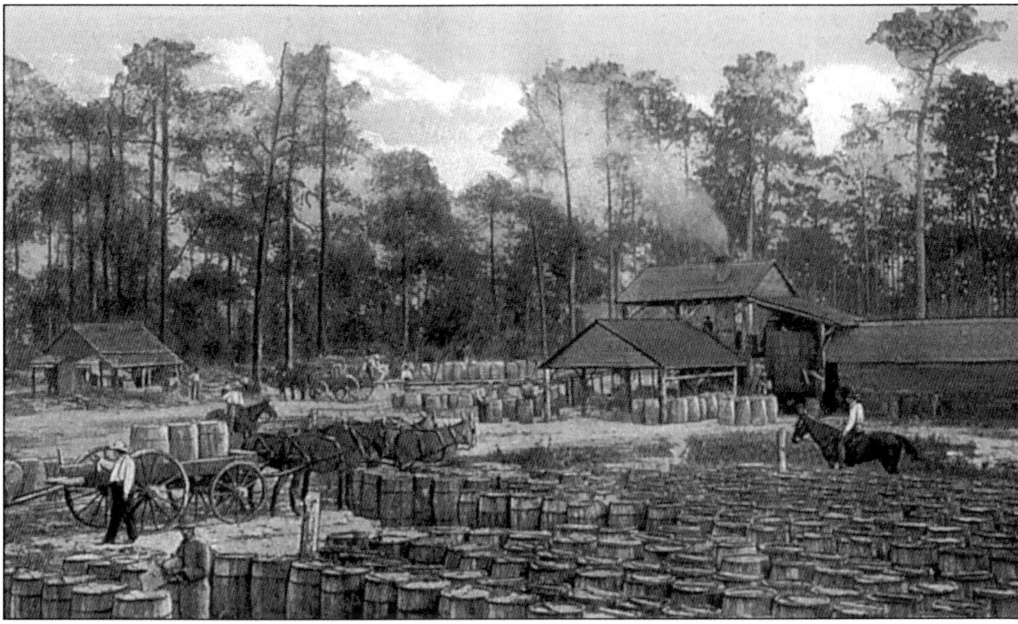

"Only" a Turpentine Still Down South. Included in the postcard are a fire still, dip wagons, woods riders, and a rosin yard, *c.* 1900.

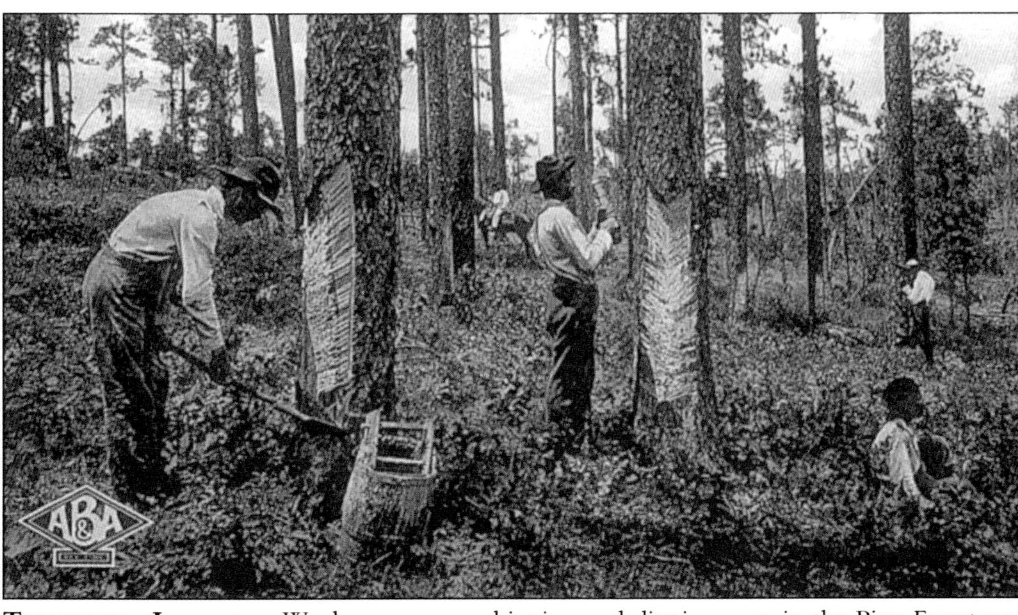

Turpentine Industry. Workers are seen chipping and dipping gum in the Pine Forest near Brunswick, Georgia. (Courtesy of Louis Harper.)

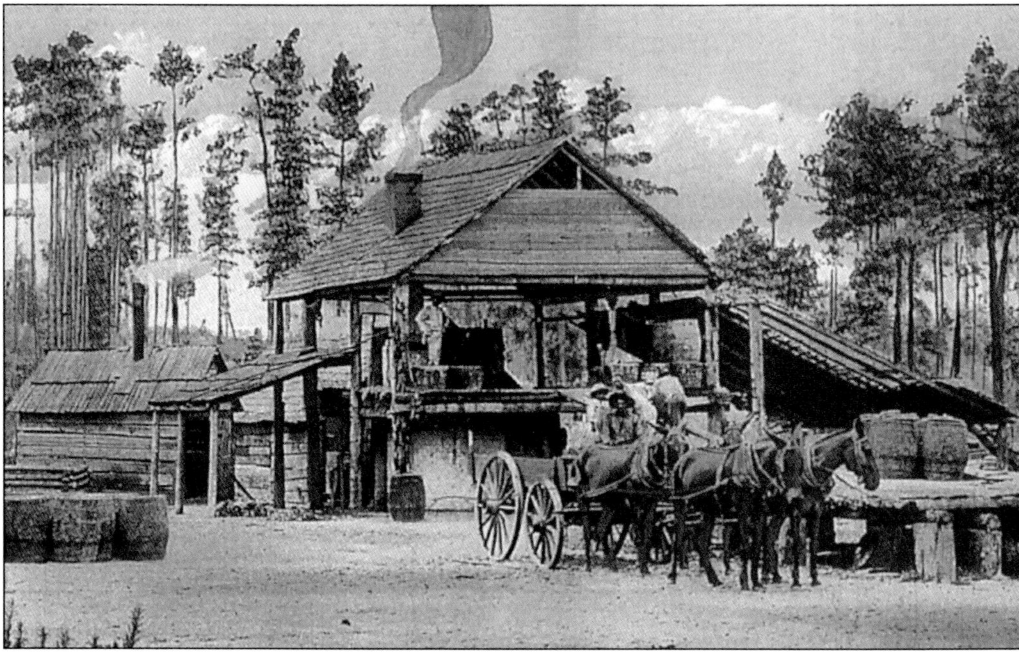

Turpentine Still. Four mules pull a dip wagon unloading raw gum or dip from the pine woods. Barrels were rolled up a two-pole ramp by hand and poured in the top of a copper kettle.

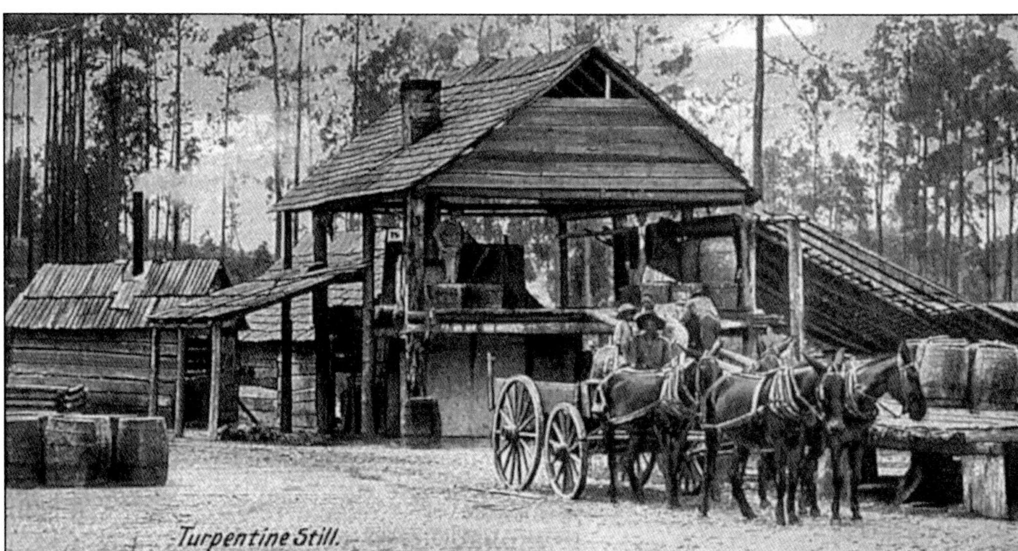

South Georgia Turpentine Still, c. 1909. The sender asked the recipient, "Of what does this remind you?"

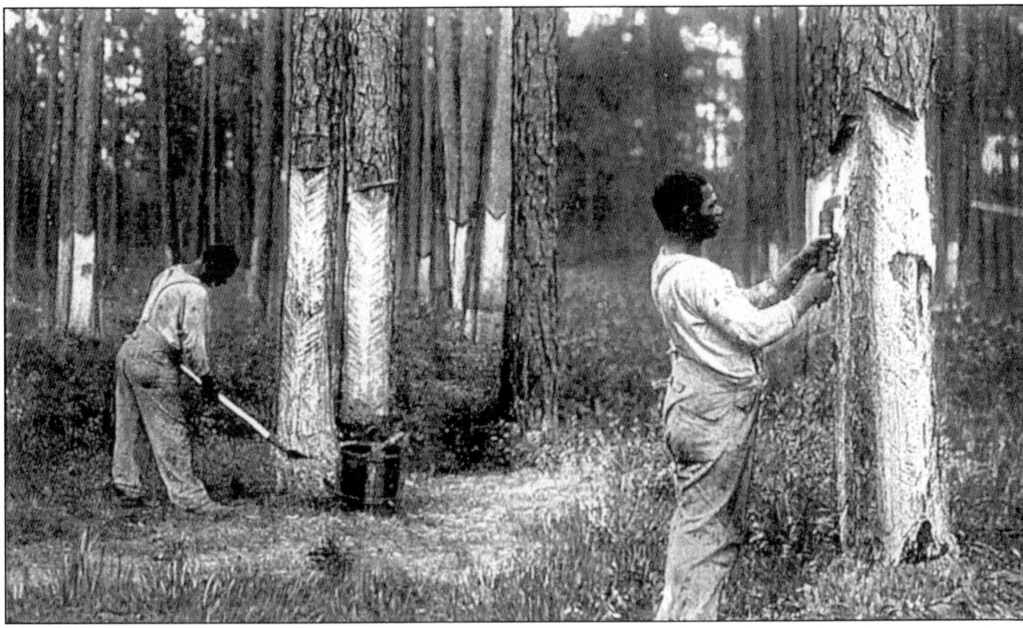

Dipping and Scraping Pine Trees, 1940s. The hand on the right is chipping or putting a "streak" on a catface. The hand on the left is scraping solidified rosin from pine faces and catching it in a bucket.

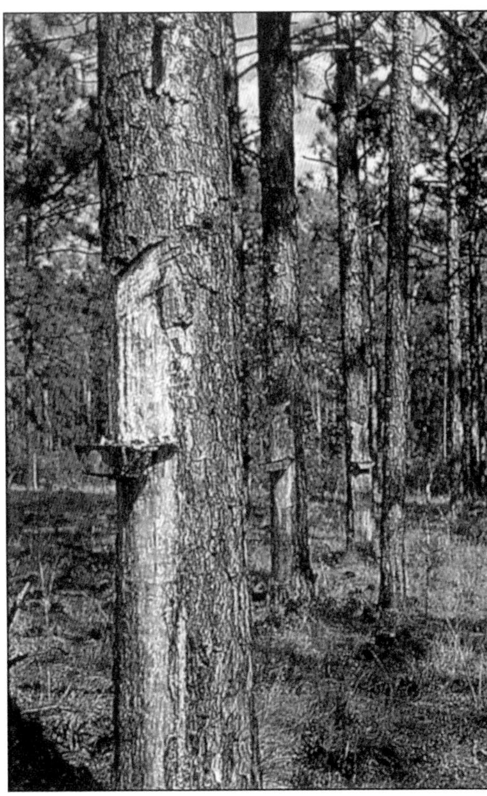

Third-year Chipping Boxes. A reddish color on the scraped areas of the trees was caused by a sulfuric acid solution sprayed on the faces to enhance gum flow. The solution wreaked havoc on a person's face and clothing on a windy day.

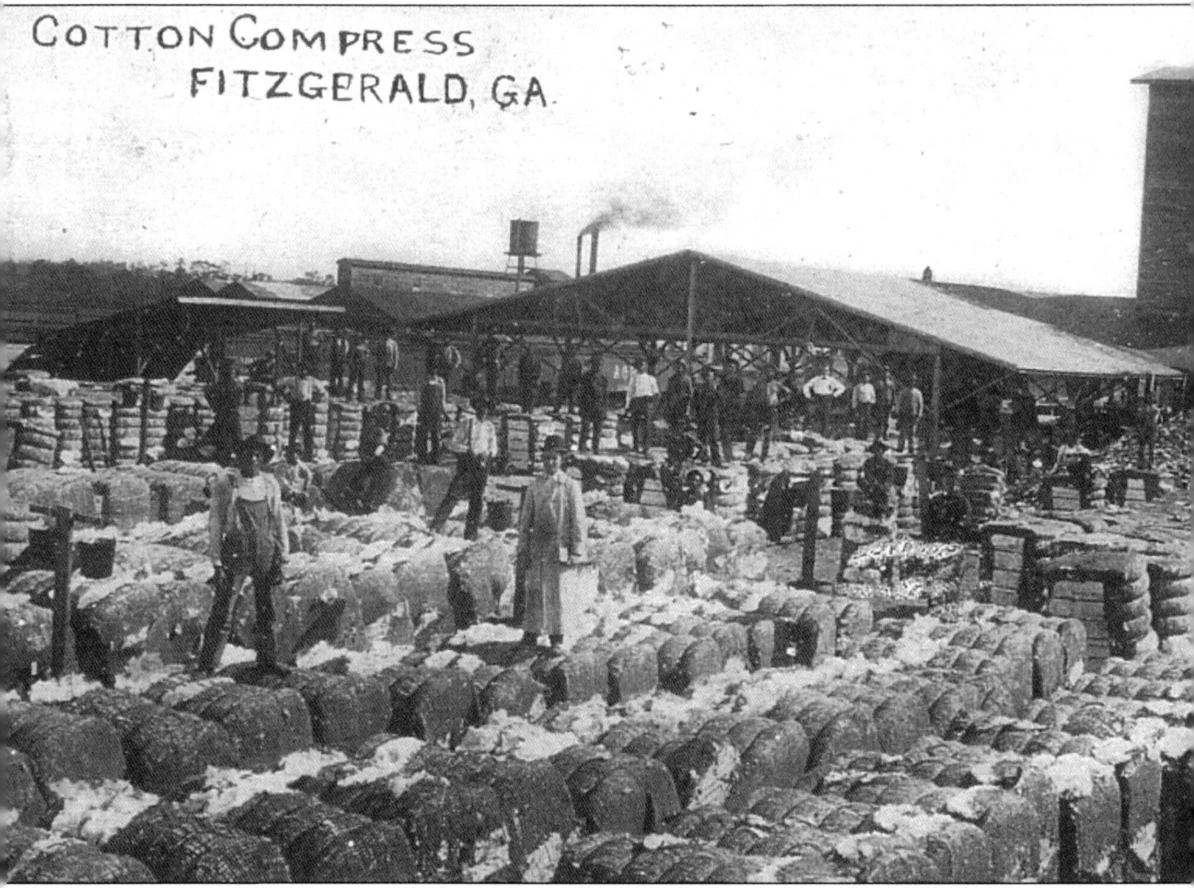

COTTON COMPRESS, FITZGERALD. Cotton seed, after ginned of their lint, were hulled and the meat cooked down to cotton seed meal. End products were hulls, meal, and cotton seed cake. This was the best smelling industry in Fitzgerald. The hulls with a sprinkling of meal were highly nutritious and were used to make cows stand still for milking. Cotton seed cake was excellent bait for fish baskets. The mill had its own deep well and water tank.

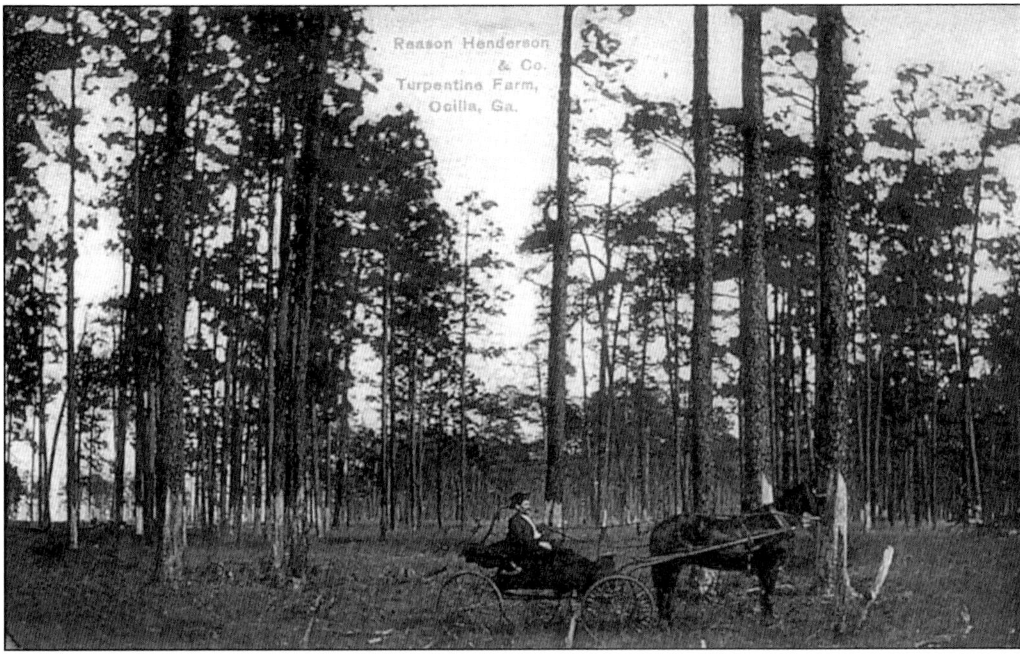

REASON HENDERSON AND COMPANY TURPENTINE FARM, OCILLA. Henderson is riding in his one-horse buggy, smoking his pipe, and inspecting this stand of virgin longleaf yellow pine. Most of the pines are well over 100 years old.

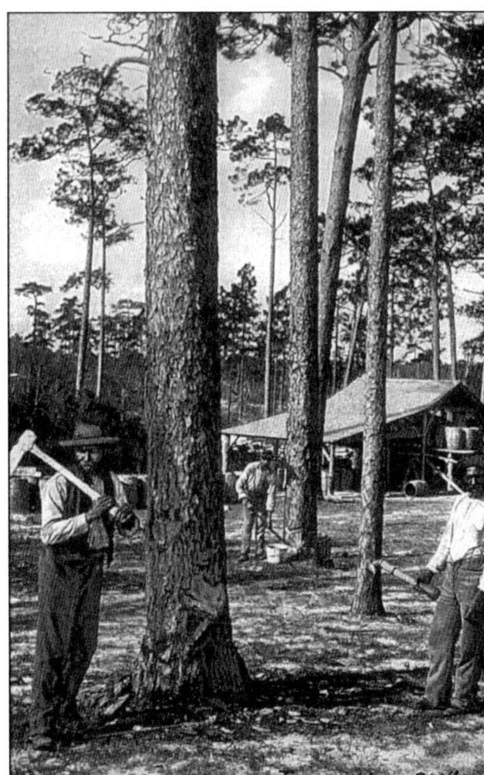

TURPENTINE STILL. The three men hold a box axe, a dip spoon, and a chipping hack, *c.* 1900.

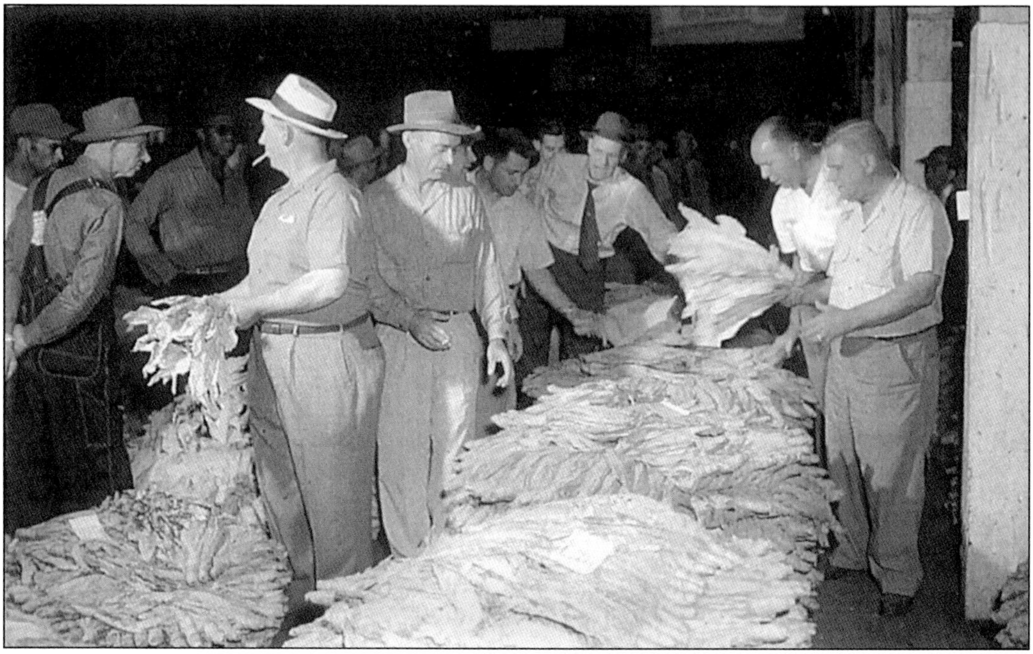

Tobacco Auction Barn, *c.* 1940s. Fitzgerald was a prominent market for the golden leaf for many years.

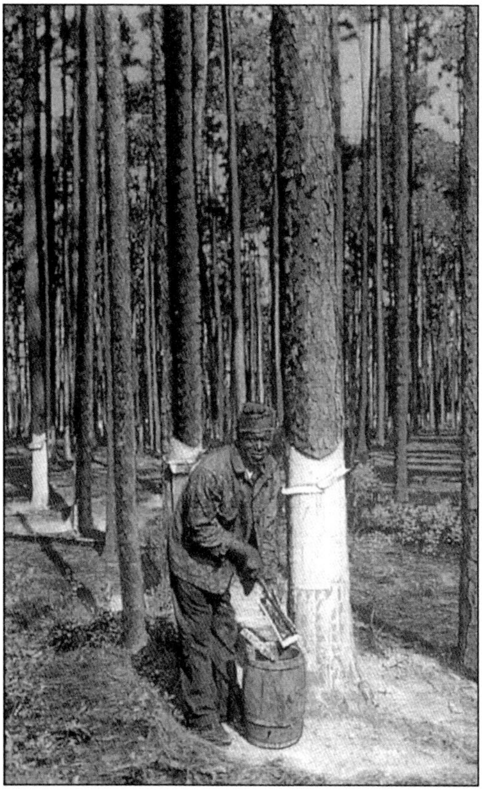

A Native of Dixieland at Work on a Turpentine Plantation. This was a major industry in the South in the 1930s.

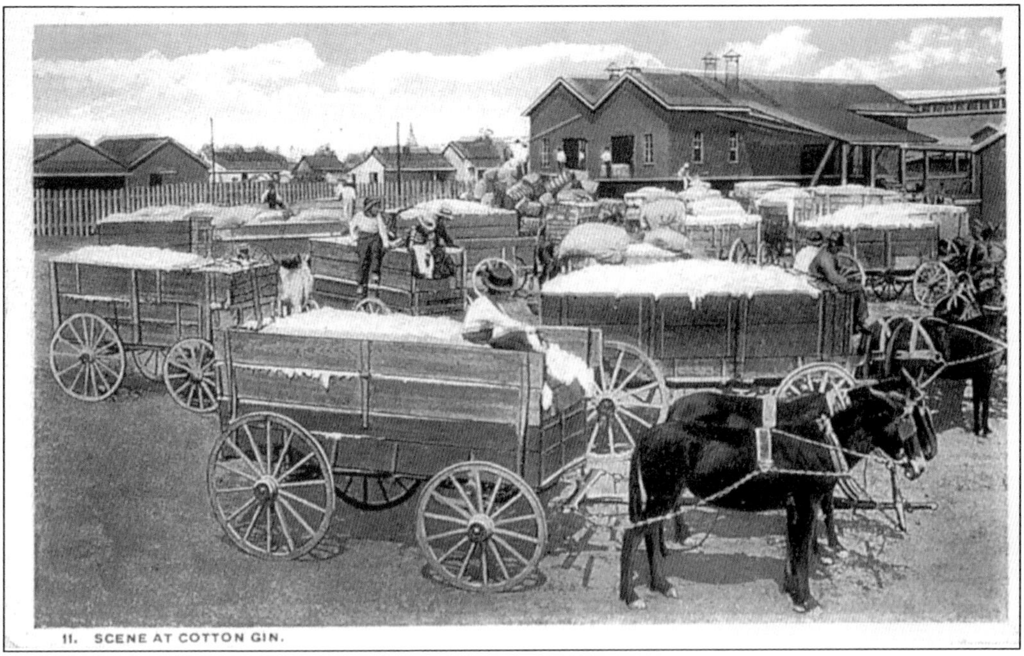

SOUTH GEORGIA COTTON GIN. The mill had no trucks—just mule-drawn wagons—in this *c.* 1920 postcard. The message written on the card read "I'm sending you a box of pecan nuts."

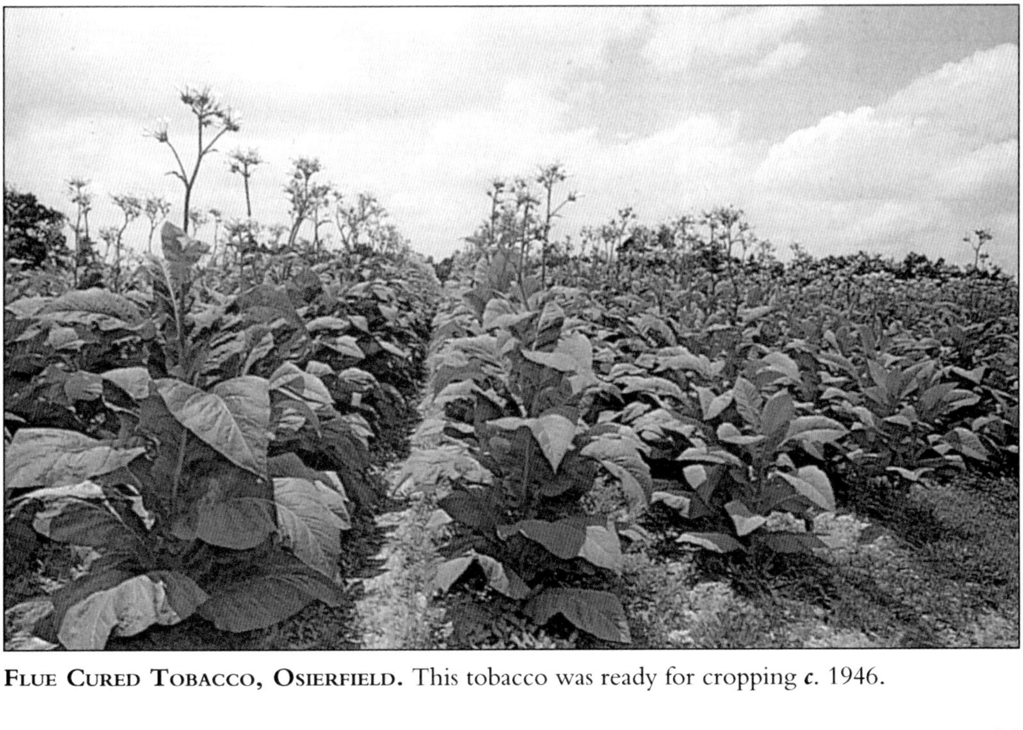

FLUE CURED TOBACCO, OSIERFIELD. This tobacco was ready for cropping *c.* 1946.

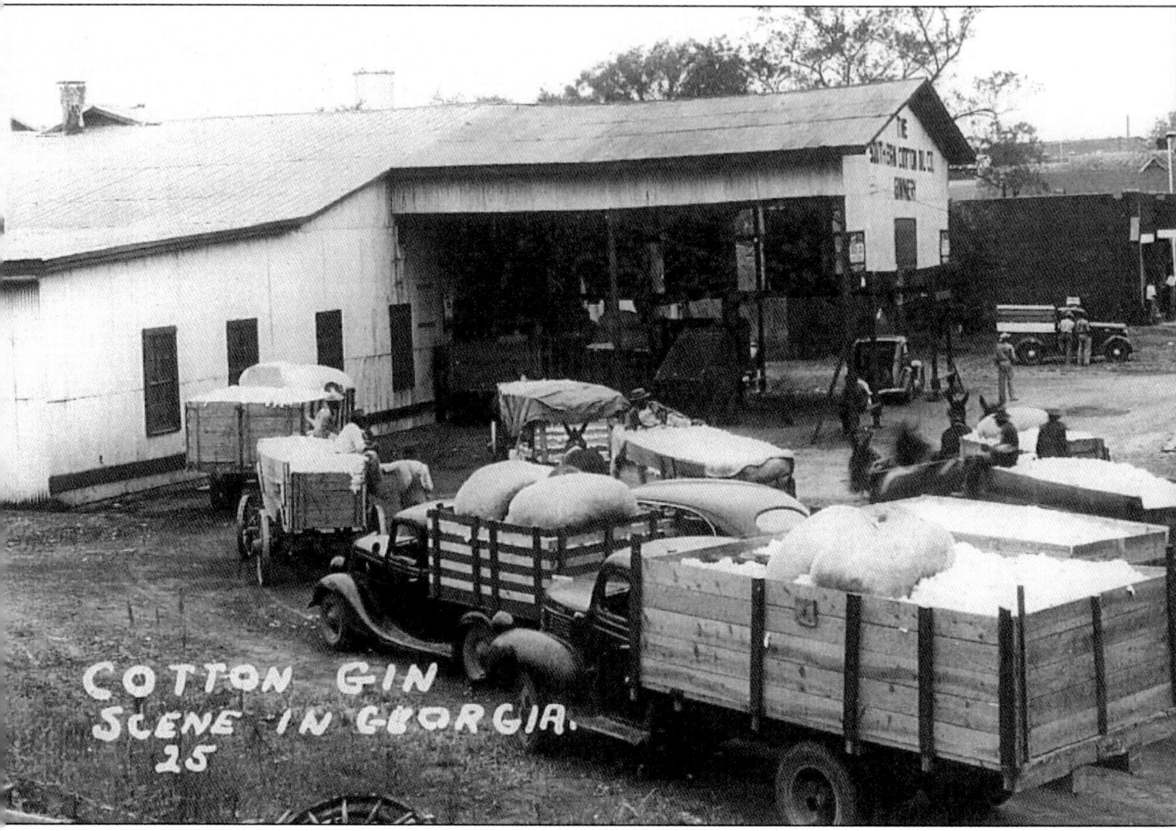

COTTON GIN, 1930s. Mules and wagons are mixed with trucks in line waiting for their turn to pull under the suction and have their seed cotton ginned.

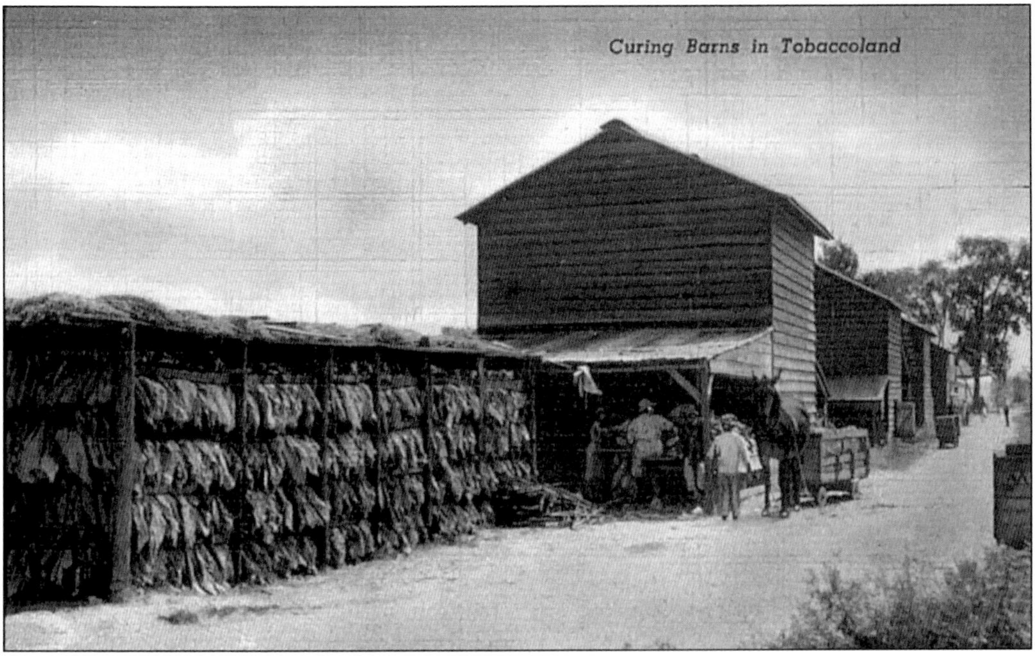

CURING BARNS IN TOBACCOLAND. Racks of green tobacco are ready to be hung in the barns in this 1930s postcard.

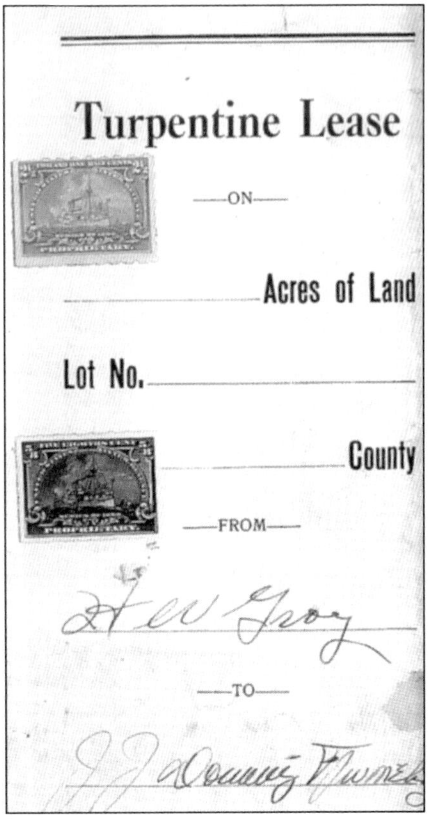

Turpentine Lease

—ON—

__________ Acres of Land

Lot No. __________

__________ County

—FROM—

H W Gray

—TO—

J J Dorminy

TURPENTINE LEASE, OSIERFIELD. This lease was issued from H.W. Gray to J.J. Dorminy and J.W. McElroy. Such agreements involved a cash payment to the landowner from the naval stores operators to "work" his timber for turpentine for a stated number of years.

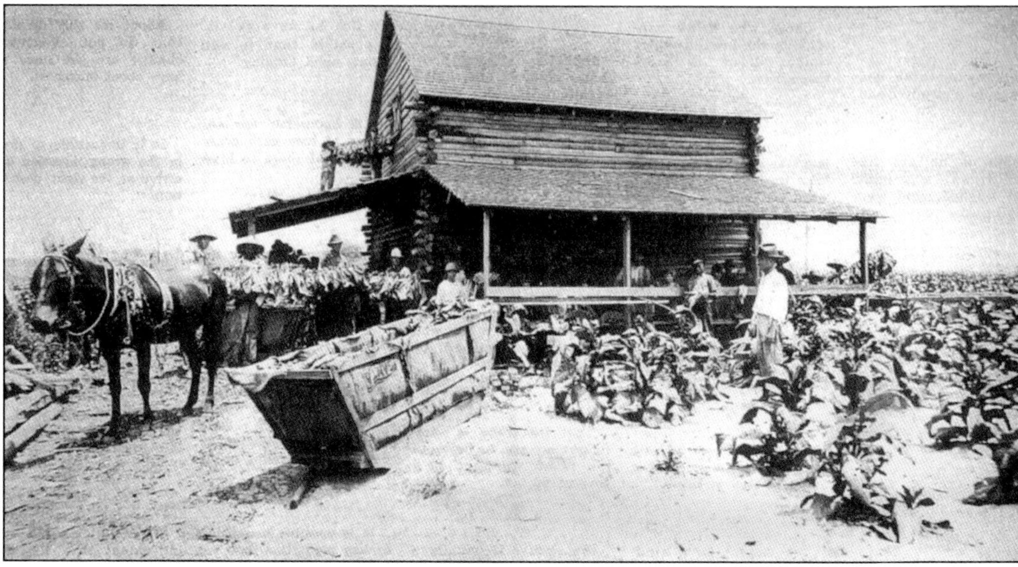

Workers Harvesting and Filling the Barn. The workers included croppers in the field, stringers, leaf handers, sled drivers, unloaders, and a crew of three or four boys to hang the finished sticks on tier poles. The barns were made of skinned pine poles and the roof was of wood shake shingles rived on the site. There was a brick furnace on one end of the barn and metal flues to carry heat throughout the barn. It was necessary for the temperature to reach over 165 degrees fahrenheit to cook the moisture from the leaf and stem. Many such barns burned down when sticks of tobacco fell on hot flues. Note the boys on the hip shelter on the left. They are passing sticks of tobacco through a top window on the barn.

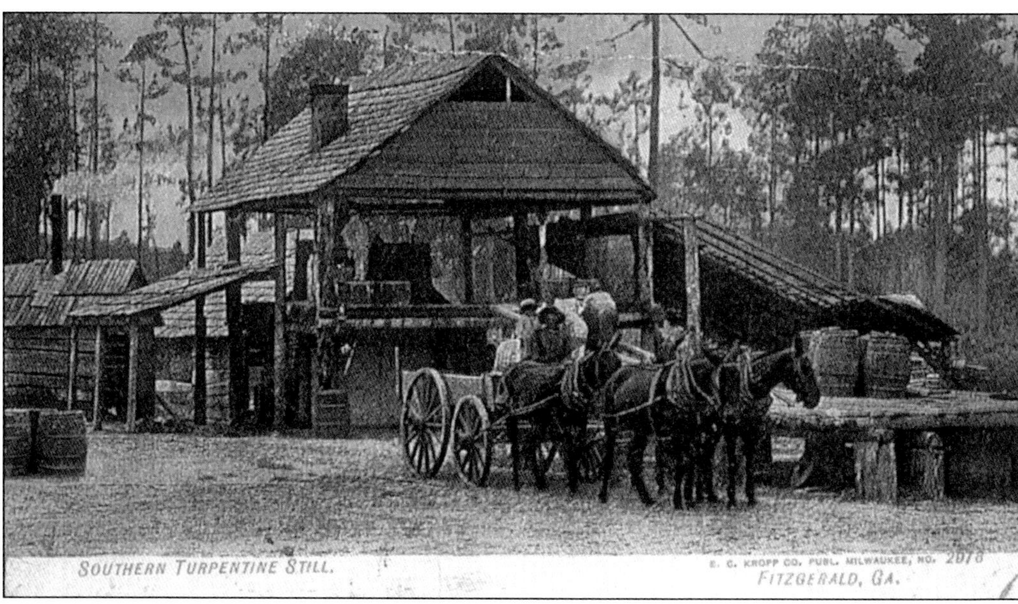

Southern Turpentine Still, Fitzgerald. This card was printed by E.C. Kropp of Milwaukee. (Courtesy of Louis Harper.)

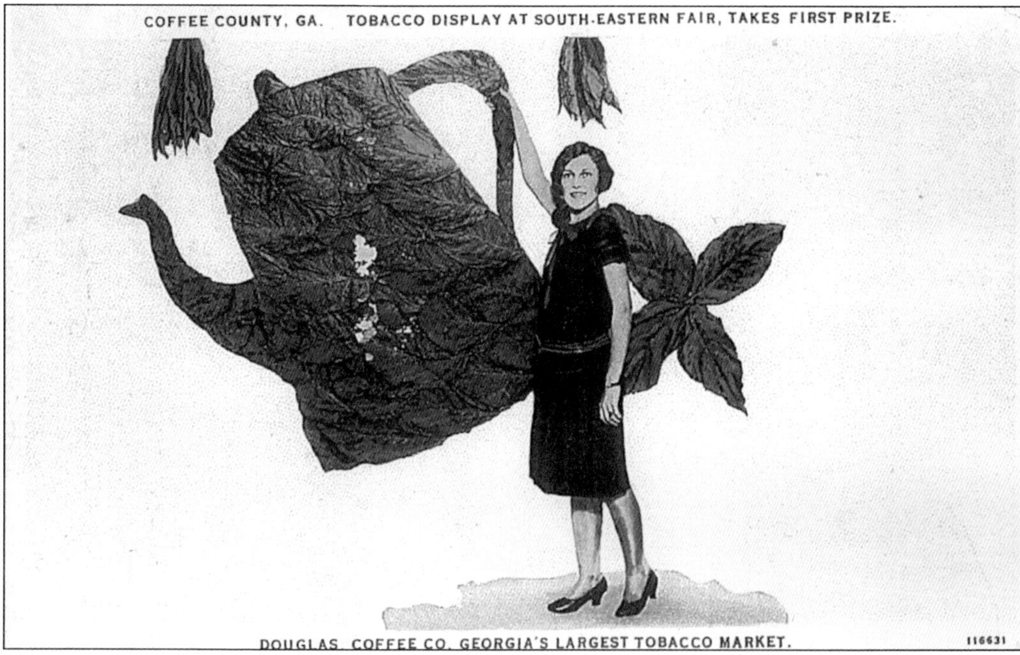

TOBACCO DISPLAY, COFFEE COUNTY, GEORGIA. This display took first prize at the Southeastern Fair held in Douglas. The card was published by the Douglas Kiwanis Club and Chamber of Commerce in the 1940s.

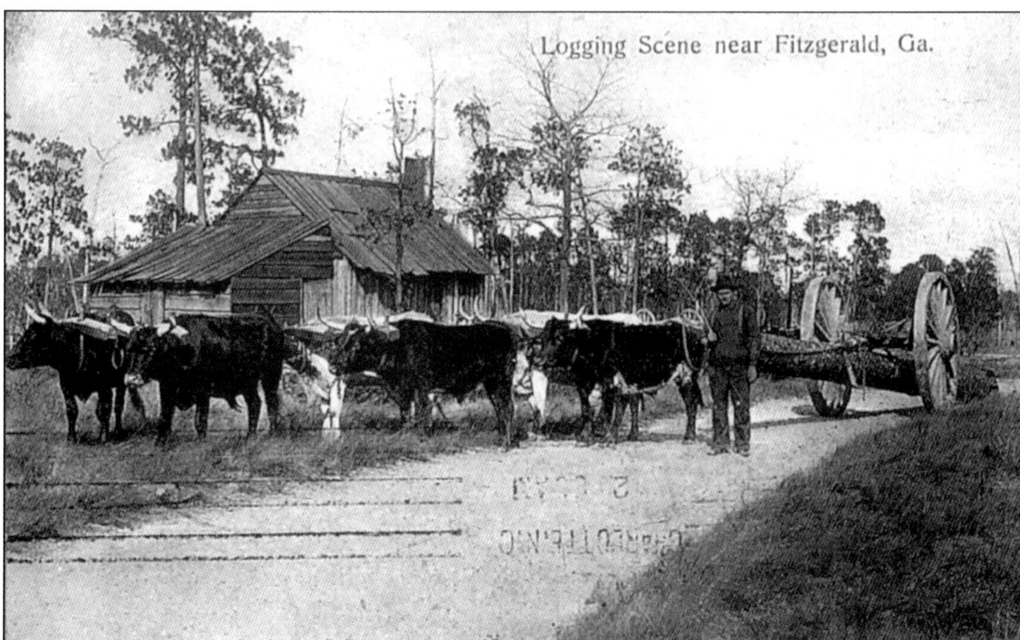

LOGGING SCENE NEAR FITZGERALD, C. 1895. Oxen were used in pairs or yolks. An oxbow was placed on the necks of a pair with an oak neck opening, then the pairs were placed in line to pull the load. This postcard shows three yolks, or six oxen.

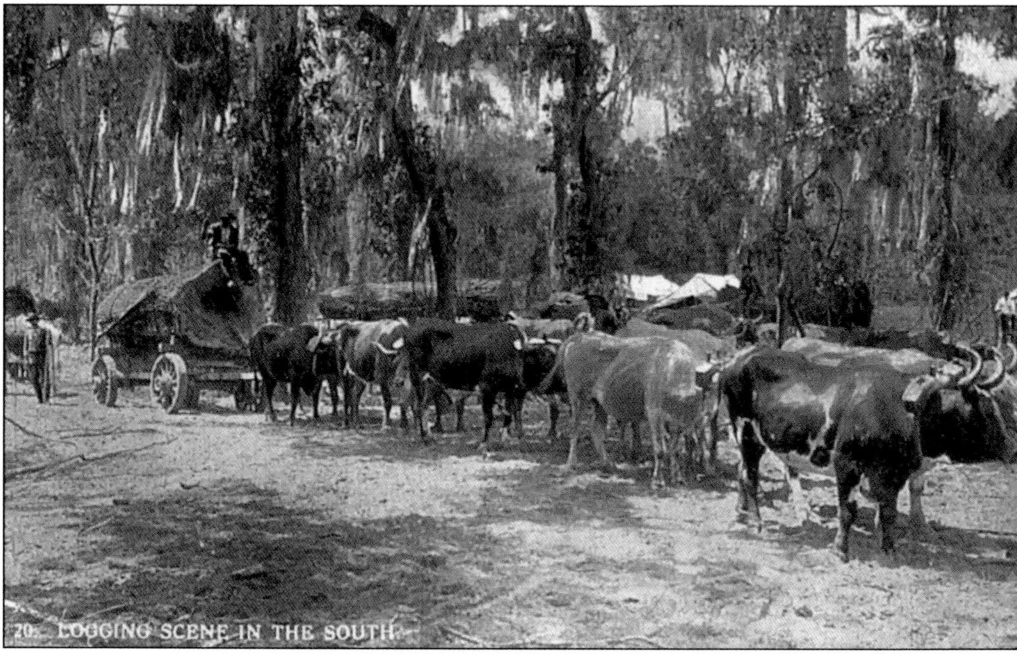

LOGGING SCENE IN THE SOUTH, *c.* 1900. Ten oxen pull what appears to be a butt cut of virgin longleaf pine or cypress log.

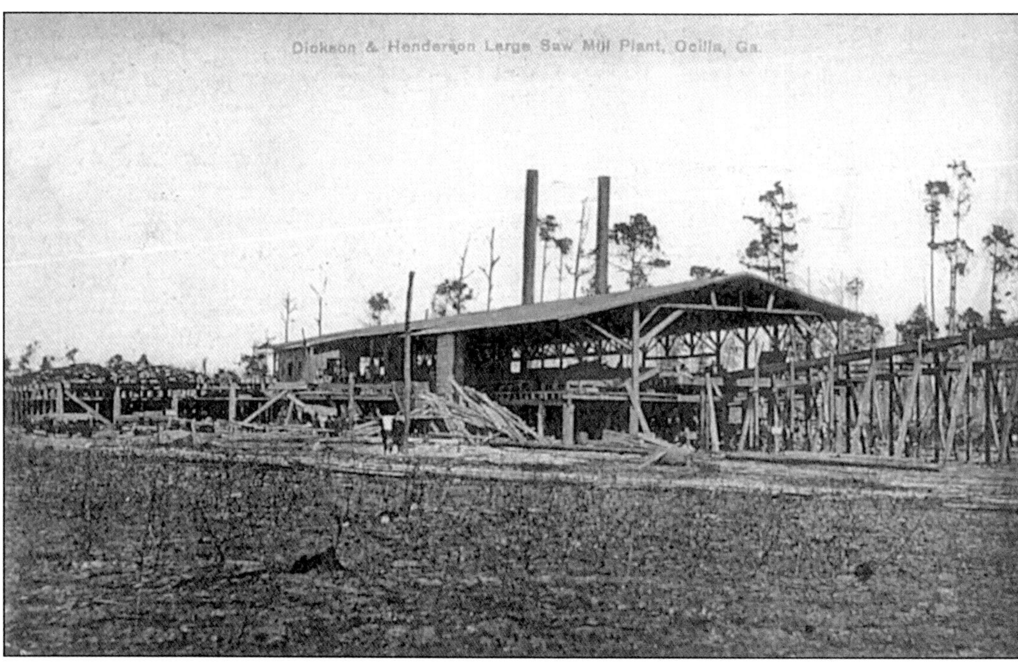

DICKSON AND HENDERSON LARGE SAWMILL PLANT, OCILLA. This card was published by the Ocilla Pharmacy and printed in Germany *c.* 1910.

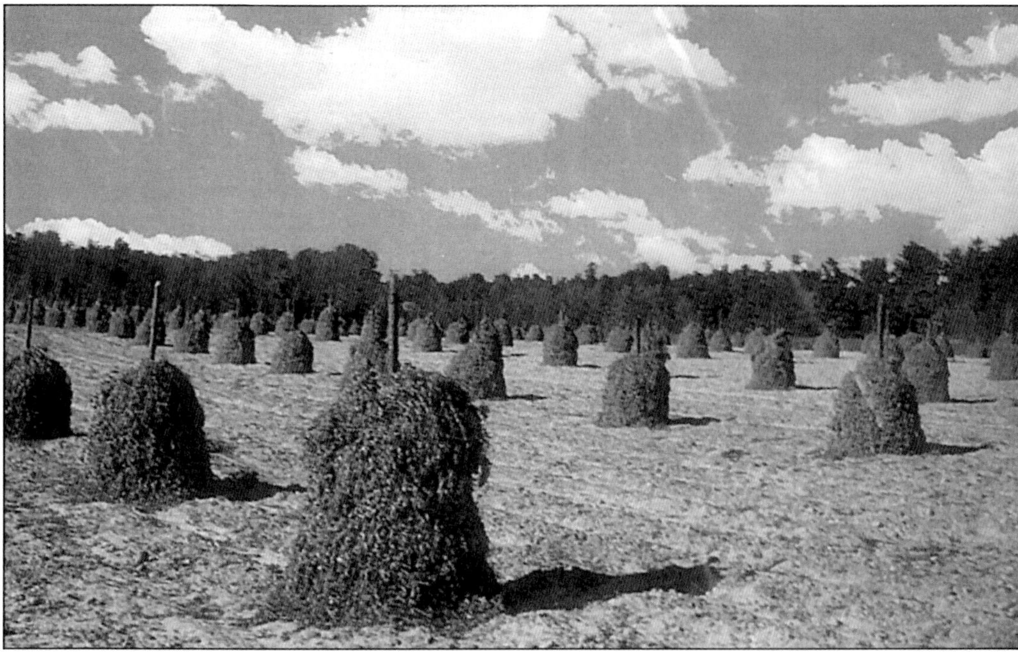

South Georgia Peanut Crop. A familiar scene in Georgia until the late 1950s, the peanut crop was dug, windrowed, and stacked on poles to dry. According to the weather they were "air" dried for about three weeks then dragged by mule or tractor to a peanut picker, which separated the peanuts from the vines.

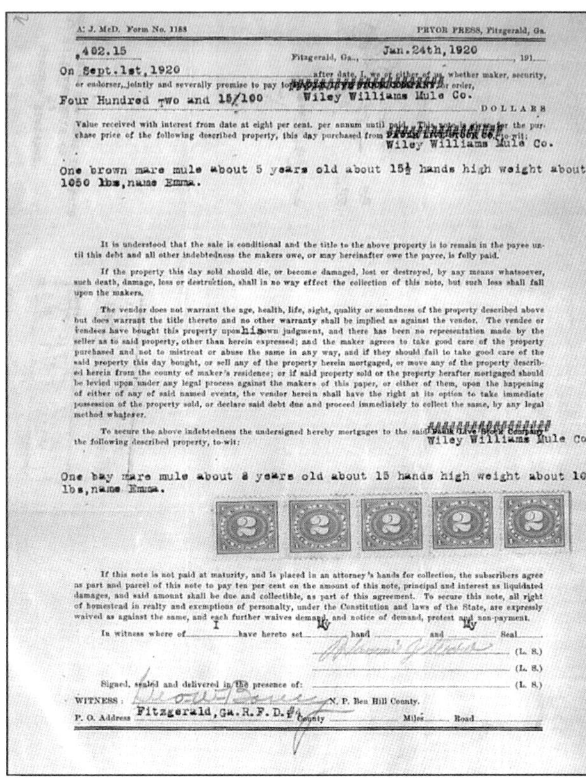

A. J. McD. Form No. 1188 PRYOR PRESS, Fitzgerald, Ga.

$492.15 Fitzgerald, Ga., Jan.24th,1920

On Sept.1st,1920 after date, I, we or either of us, whether maker, security, or endorser, jointly and severally promise to pay to Wiley Williams Mule Co. or order,

Four Hundred Two and 15/100 DOLLARS

Value received with interest from date at eight per cent. per annum until paid. This note is given for the purchase price of the following described property, this day purchased from Wiley Williams Mule Co. to-wit:

One brown mare mule about 5 years old about 15½ hands high weight about 1050 lbs, name Emma.

It is understood that the sale is conditional and the title to the above property is to remain in the payee until this debt and all other indebtedness the makers owe, or may hereinafter owe the payee, is fully paid.

If the property this day sold should die, or become damaged, lost or destroyed, by any means whatsoever, such death, damage, loss or destruction, shall in no way effect the collection of this note, but such loss shall fall upon the makers.

The vendor does not warrant the age, health, life, sight, quality or soundness of the property described above but does warrant the title thereto and no other warranty shall be implied as against the vendor. The vendee or vendees have bought this property upon his own judgment, and there has been no representation made by the seller as to said property, other than herein expressed; and the maker agrees to take good care of the property purchased and not to mistreat or abuse the same in any way, and if they should fail to take good care of the said property this day bought, or sell any of the property herein mortgaged, or move any of the property described herein from the county of maker's residence; or if said property sold or the property herafter mortgaged should be levied upon under any legal process against the makers of this paper, or either of them, upon the happening of either of any of said named events, the vendor herein shall have the right at its option to take immediate possession of the property sold, or declare said debt due and proceed immediately to collect the same, by any legal method whatever.

To secure the above indebtedness the undersigned hereby mortgages to the said Wiley Williams Mule Co. the following described property, to-wit:

One bay mare mule about 8 years old about 15 hands high weight about 100[illegible] lbs, name Emma.

If this note is not paid at maturity, and is placed in an attorney's hands for collection, the subscribers agree as part and parcel of this note to pay ten per cent on the amount of this note, principal and interest as liquidated damages, and said amount shall be due and collectible, as part of this agreement. To secure this note, all right of homestead in realty and exemptions of personalty, under the Constitution and laws of the State, are expressly waived as against the same, and each further waives demand, and notice of demand, protest and non-payment.

In witness where of I have hereto set My hand and My Seal.

[illegible] (L. S.)

(L. S.)

Signed, sealed and delivered in the presence of: (L. S.)

WITNESS: [illegible] N. P. Ben Hill County.

P. O. Address Fitzgerald, Ga. R. F. D. #4 County Miles Road

A Mule Note. Fitzgerald had several mule barns through the 1940s until the mule was replaced by the tractor. Wiley Williams and George Boney were prominent mule dealers. The mule here was described as "one bay mare mule about 8 years old about 15 hands high, weight about 1,000 pounds, name Emma."

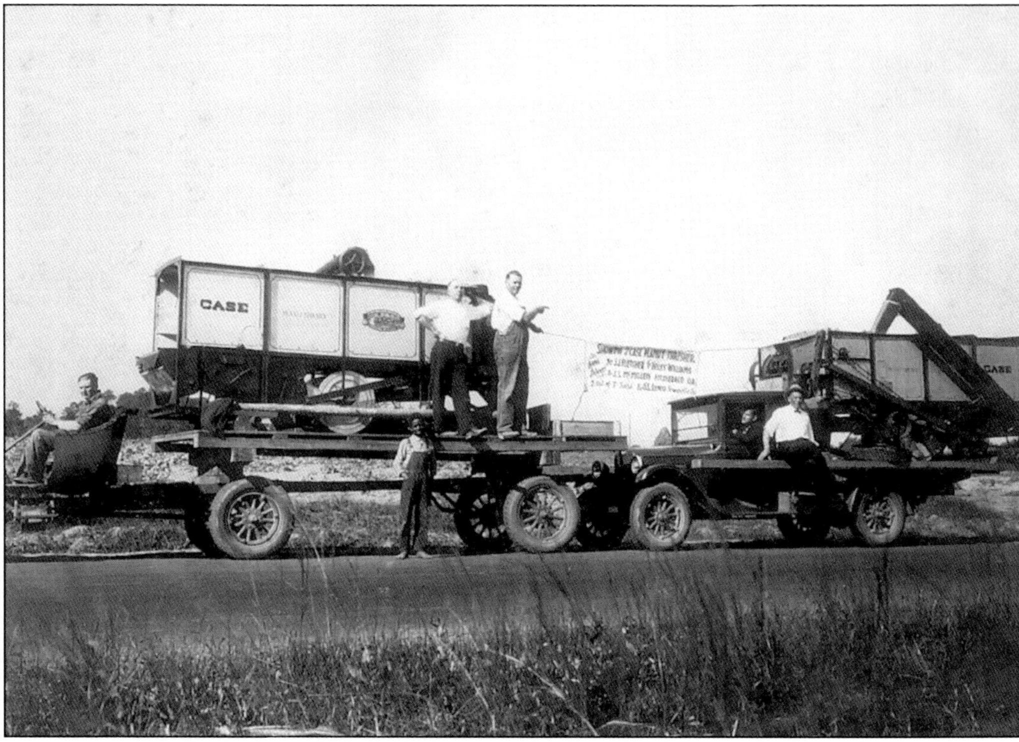

CASE PEANUT THRESHERS. The threshers are being delivered by J.J. Fletcher, Wiley Williams, and J.L. McMillen of Fitzgerald. These threshers were run by belt pulleys on tractors but still had to be fed by hand-held pitchforks. (Courtesy of Louis Harper.)

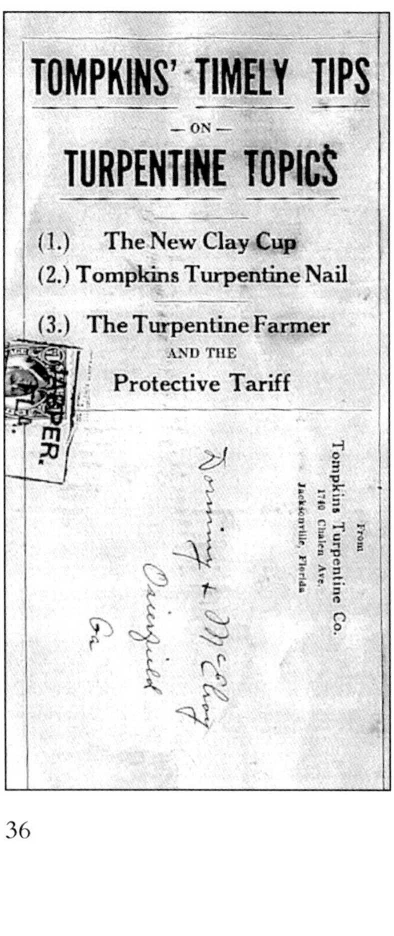

TOMPKINS' TIMELY TIPS

— ON —

TURPENTINE TOPICS

(1.) The New Clay Cup
(2.) Tompkins Turpentine Nail
(3.) The Turpentine Farmer
AND THE
Protective Tariff

From
Tompkins Turpentine Co.
Jacksonville, Florida

Dorminy & McElroy
Osierfield
Ga

TURPENTINE ADVERTISEMENT. This advertisement, touting turpentine cups and hardware, was sent to Dorminy and McElroy at Osierfield *c.* 1928.

Three

Railroads and Transportation

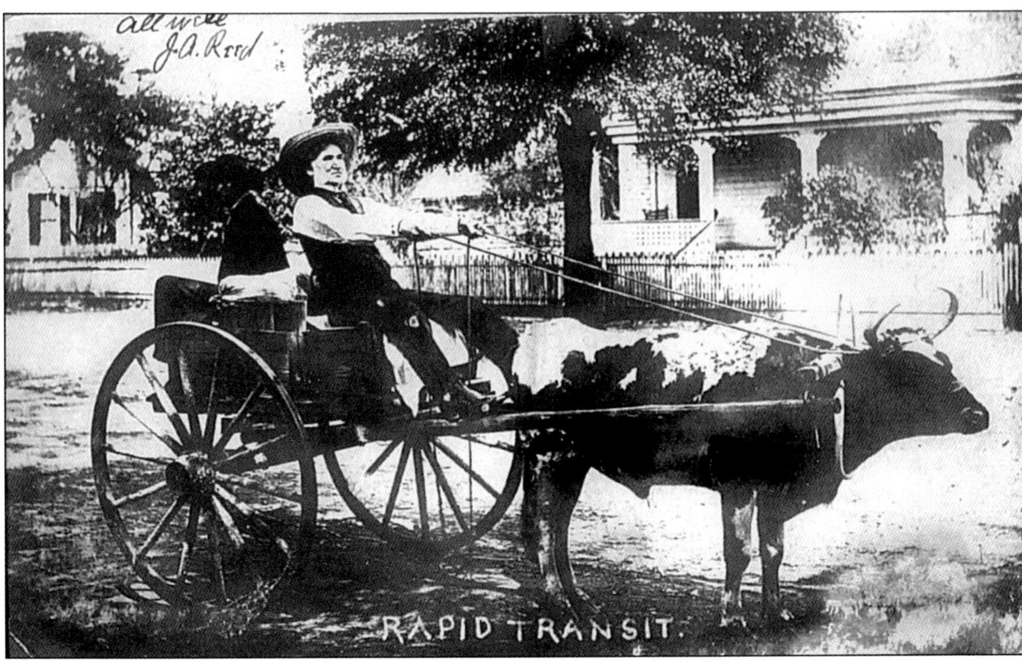

Rapid Transit. This spoof on taxi service was an early Fitzgerald card sold by Adams Candy Kitchen *c.* 1900.

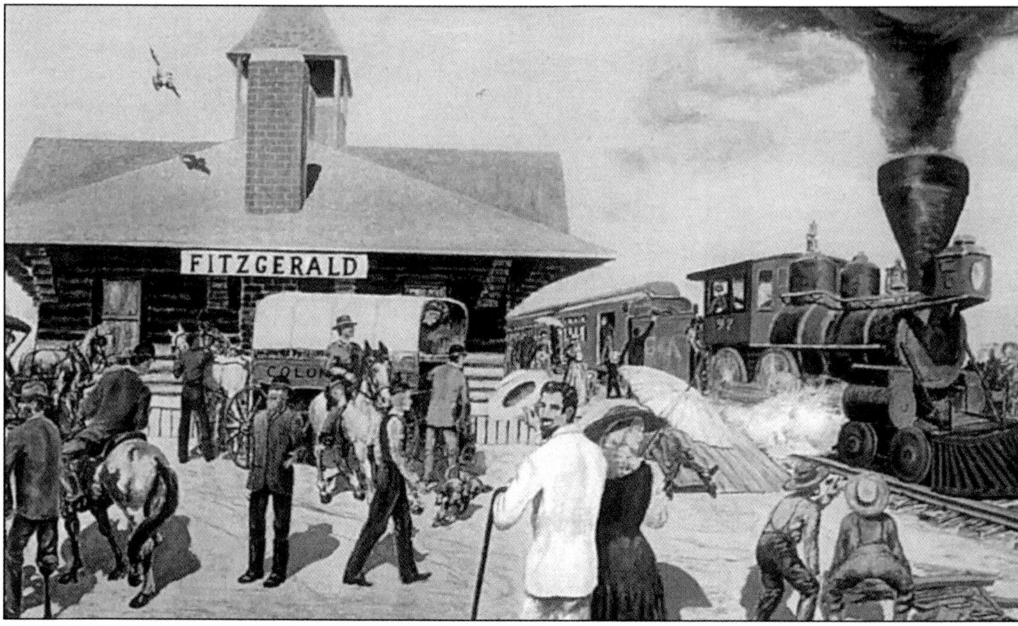

First Train Arrives in Fitzgerald, 1896. Local artist David Jay created this image of the first train to arrive in Fitzgerald, pulled by a Georgia and Alabama Railroad engine from Abbeville and points north. The original painting hangs today in the Blue and Gray Museum in Fitzgerald.

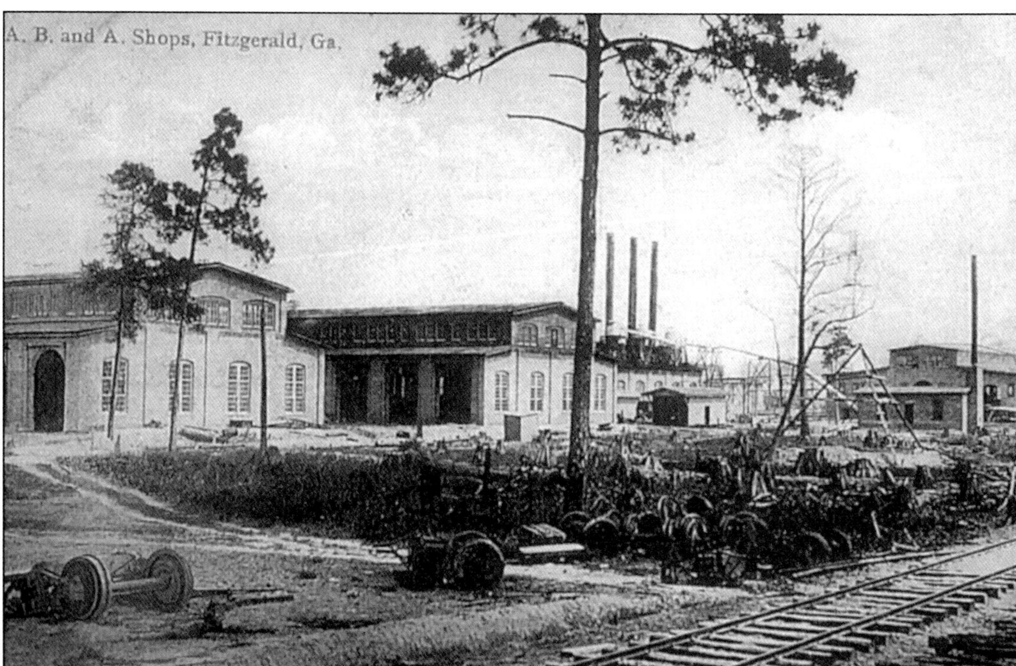

Atlanta, Birmingham, and Atlantic (A. B. & A.) Shops at Fitzgerald. The shops were located about two miles west of Fitzgerald at "Westwood."

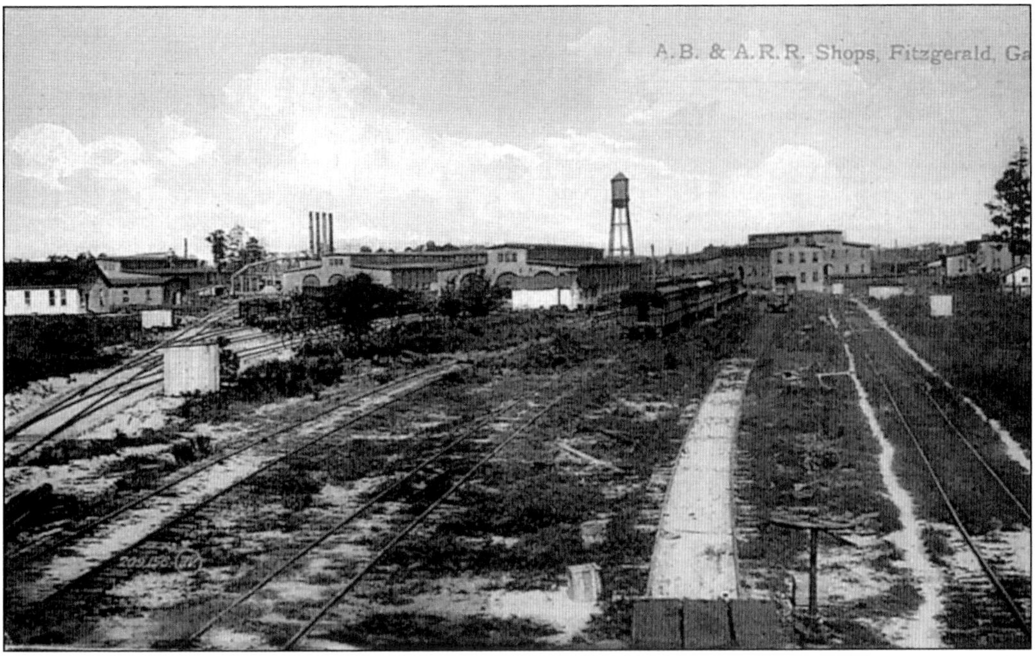

Westwood, Early 1900s. The A. B. & A. Railroad shops were located here in Fitzgerald. Several of these buildings still stand in 2001. The shops were closed for the most part in the 1950s and moved to Waycross, Georgia.

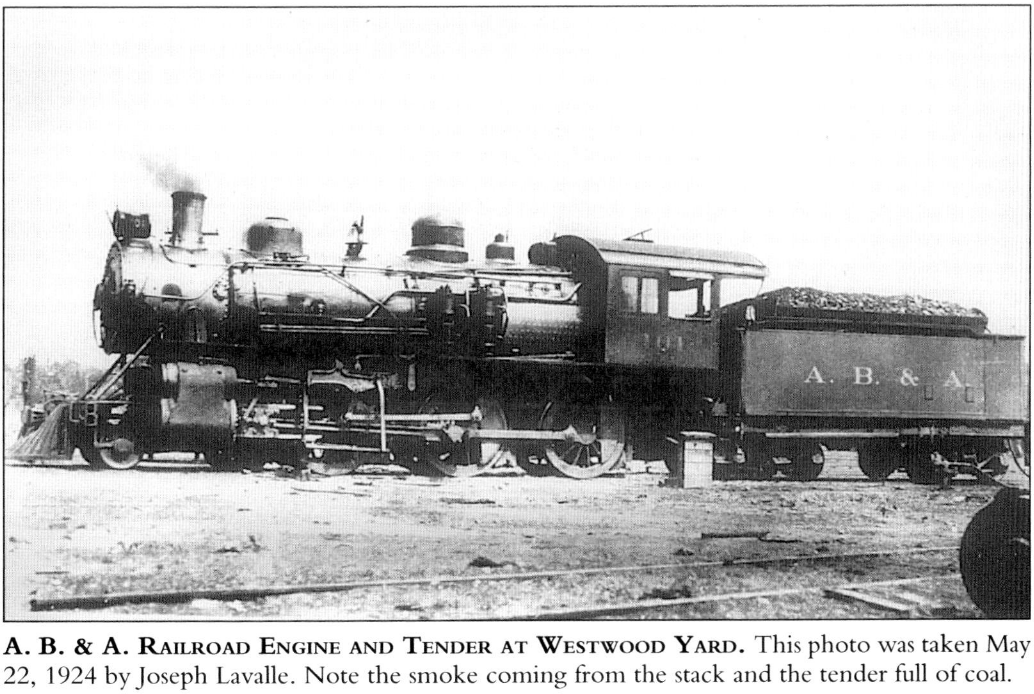

A. B. & A. Railroad Engine and Tender at Westwood Yard. This photo was taken May 22, 1924 by Joseph Lavalle. Note the smoke coming from the stack and the tender full of coal.

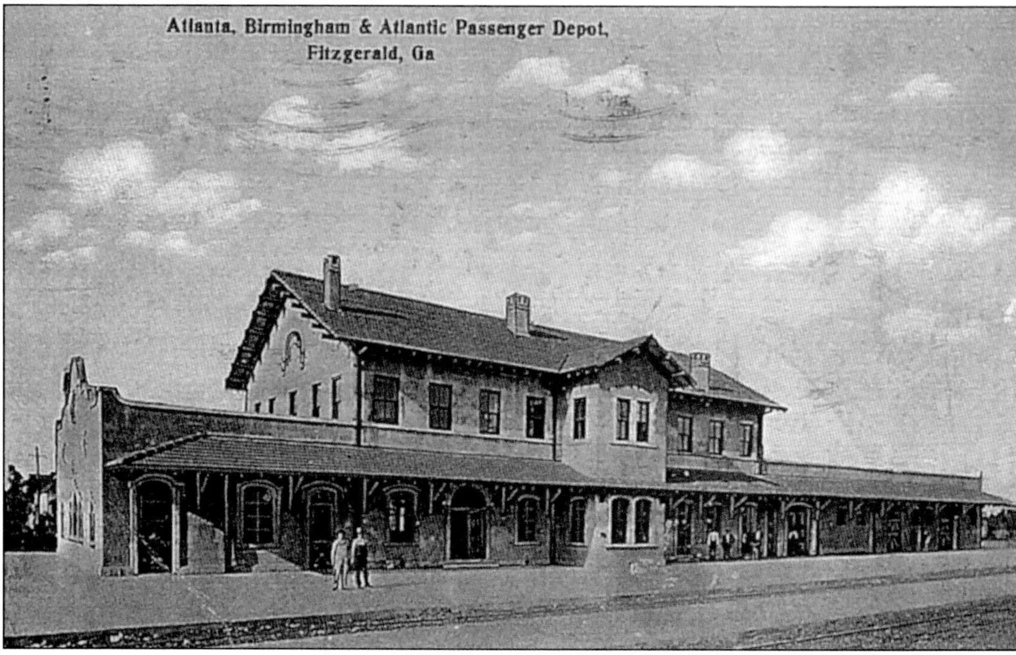

A. B. & A. Passenger Depot, Fitzgerald. The depot is pictured in the early 1900s. (Courtesy of Louis Harper.)

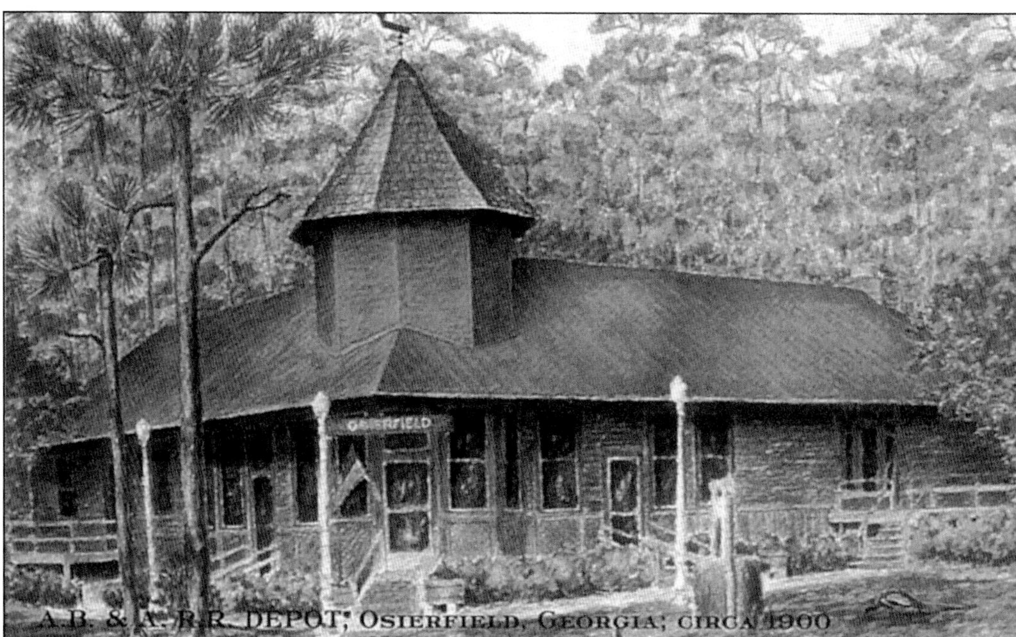

A. B. & A. Depot, Osierfield, Early 1900s. This original painting by R.A. Parks was made into a postcard.

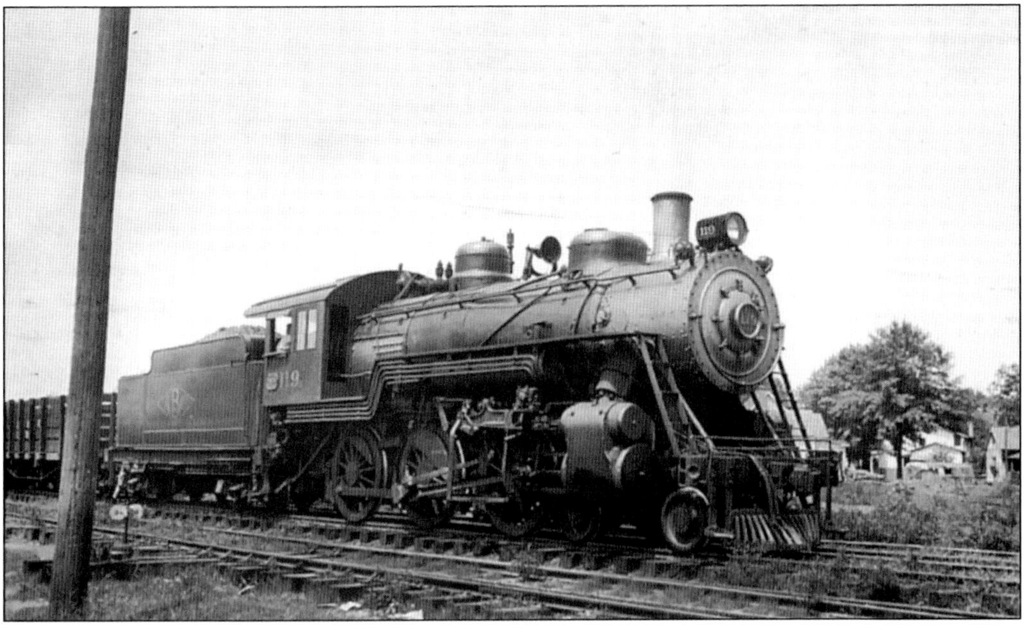

ATLANTA, BIRMINGHAM, & COAST (FORMERLY A. B. & A.) RAILROAD. Engine No. 119 is seen at Waycross, Georgia in the 1920s.

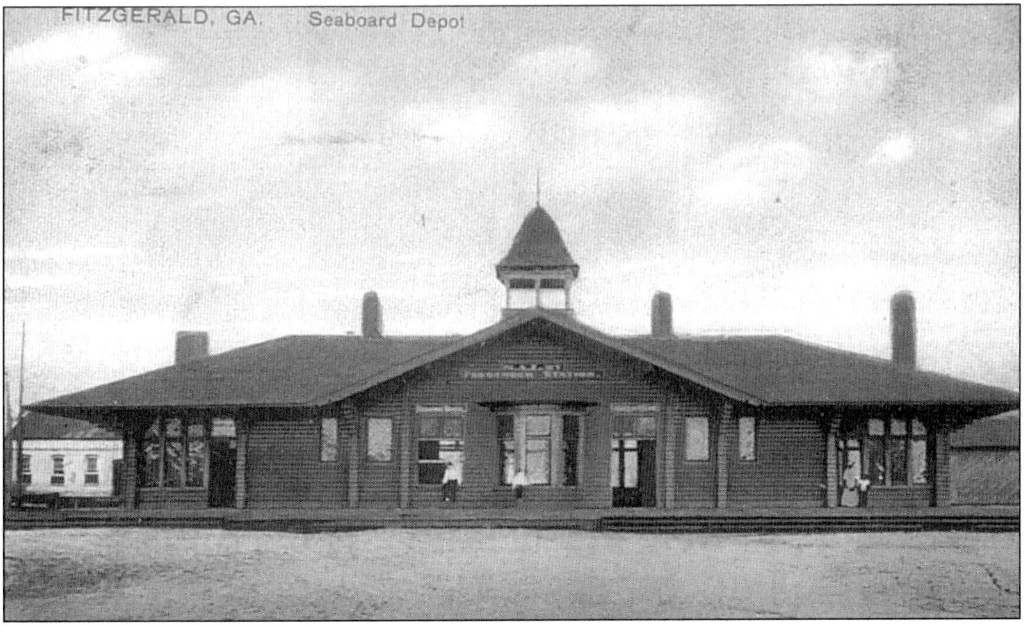

SEABOARD DEPOT, FITZGERALD. This beautiful depot was torn down in the late 1930s ostensibly to straighten a curve in U.S. 319. The curve is still there in 2001. The Georgia and Alabama Railroad from Abbeville was the first railroad to reach Fitzgerald in 1896. It later had a dead-end spur to Ocilla, Georgia, nine miles south.

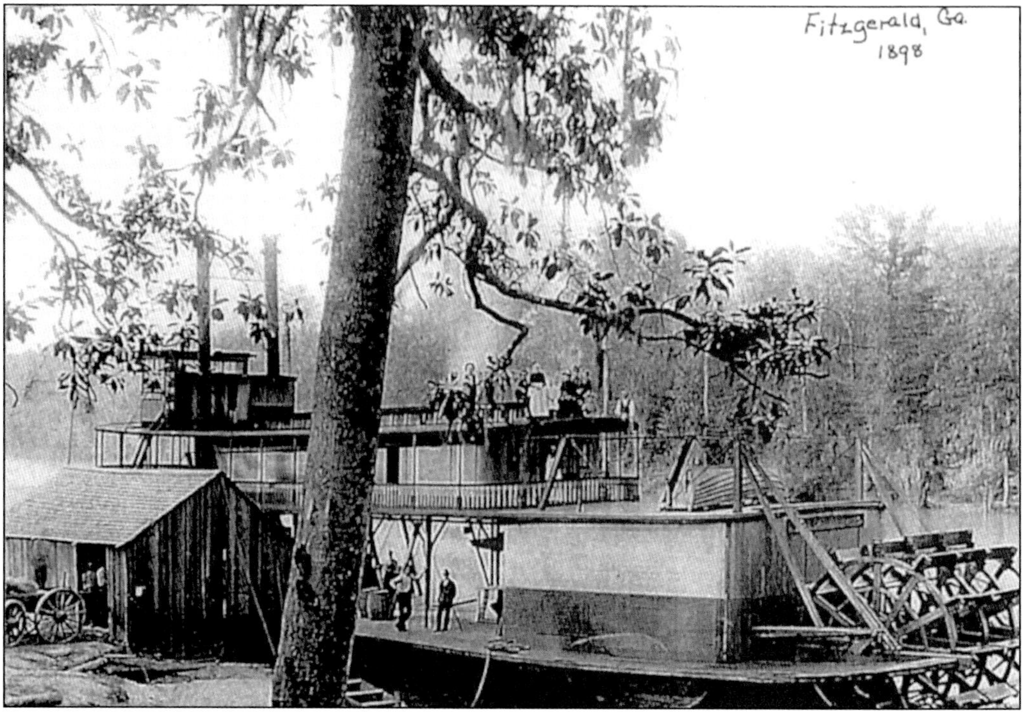

STEAMBOAT AT CAMP BROOKLYN. This photograph was made on the Ocmulgee River in 1898. (Courtesy of Louis Harper.)

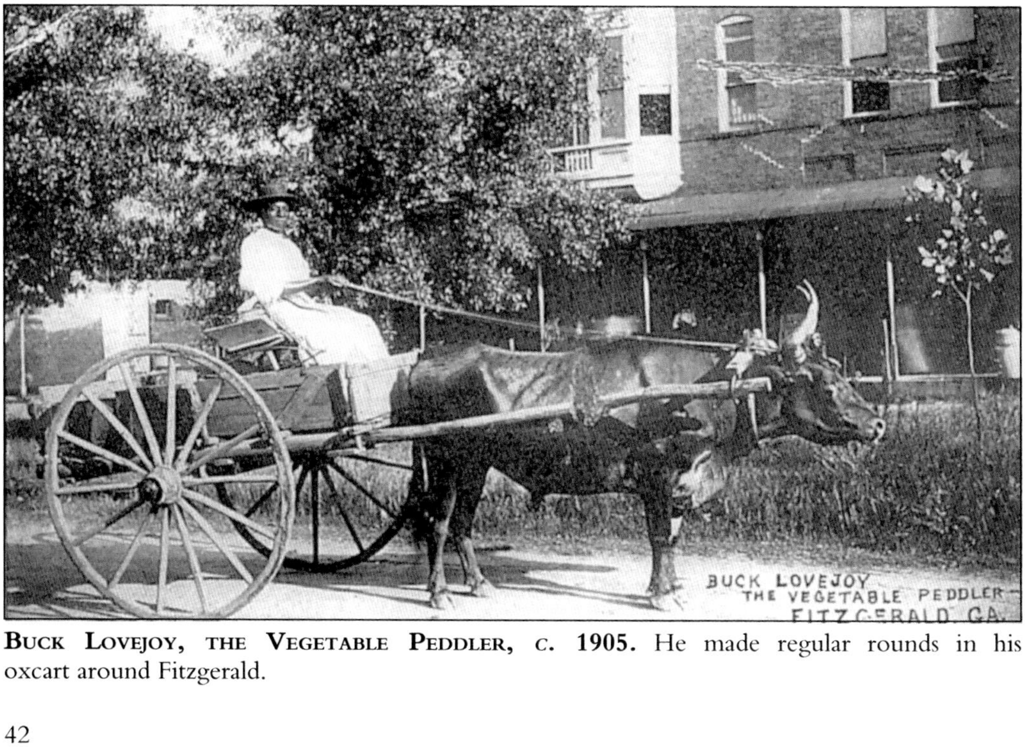

BUCK LOVEJOY, THE VEGETABLE PEDDLER, *c.* 1905. He made regular rounds in his oxcart around Fitzgerald.

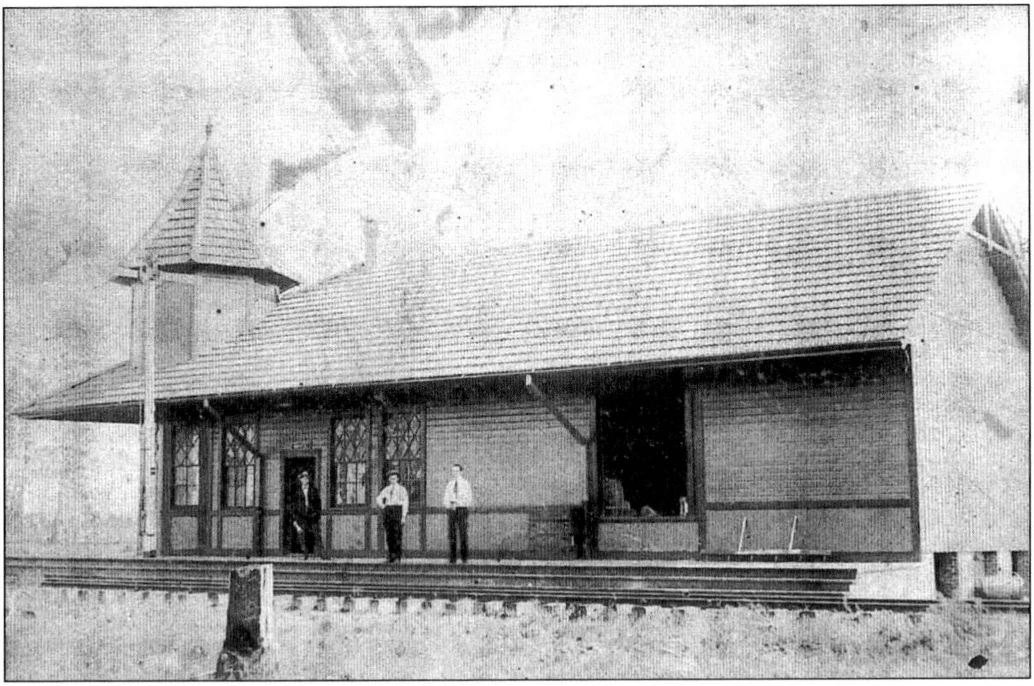

A. B. & A. Depot at Osierfield. The ticket collector stands with gentlemen in front of the depot and freight is stored in the open room in this early 1900s view.

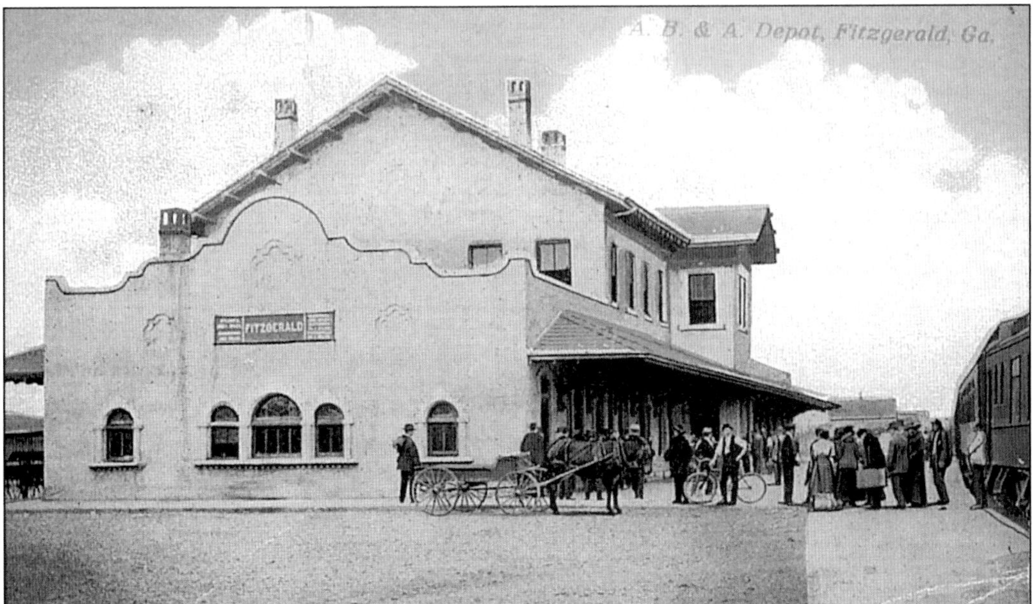

A. B. & A. Depot, Fitzgerald. Built about 1909 in Spanish architectural style, the depot had a red Ludowici clay tile roof cast along the Altamaha River by Dixie Tile Company. The building is currently used as Fitzgerald municipal offices, with the Blue and Gray Museum housed in the west end. In 1933 the author stood on Johnston Street holding his father's hand when Franklin D. Roosevelt made a whistle stop here.

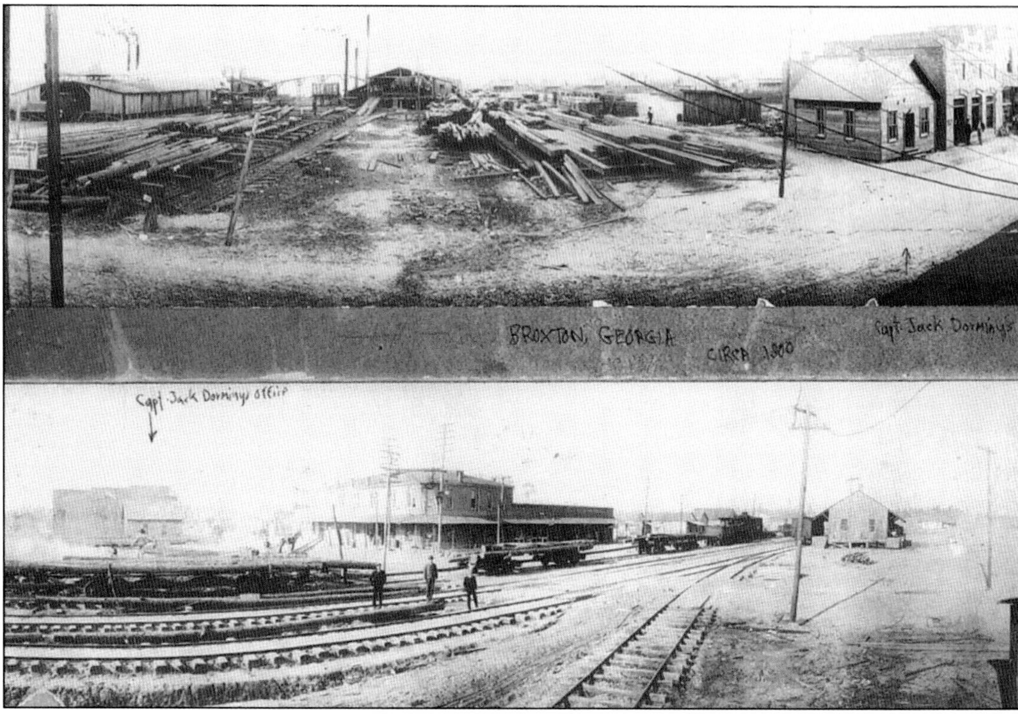

Dorminy Sawmill, Broxton. The top view shows the sawmill and the bottom view shows the railroad tracks that ran adjacent to the mill. In both views an arrow points to Capt. Jack Dorminy's office.

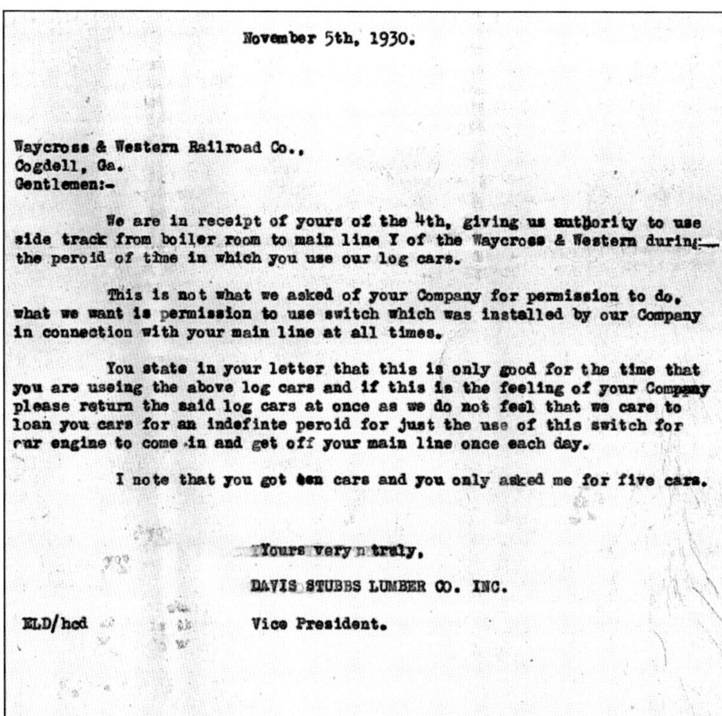

November 5th, 1930.

Waycross & Western Railroad Co.,
Cogdell, Ga.
Gentlemen:-

We are in receipt of yours of the 4th, giving us authority to use side track from boiler room to main line Y of the Waycross & Western during the peroid of time in which you use our log cars.

This is not what we asked of your Company for permission to do, what we want is permission to use switch which was installed by our Company in connection with your main line at all times.

You state in your letter that this is only good for the time that you are useing the above log cars and if this is the feeling of your Company please return the said log cars at once as we do not feel that we care to loan you cars for an indefinte peroid for just the use of this switch for our engine to come in and get off your main line once each day.

I note that you got ten cars and you only asked me for five cars.

Yours very truly,

DAVIS STUBBS LUMBER CO. INC.

ELD/hcd Vice President.

Letter to Waycross and Western Railroad Company. This November 5, 1930 letter was sent from the Davis Stubbs Lumber Company addressing concerns about railroad use. Davis Stubbs Lumber Company had lent the railroad company log cars but asked that they be returned if the lumber company could not have full access to Waycross and Western's main line.

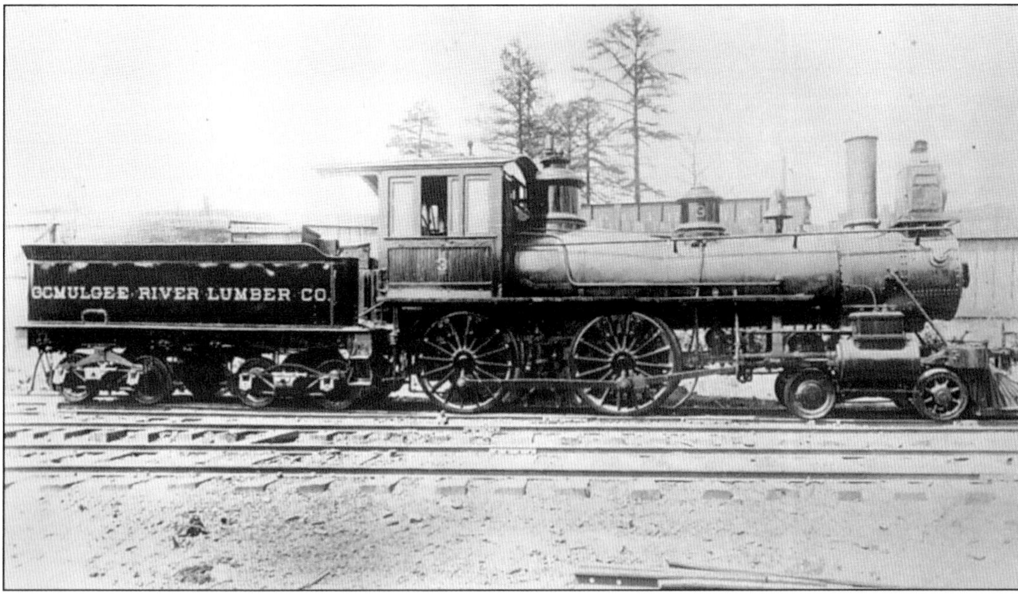

Ocmulgee River Lumber Company Engine #3. This engine was formerly Southern Iron and Equipment Company #497. (Courtesy of Don Hensley.)

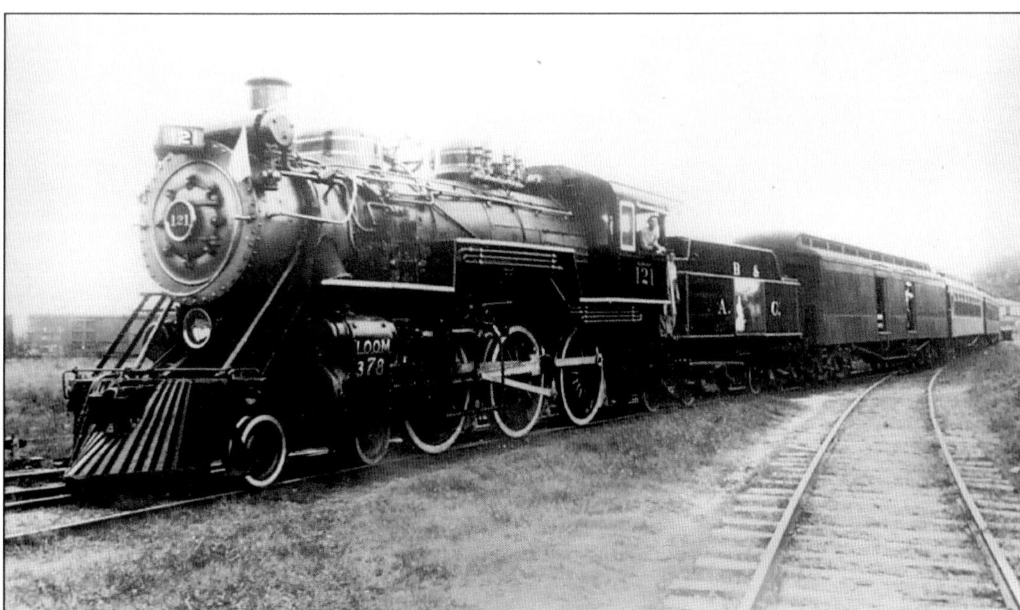

A. B. & A. Railroad Baggage Car and Passenger Train. Almost all makeups had a railroad post office where anyone could post a letter in a slot on the mail car. Nearly all U.S Post Office mail was transported by rail in the 1930s.

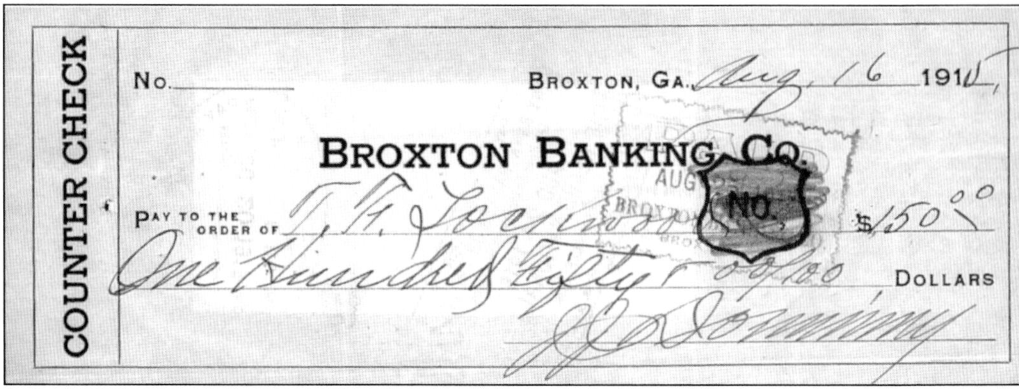

COUNTER CHECK

No.______ BROXTON, GA. Aug. 16 1915

BROXTON BANKING CO.

PAY TO THE ORDER OF T.H. Lockwood $150.00

One Hundred Fifty & 00/100 DOLLARS

J.J. Dorminy

Counter Check, Broxton Banking Company. This check was tendered to T.H. Lockwood by J.J. Dorminy *c.* 1915.

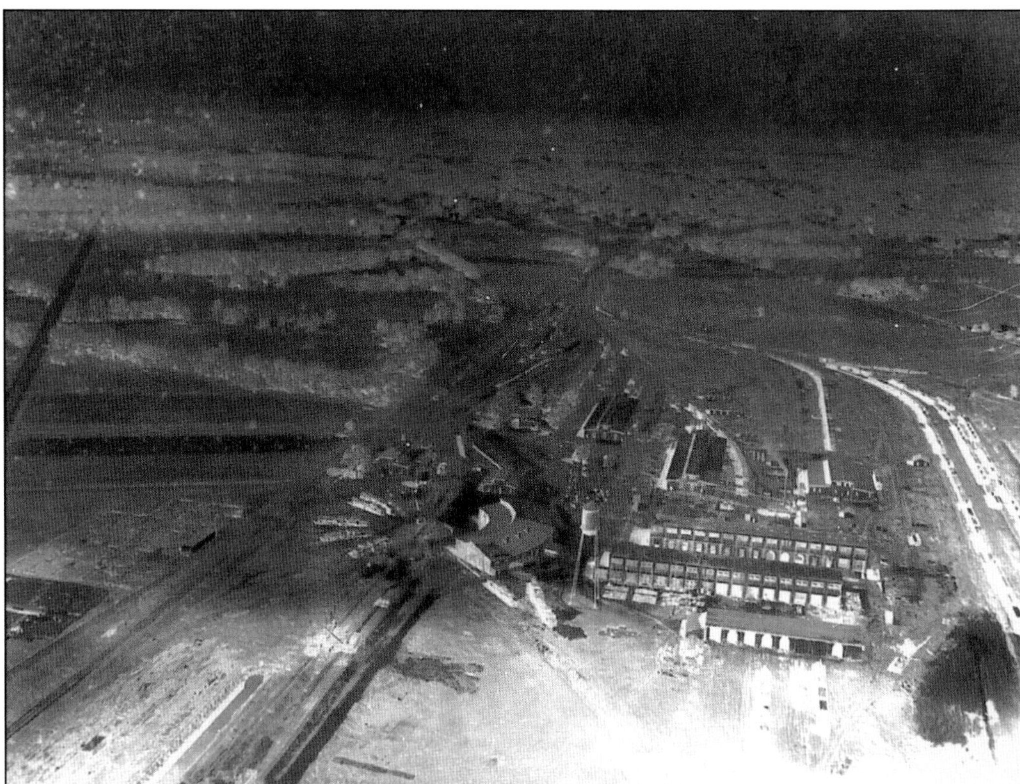

Westwood Shop Complex, Fitzgerald. An aerial view shows the complex c. late 1940s. Around the tracks can be seen several steam engines and tenders waiting their turns to go into the roundhouse for repairs. (Courtesy of Jack Paulk.)

Four

Capture of Jefferson Davis

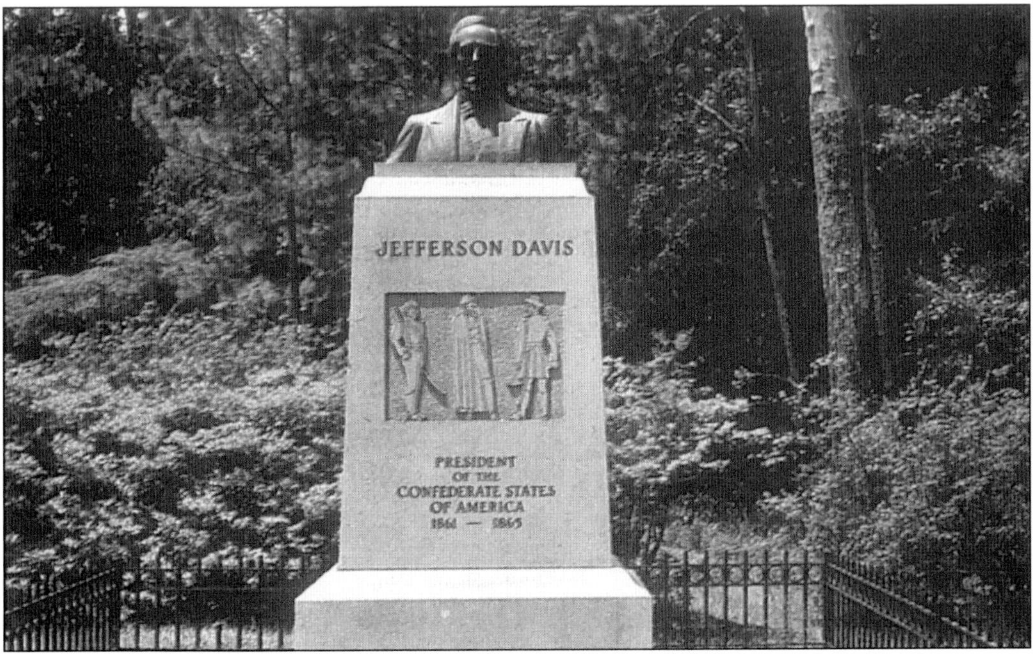

Monument at Jefferson Davis Park. This monument is located at the Jefferson Davis State Park west of Fitzgerald in Irwinville, Georgia.

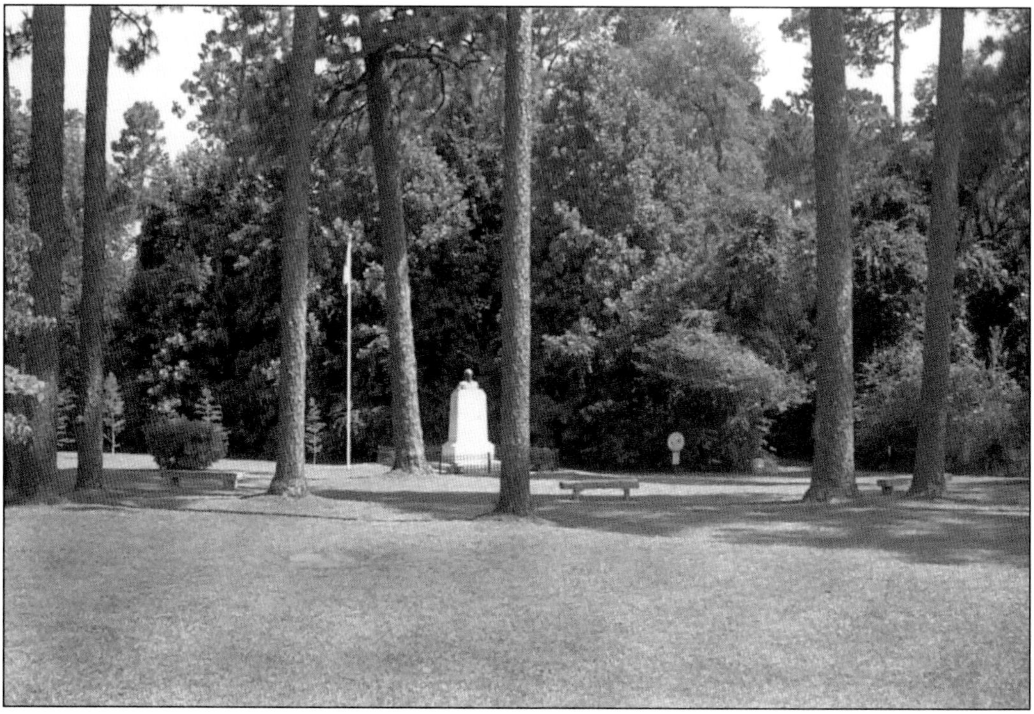

ANOTHER VIEW OF JEFFERSON DAVIS AT IRWINVILLE, GEORGIA. Judge J.B. Clements deeded the site to the state of Georgia. His father, R.W. Clements, vowed he would own the sacred spot as soon as he was financially able. When he purchased the land he said "no Yankee would ever own it."

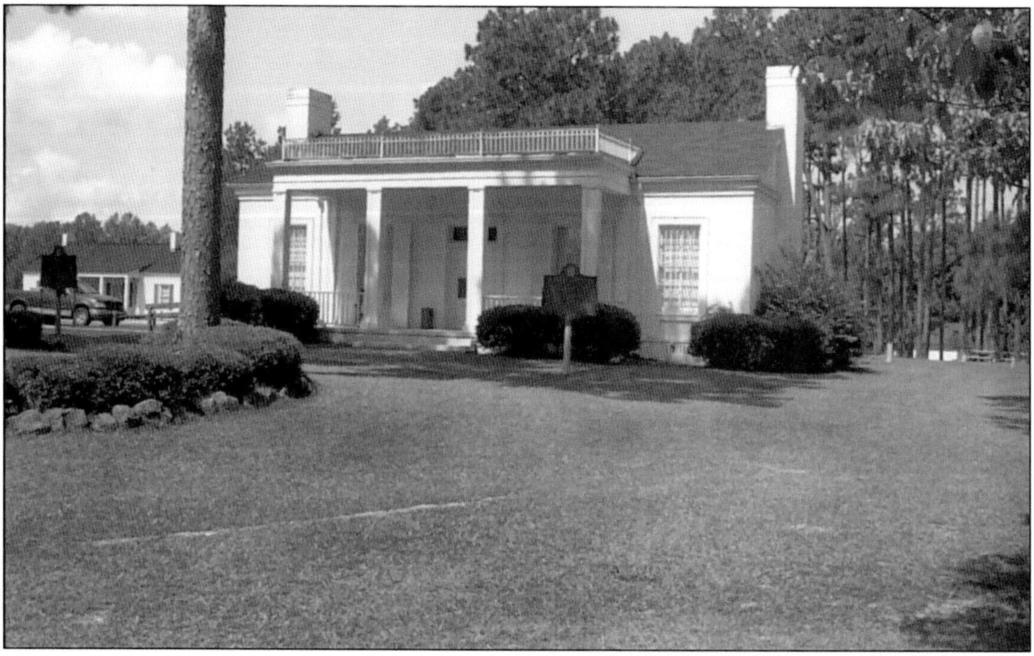

JEFFERSON DAVIS STATE PARK. The museum on the park grounds is pictured in 2001.

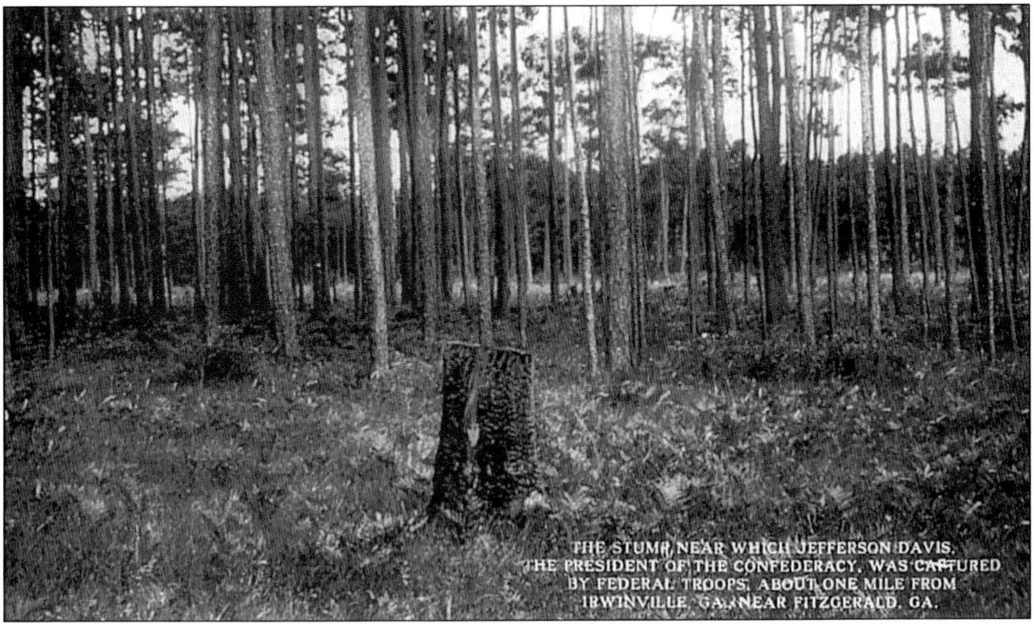

JEFFERSON DAVIS CAPTURE SITE. The stump is located near the site where Jefferson Davis was captured by Federal troops on May 10, 1865.

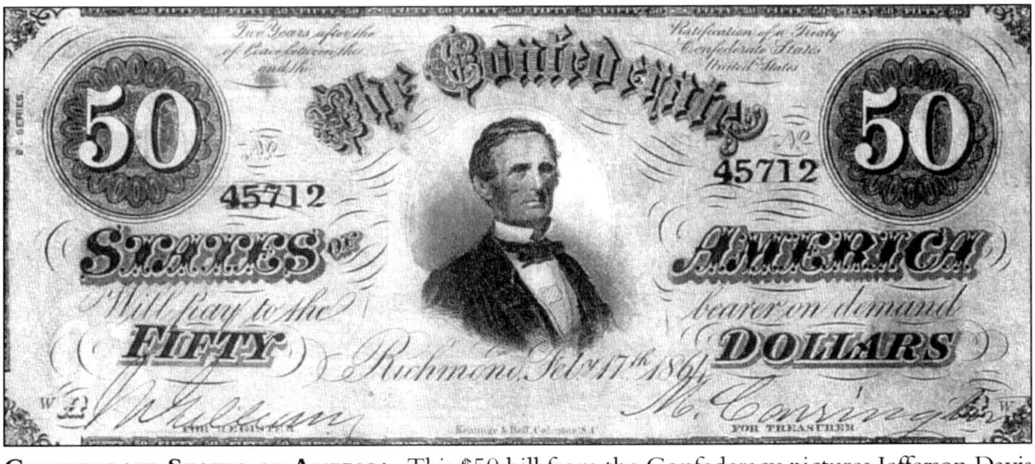

CONFEDERATE STATES OF AMERICA. This $50 bill from the Confederacy pictures Jefferson Davis and was made in Richmond, Virginia in 1864. Most CSA notes had printed on their faces the following: "Two years after ratification of a treaty of peace between the Confederate states and the United States . . . will pay to the bearer . . . ."

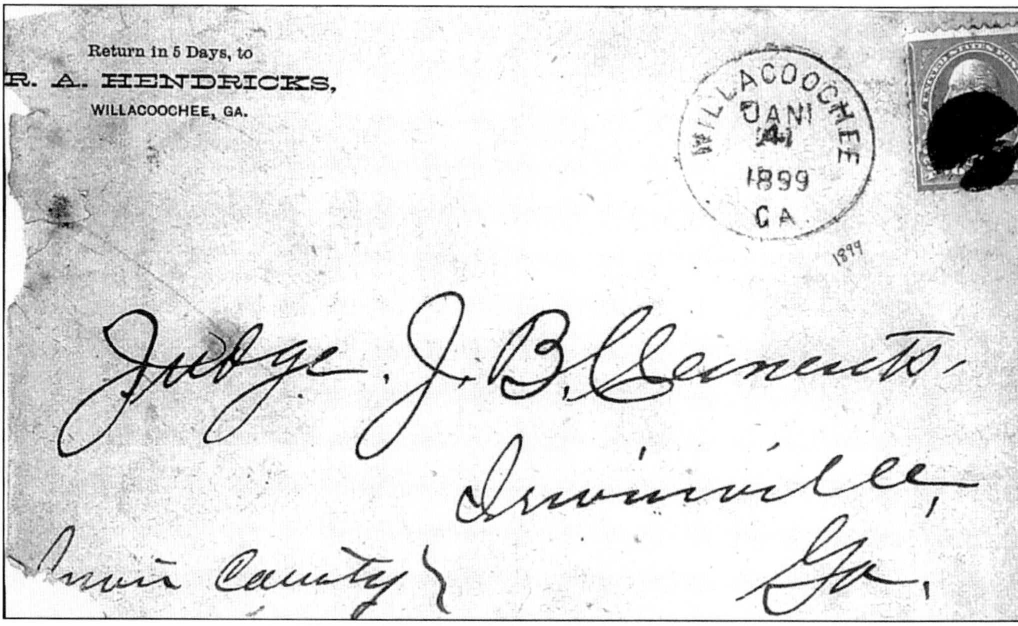

Judge J.B. Clements. Clements, the recipient of this letter postmarked in Willacoochee, Georgia, in January 1899, owned the land where Jefferson Davis was captured. It is rumored that Clements stated in his will that the hallowed ground was "never to be sold to a Yankee." Judge Clements is the author of *A History of Irwin County*.

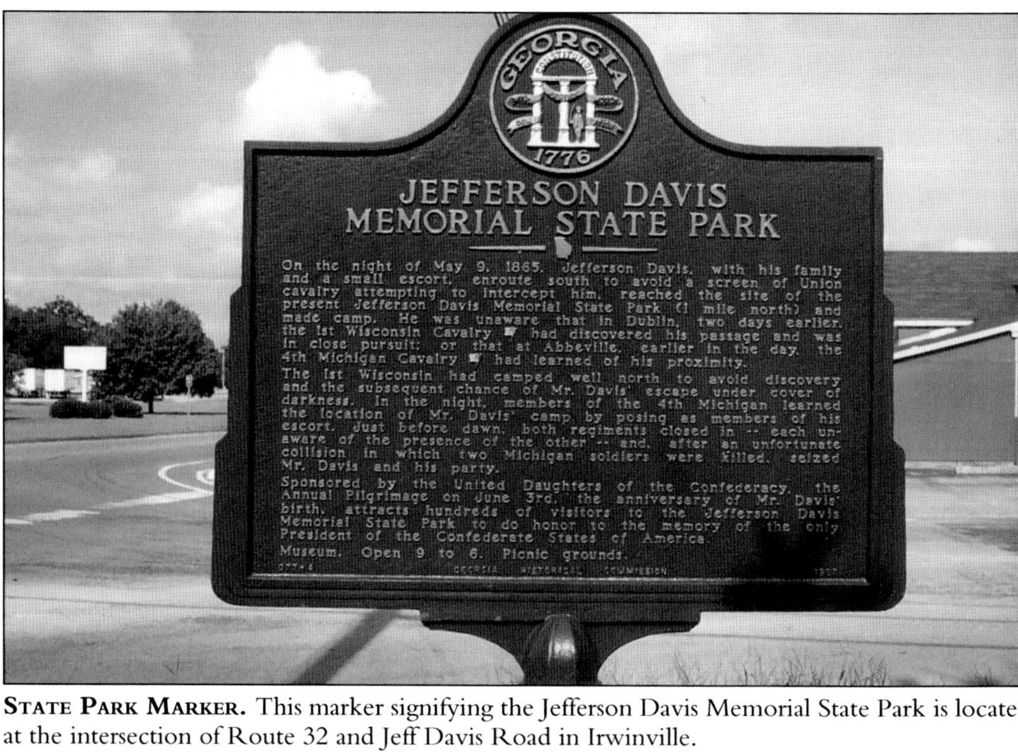

State Park Marker. This marker signifying the Jefferson Davis Memorial State Park is located at the intersection of Route 32 and Jeff Davis Road in Irwinville.

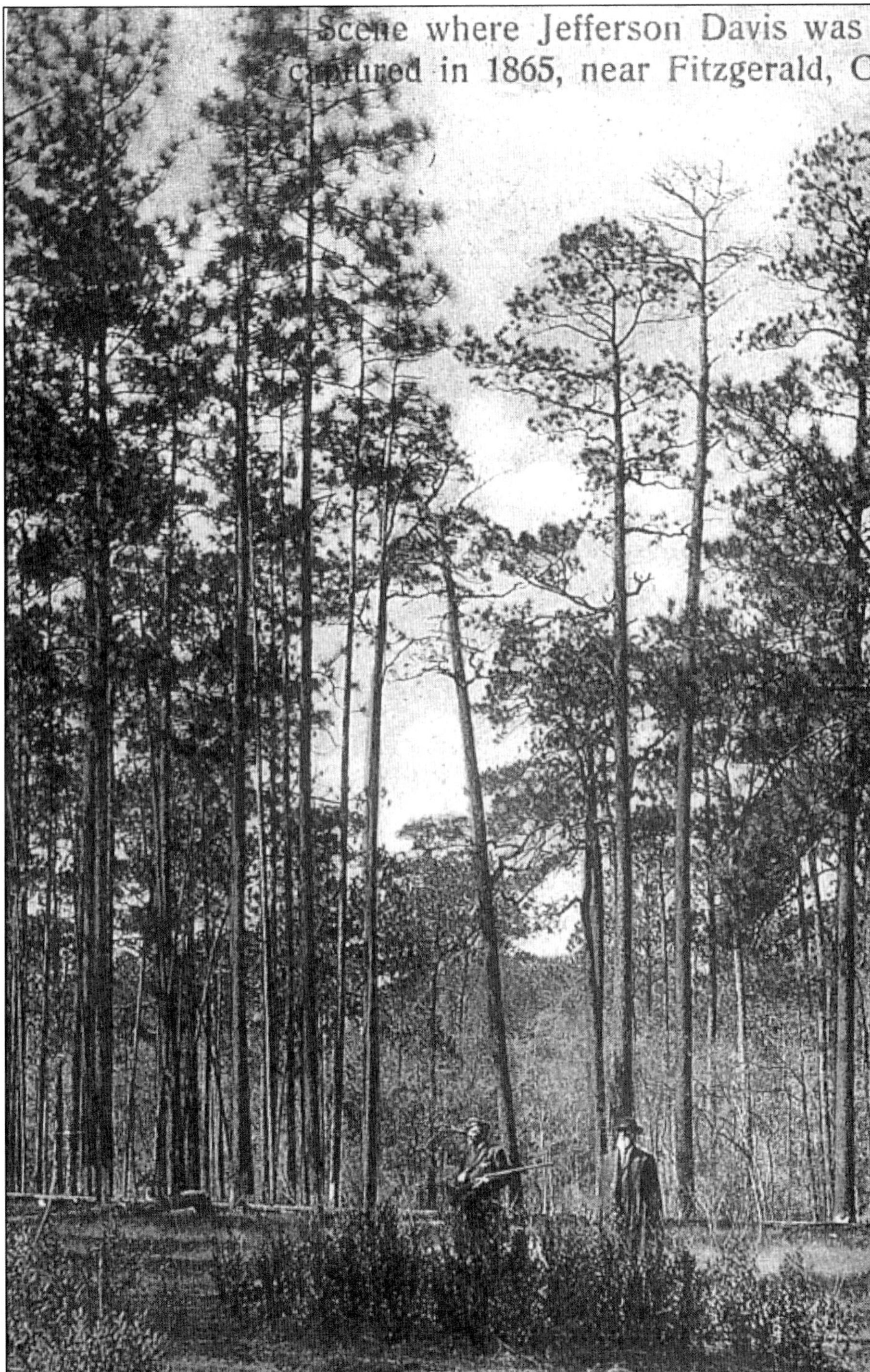

Scene of Jefferson Davis Capture. Paul Trouche of Charleston, South Carolina published this card depicting the scene where Davis was captured in 1865 near Fitzgerald. (Courtesy of Louis Harper.)

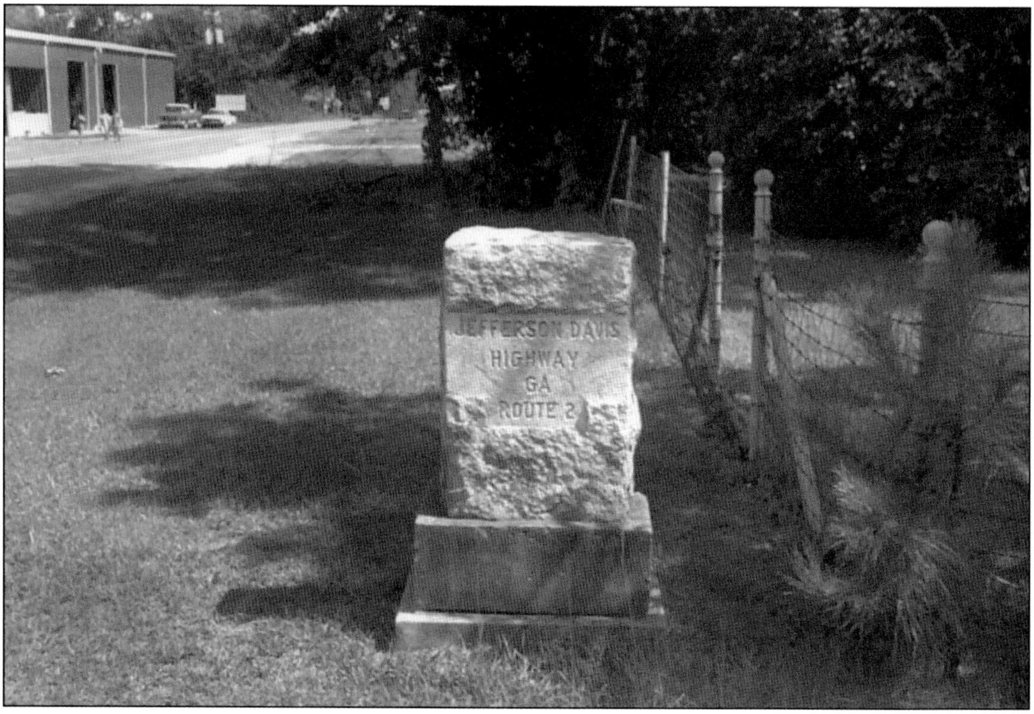

Jefferson Davis Highway. Another marker in Irwinville denotes the highway named in honor of the president of the Confederacy.

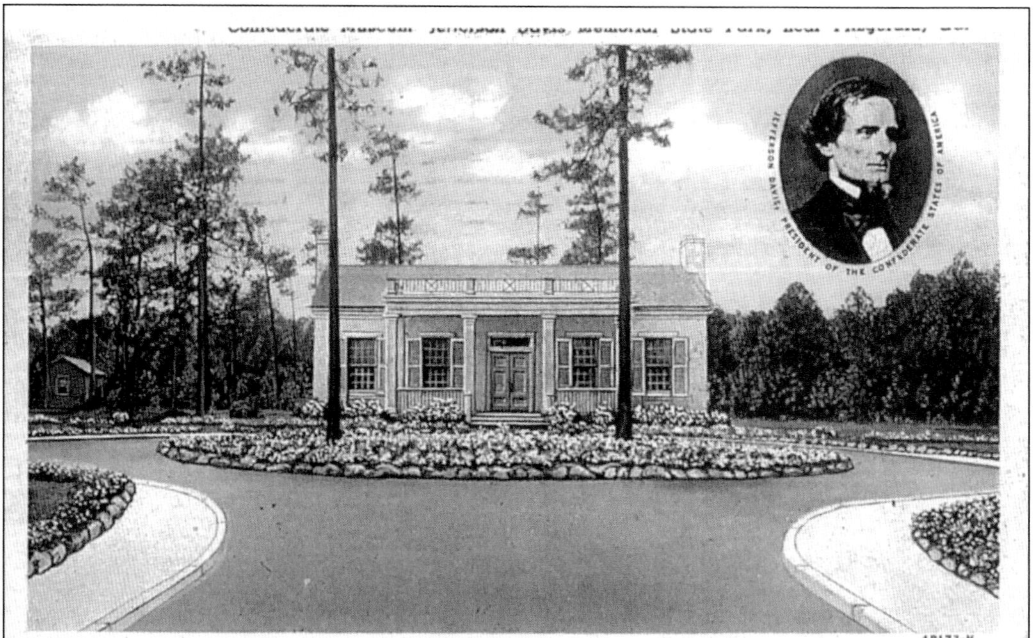

Confederate Museum. A postcard depicts the museum located in the Jefferson Davis State Park near Fitzgerald. The caption around the inset photograph reads "Jefferson Davis, President of the Confederate States of America."

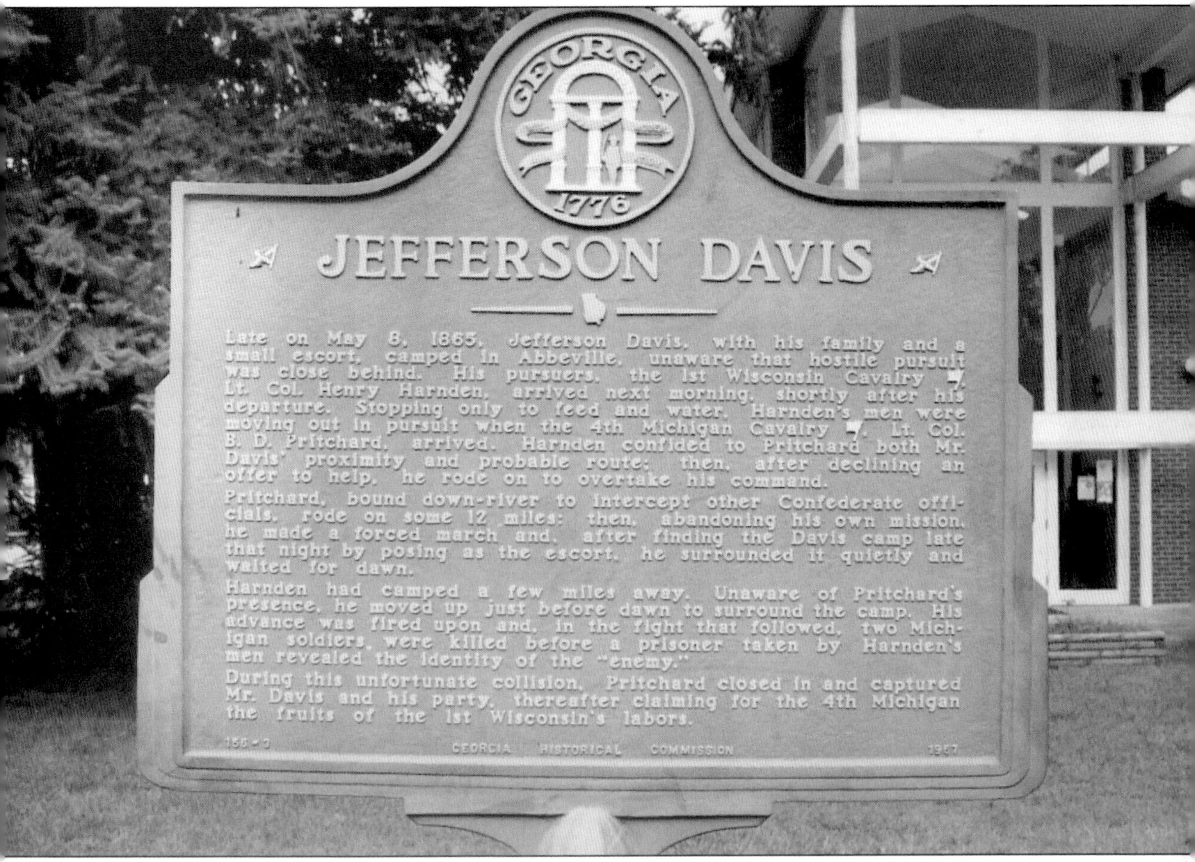

Abbeville Marker. Situated across U.S. 129 in Abbeville, Georgia from the town's courthouse, this historic marker recounts Jefferson Davis and his party spending the night here on May 8, 1865, the night before Davis was captured.

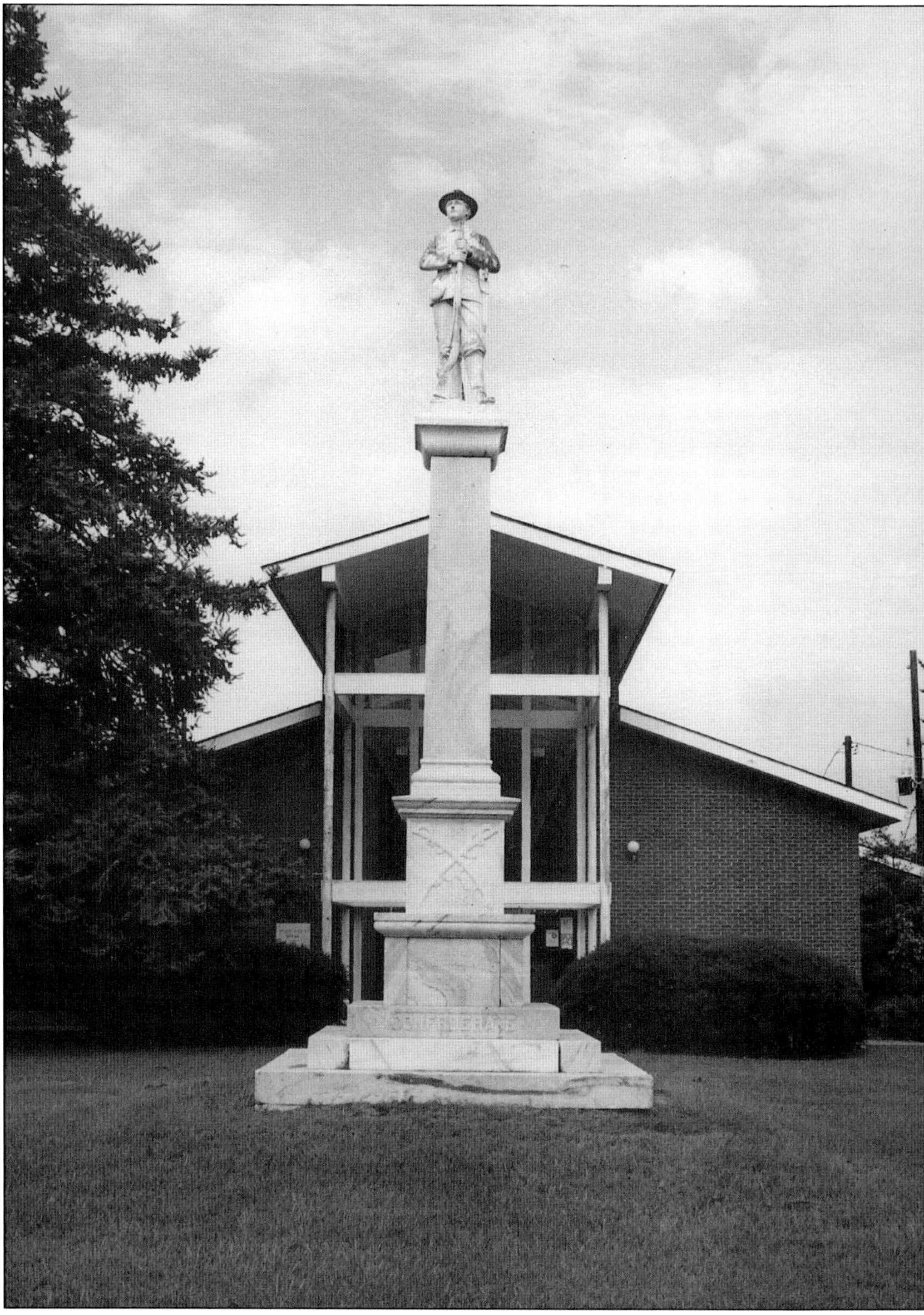

ABBEVILLE MONUMENT. Also located across from the Abbeville Courthouse on U.S. 129, this Confederate monument boasts an interesting characteristic—while most Confederate monuments face north, this one faces east.

OCILLA MEMORIAL. The courthouse lawn in Ocilla, Georgia, is the site of this majestic Confederate monument, facing north. The inscription reads

Tell it as you may
It can never be told
Sing it as you will
It can never be sung
The story of the glory
Of the men who wore the gray.

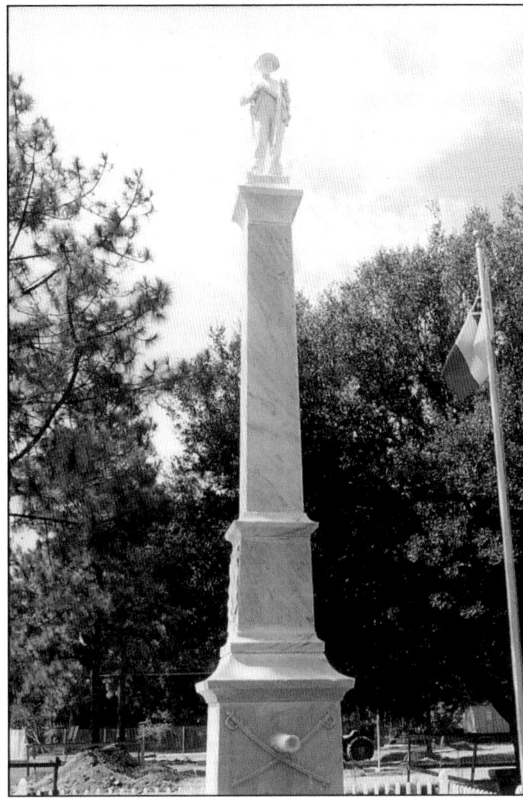

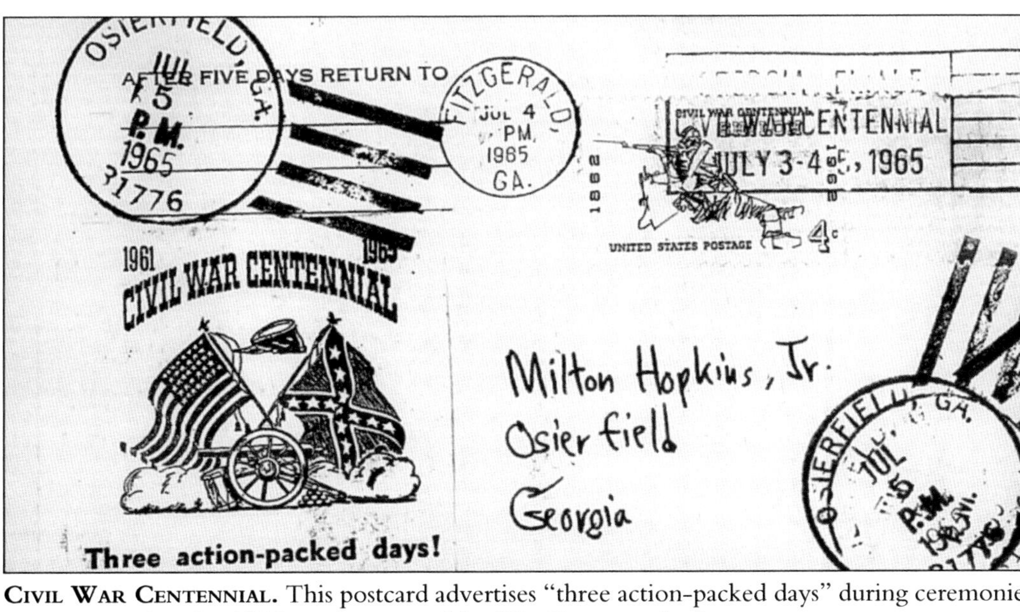

CIVIL WAR CENTENNIAL. This postcard advertises "three action-packed days" during ceremonies commemorating the 100th anniversary of the War Between the States.

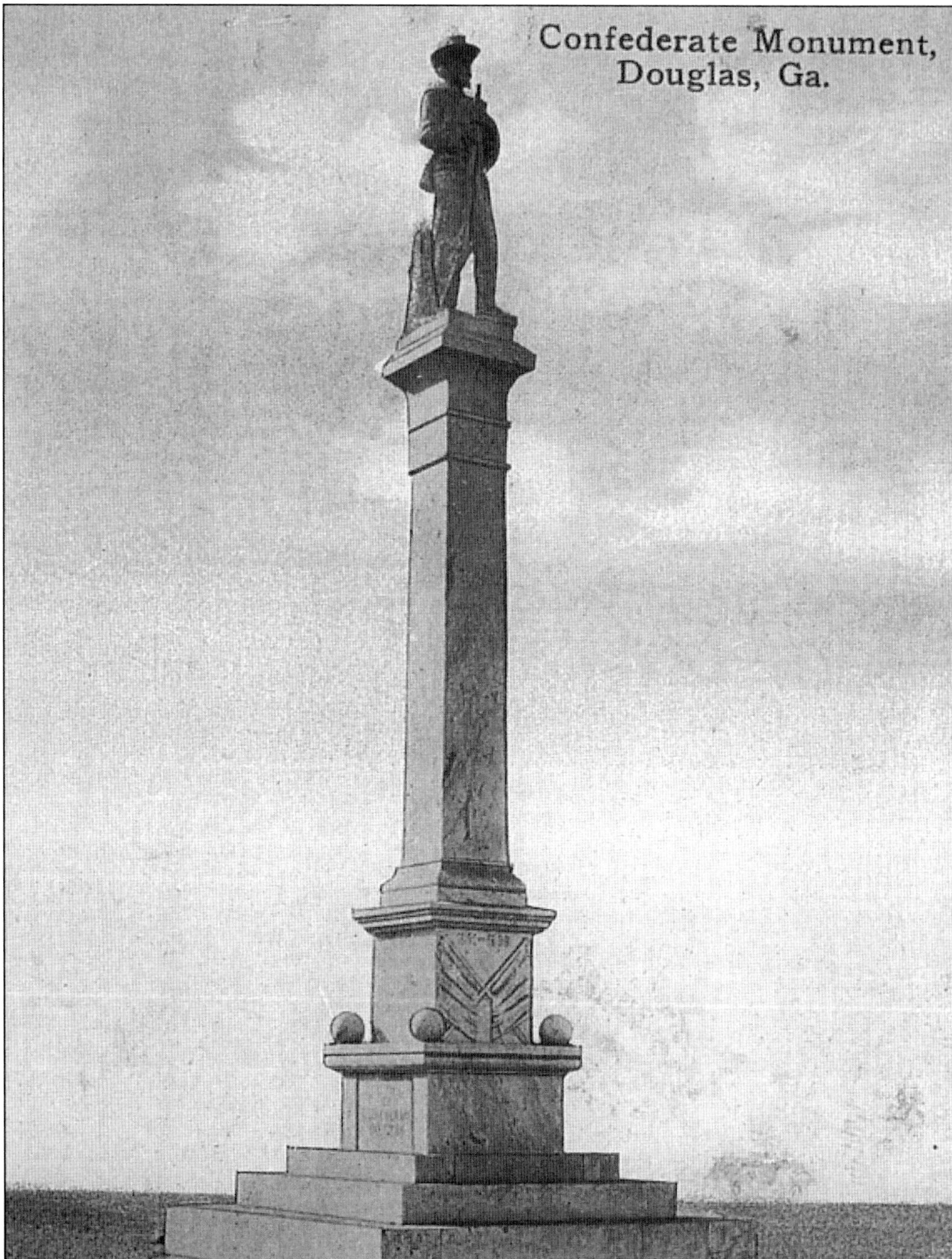

CONFEDERATE MONUMENT. In Douglas, Georgia, this Confederate monument faces north. Celestine Sibley, a famous Atlanta newspaper writer, wrote of waking up one morning in her Douglas, Georgia hotel room and staring out the open window to the face of the Confederate soldier. Most Confederate monuments were originally placed at Main Street intersections but later moved to courthouse lawns and parks.

Five

Residences and Street Scenes

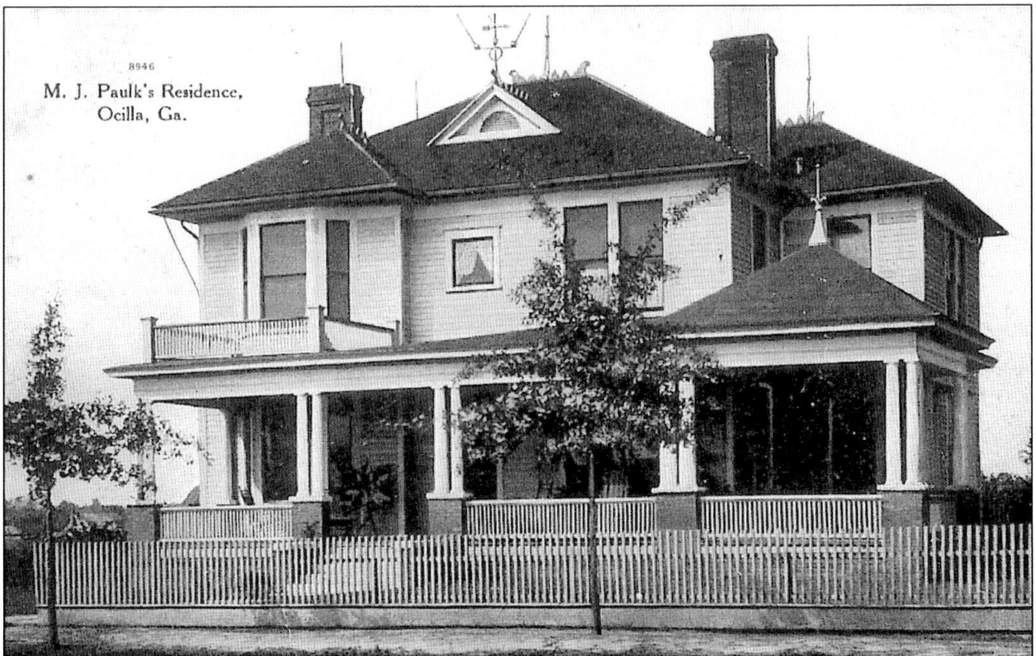

M.J. Paulk Residence. This home in Ocilla is pictured *c.* 1900.

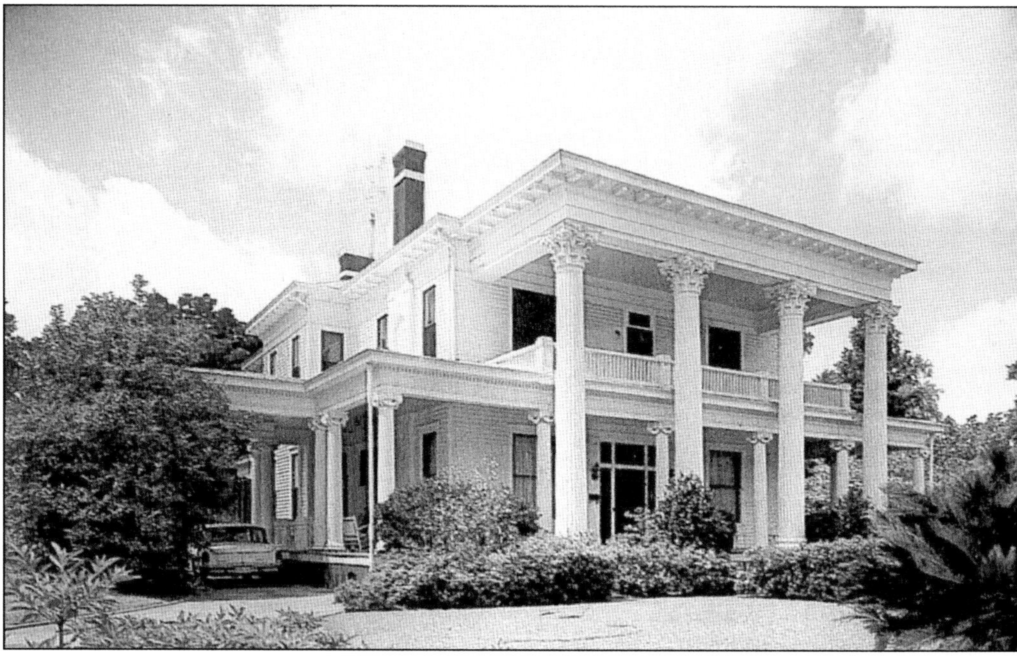

Home of Capt. J.J. Dorminy. The Dorminy family resided on West Central Avenue in Fitzgerald. (Courteys of Louis Harper.)

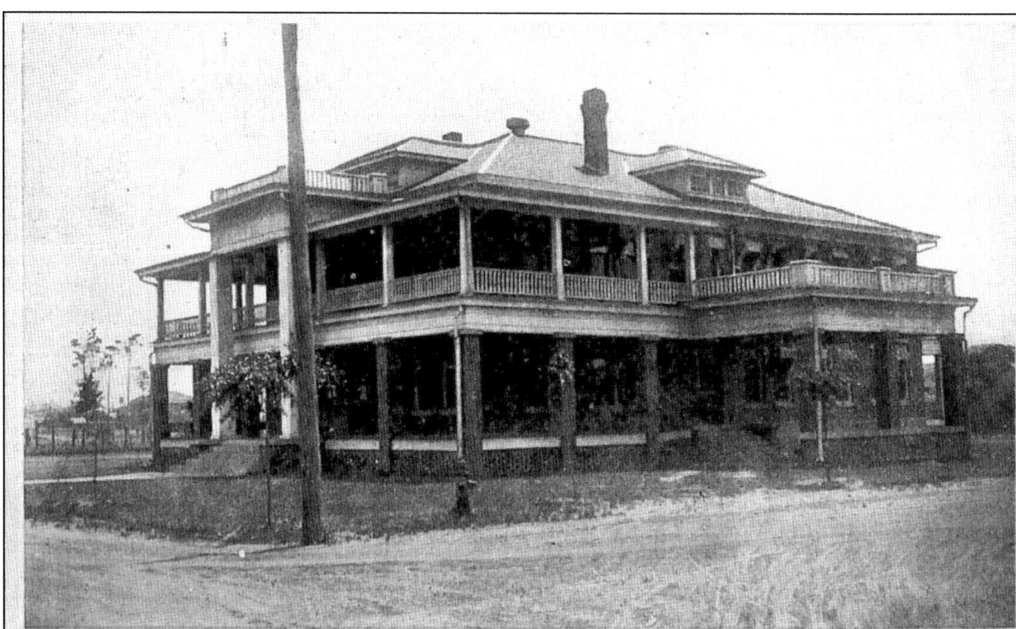

Dismuke & Willis Sanitarium. This facility was located on the old Ocilla-Fitzgerald Road in Ocilla, Georgia.

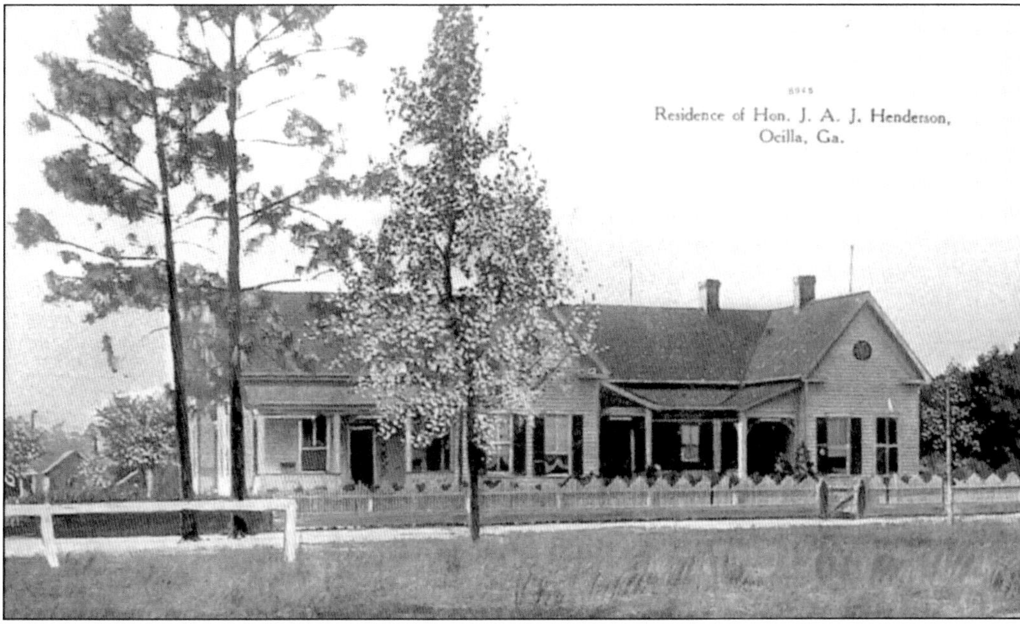

HON. J.A.J. HENDERSON HOME. Located in Ocilla, the home is depicted on a postcard in the early 1900s. (Courtesy of Gussie Hingson.)

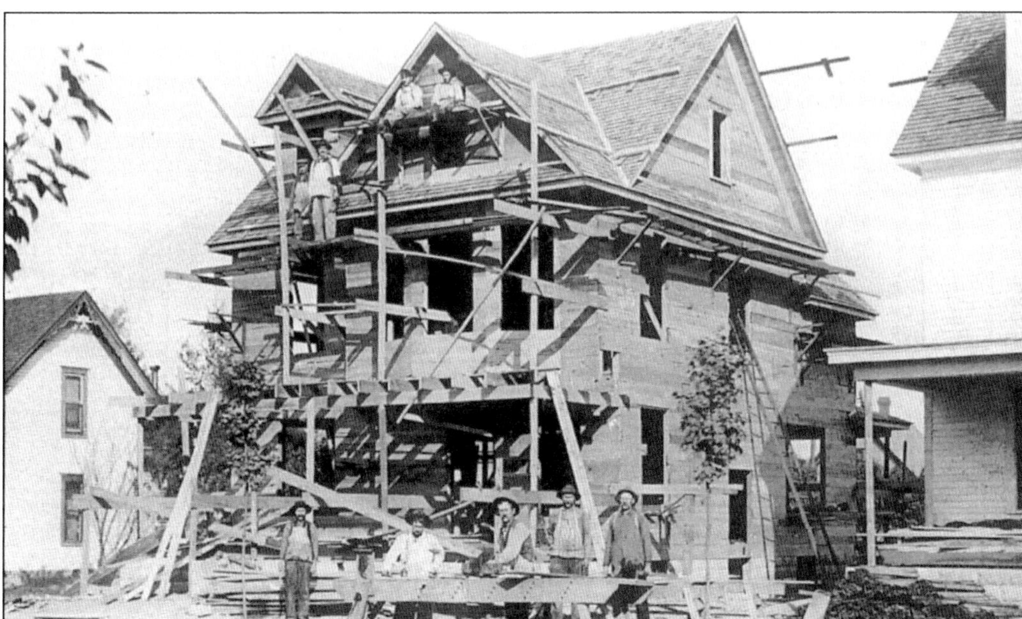

UNDER CONSTRUCTION, *c.* 1900. This Fitzgerald home is being constructed by nine carpenters, three of whom are perched high on the scaffolding. Apparently the house on the right was also under construction as toe boards on the roof are still in place.

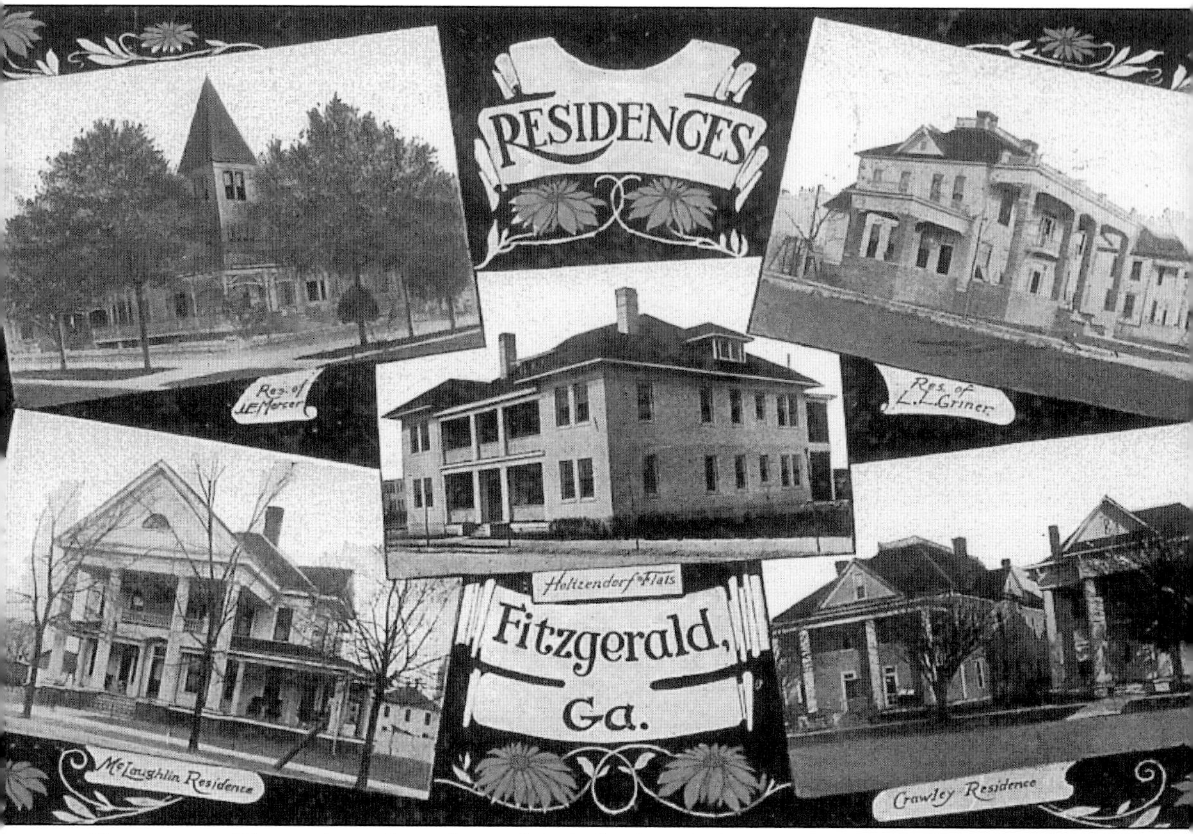

RESIDENCES. Those pictured on the card include, from left to right, (top) J.E. Mercer and L.L. Griner; (middle) Holtzendorf Flats; (bottom) McLaughlin and Crawley.

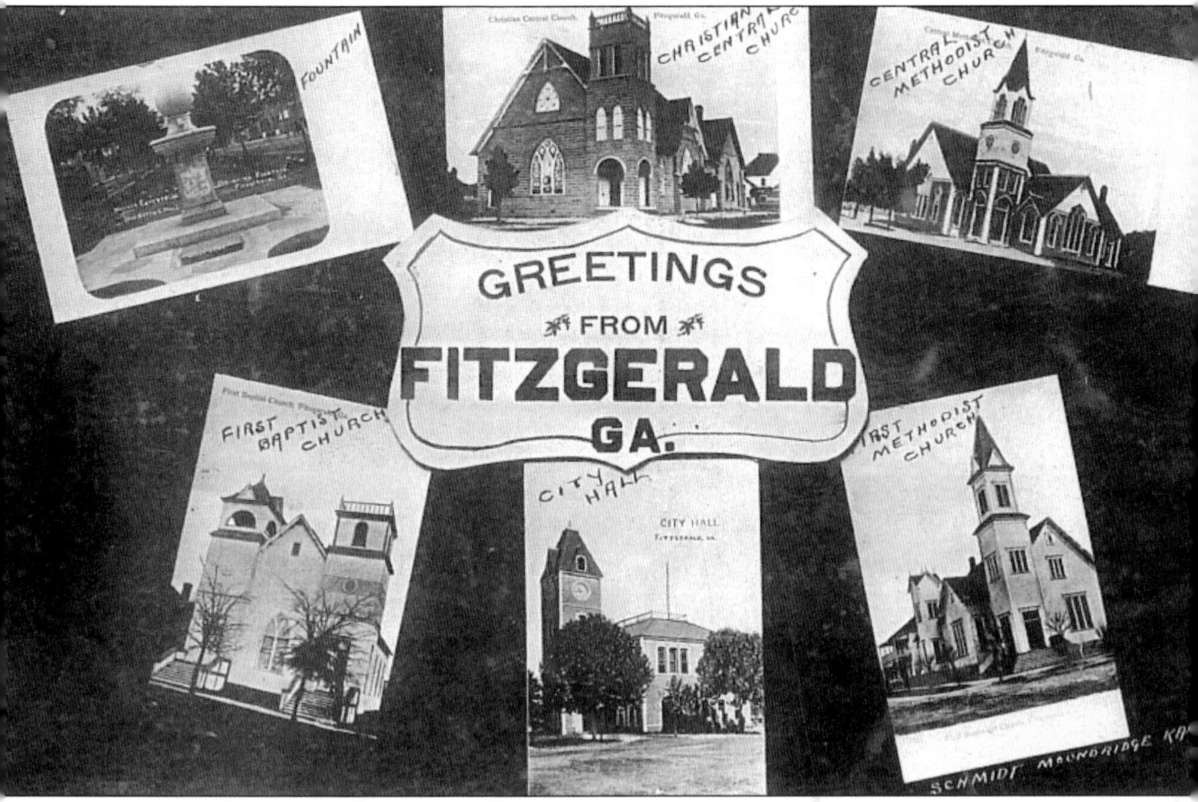

GREETINGS FROM FITZGERALD. In this c. 1910 postcard, the following local landmarks are pictured, from left to right: (top) Mother Enterprise Fountain, Central Christian Church, and Central Methodist Church; (bottom) First Baptist Church, City Hall, and First Methodist Church.

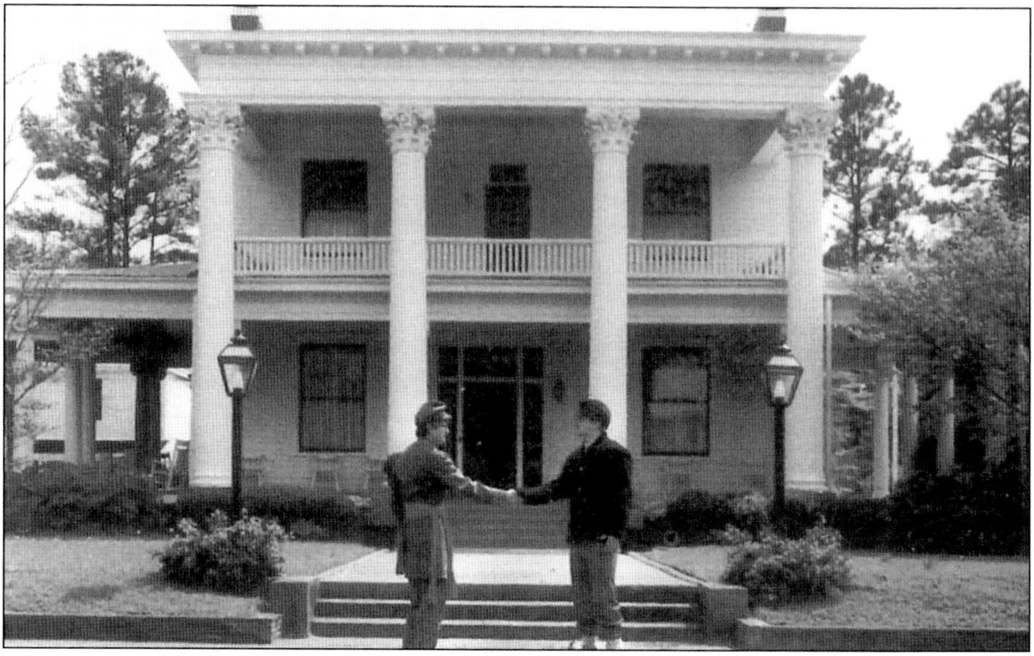

Dorminy-Massee Home. Capt. J.J. Dorminy moved from Broxton, Georgia about 1915 and built this home on West Central Avenue. His daughter Eulalie Dorminy Massee lived here for many years. It has been restored by his grandson and great-grandson and is now a bed-and-breakfast inn.

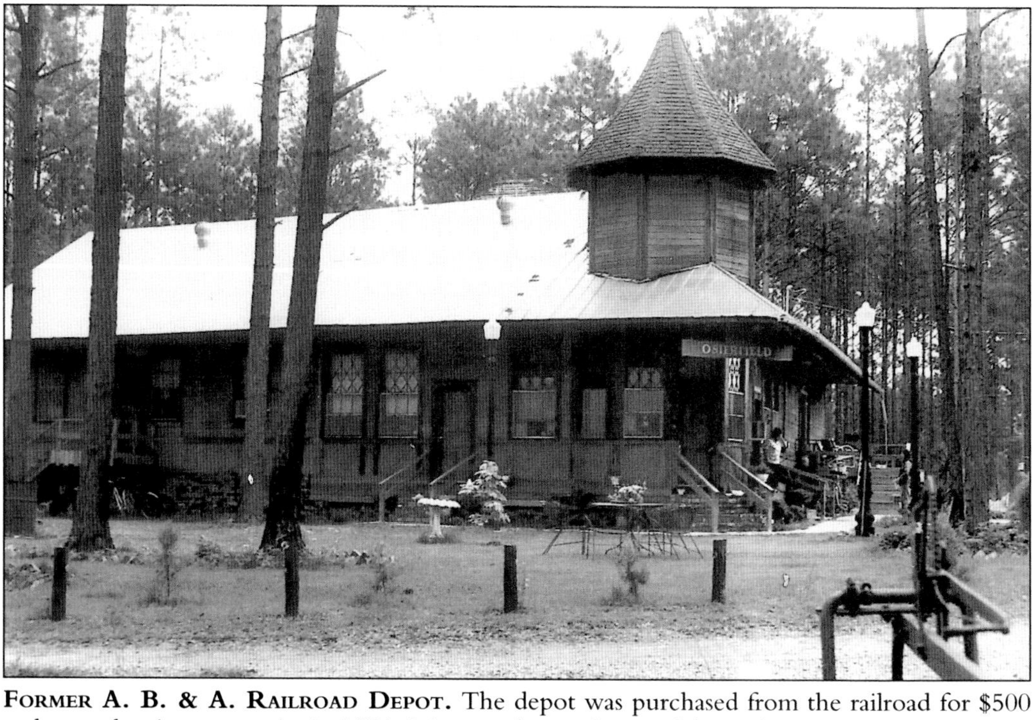

Former A. B. & A. Railroad Depot. The depot was purchased from the railroad for $500 and moved to its present site in 1974. It is now the residence of the author.

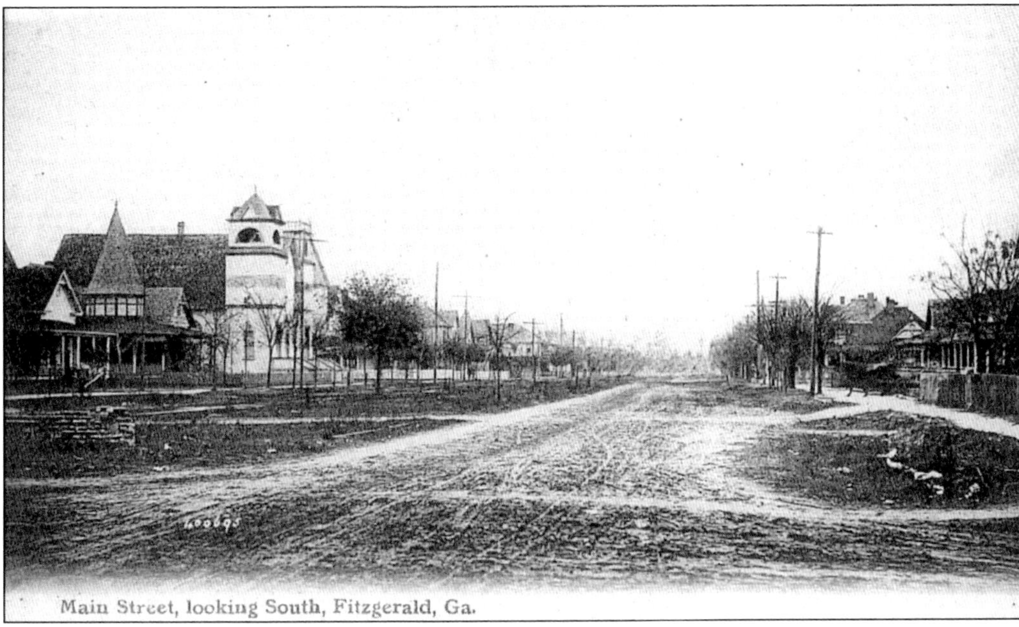

Main Street, Fitzgerald. An unpaved Main Street is seen looking south in this early 1900s view.

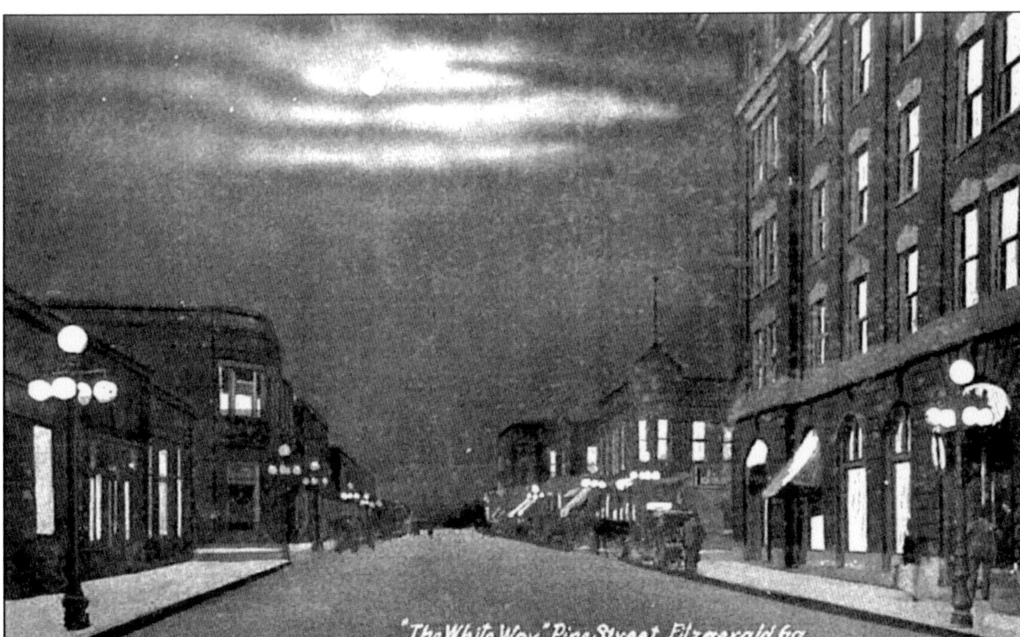

Pine Street Looking West. Postcard peddlers favored nighttime views such as this one with a full moon and bright streetlights.

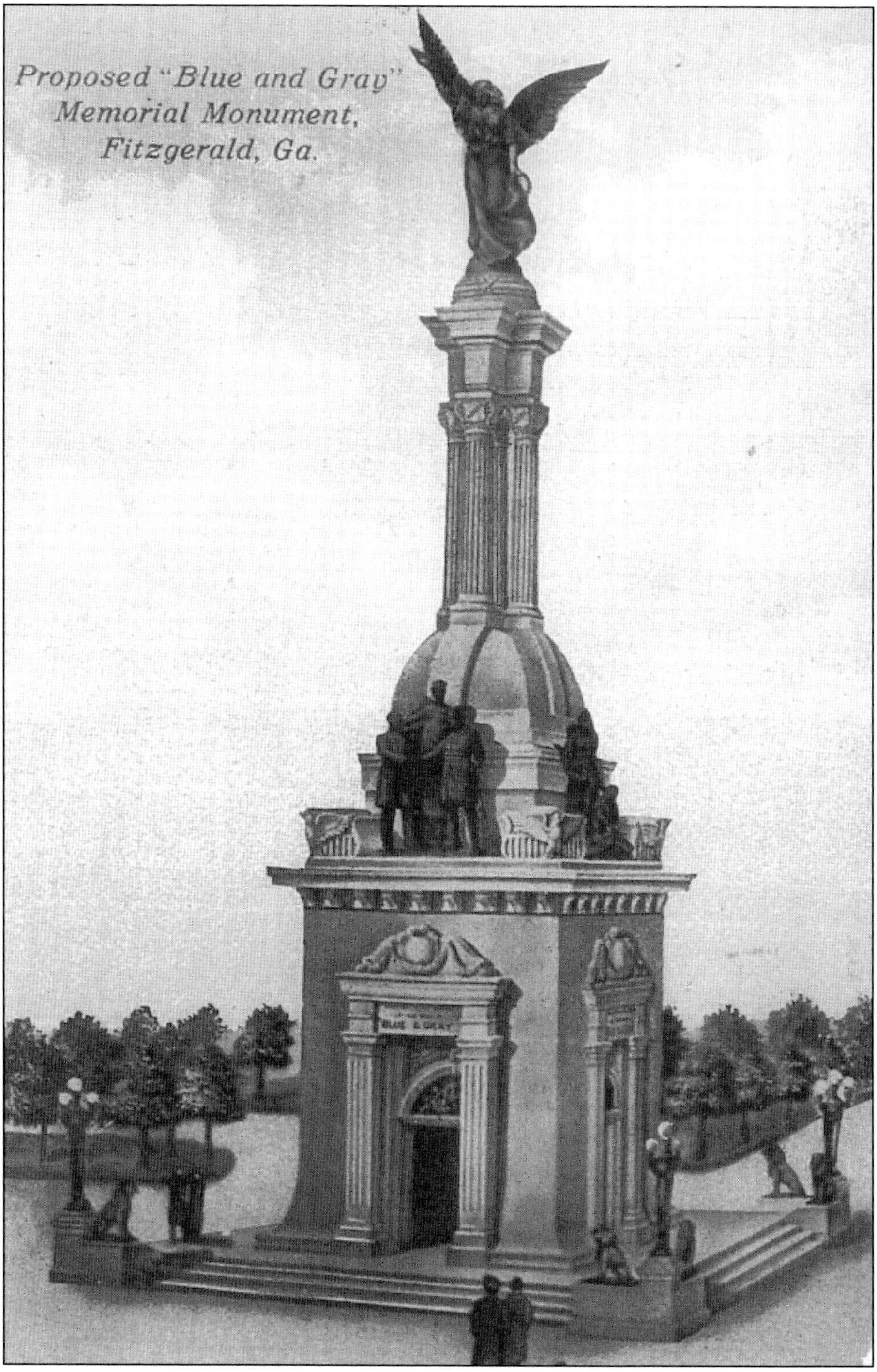

PROPOSED BLUE AND GRAY MONUMENT, FITZGERALD. Funds were solicited from all states, but this memorial was never built. It was to be 125 feet tall and expected to cost $125,000 to construct. The monument would boast the image of Union and Confederate soldiers shaking hands.

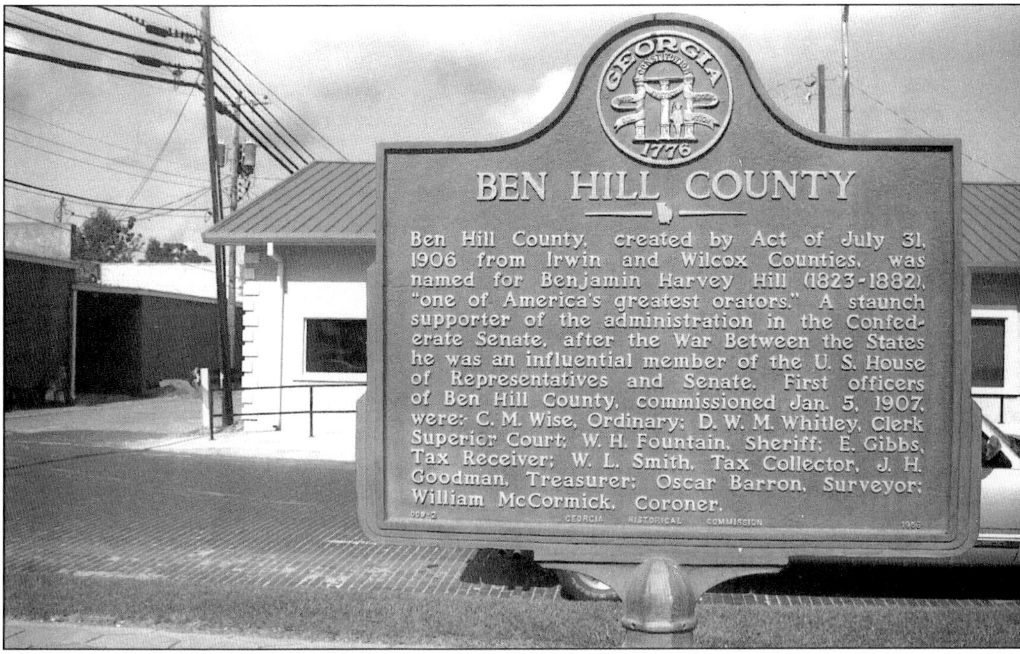

Ben Hill County. This marker is located on the lawn of the Ben Hill County Courthouse on East Central Avenue. The county was created in 1906 from Irwin and Wilcox Counties and named for Benjamin Harvey Hill (1823–1882).

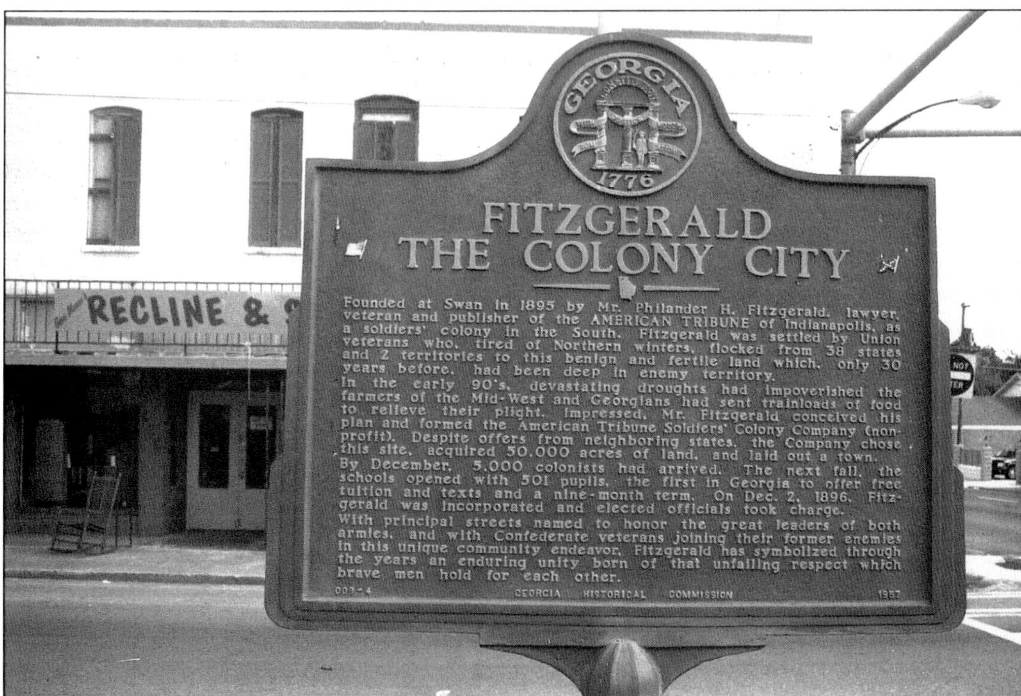

Fitzgerald, the Colony City. This marker is located at the intersection of Central Avenue and Grant Street.

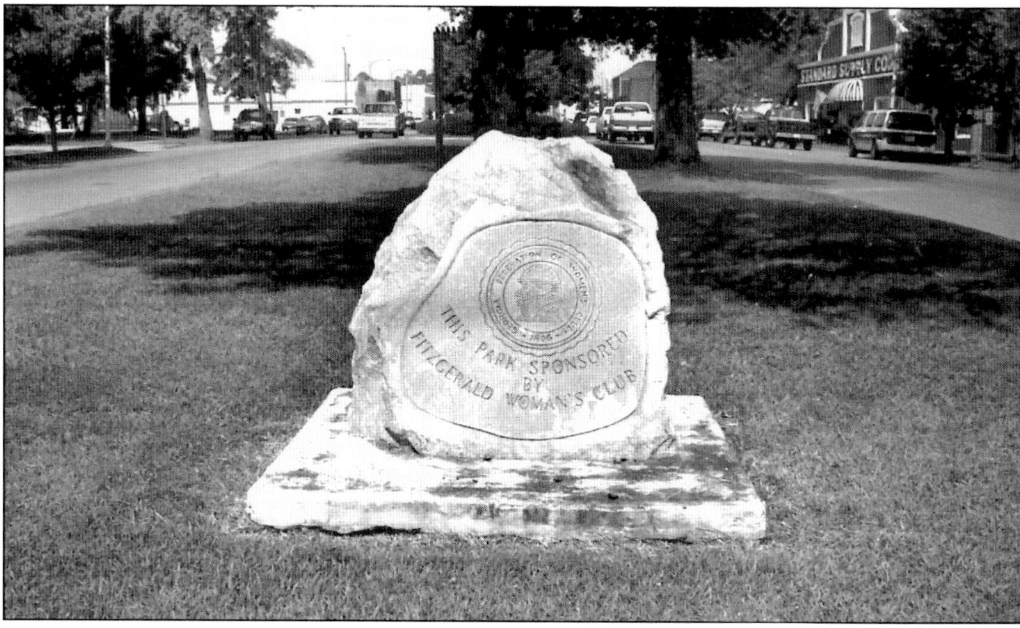

GEORGIA FEDERATION OF WOMENS CLUBS. The granite marker represents a park sponsored by the Fitzgerald Women's Club. It originally sat at a state highway roadside park about four miles east, and has since been moved to the intersection of Sheridan Street and East Central Avenue.

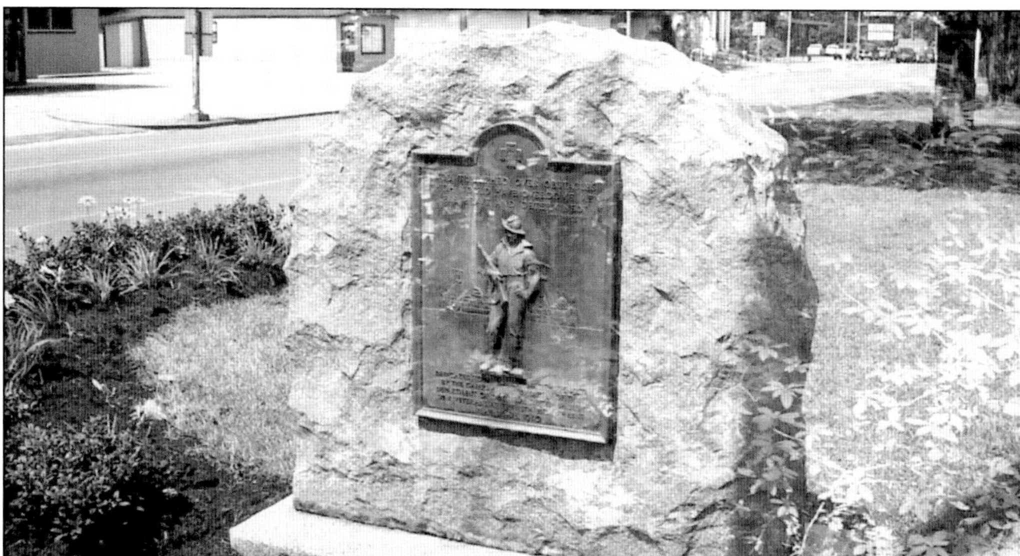

VETERANS MONUMENT. Made of Stone Mountain granite and facing east, this monument is located at the intersection of Main Street and Central Avenue in Fitzgerald and reads "You triumphed over obstacles which would have overcome men less brave and determined. —President McKinley." It was dedicated to the veterans of 1898-1902 by the camps and auxiliaries of the Department of Georgia World War Veterans at the 18th encampment May 26-28, 1940.

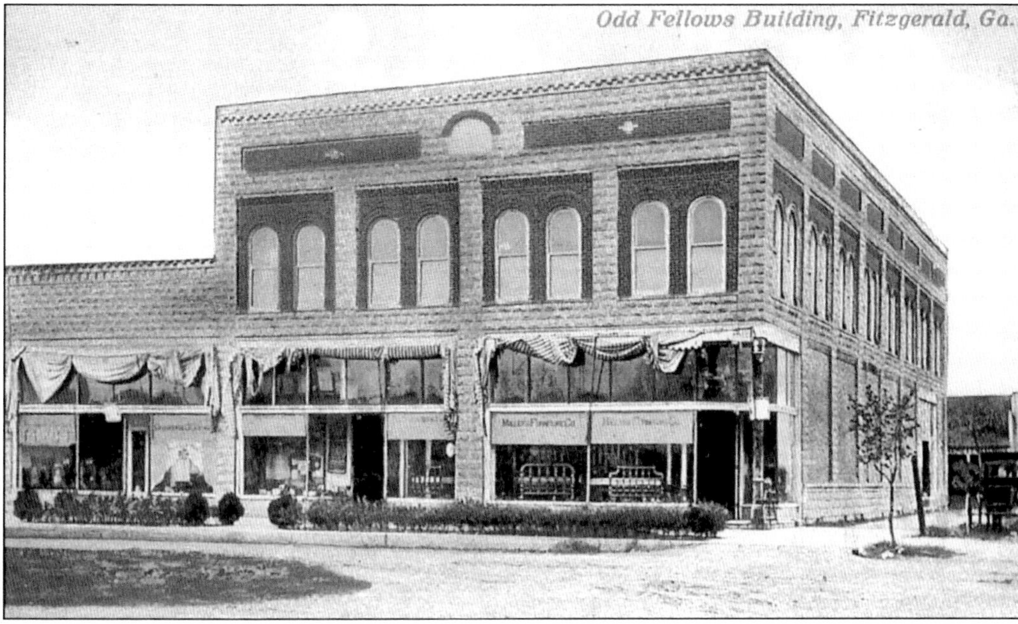

Odd Fellows Building, Fitzgerald. Still standing in 2001, the lower floor was occupied by Miller Furniture Company in the early 1900s.

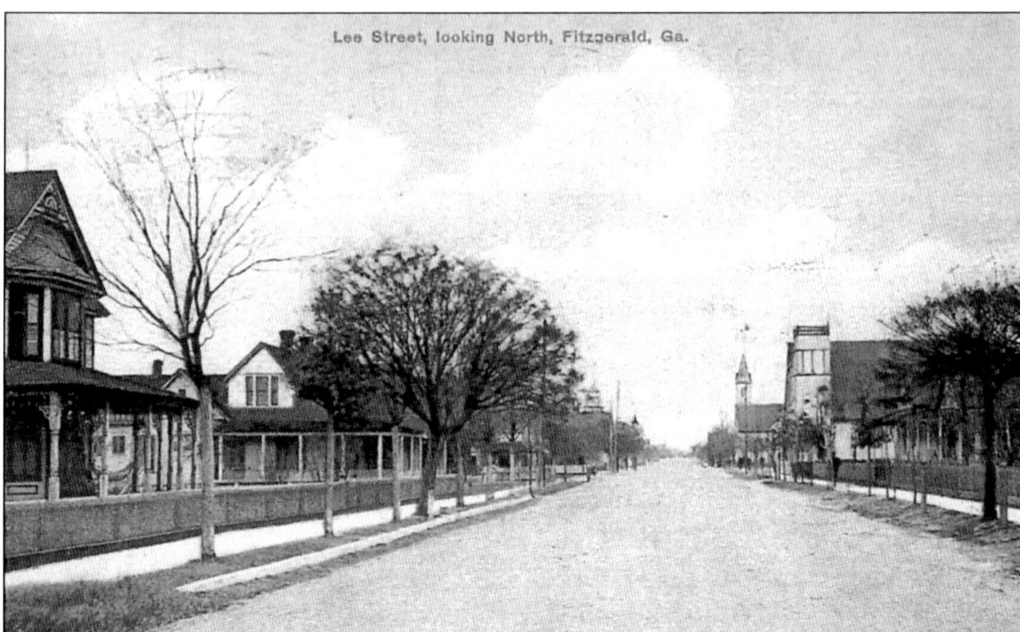

Lee Street, Fitzgerald. In this view, looking north, sidewalks have been paved but the street is still dirt.

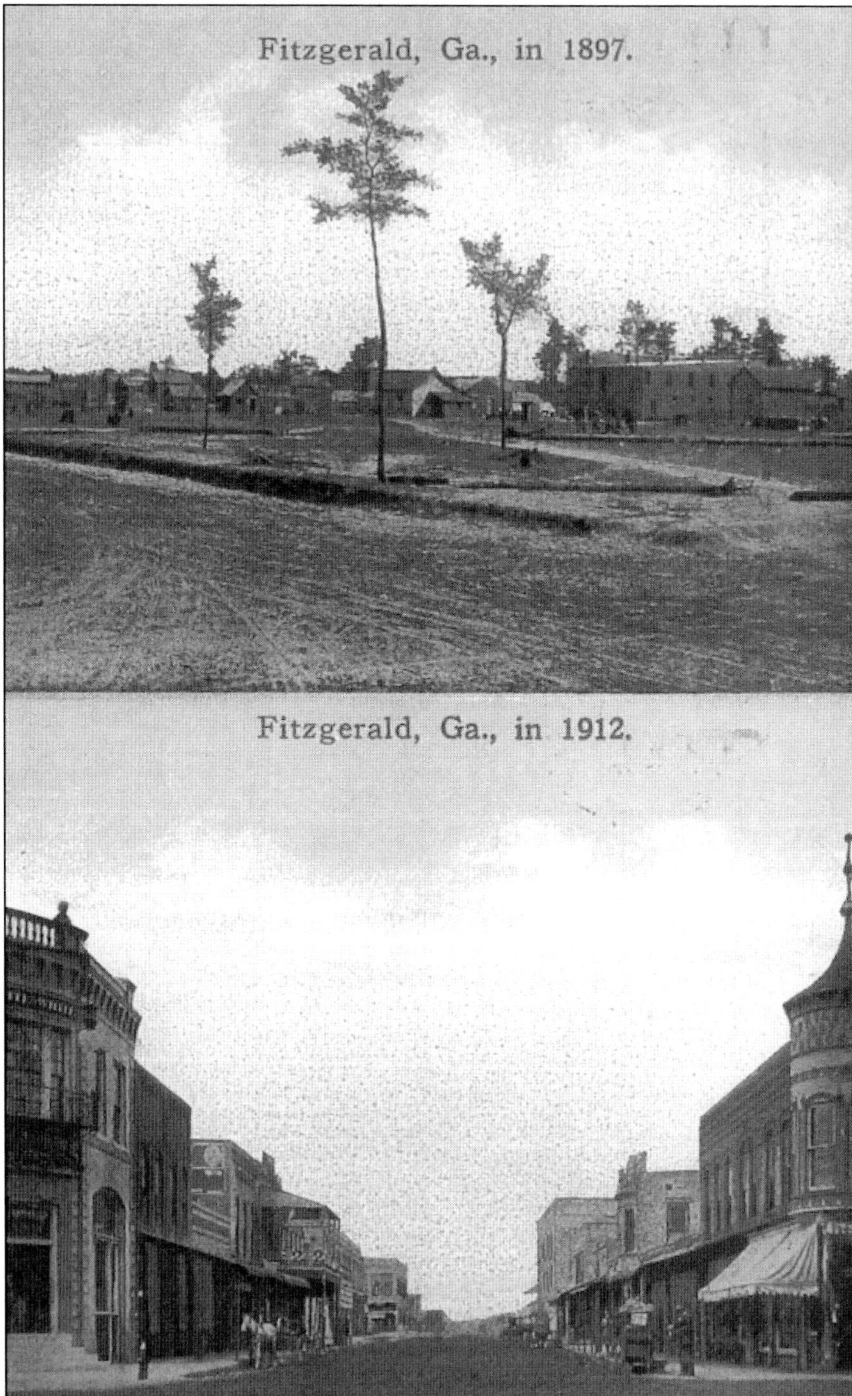

VIEWS FROM TWO CENTURIES. The top view on this postcard shows Fitzgerald in 1897; the bottom view captures a 1912 scene looking west on Pine Street. The postcard was mailed from California in 1915 and its postmark advertised the World's Panama-Pacific Exposition in San Francisco.

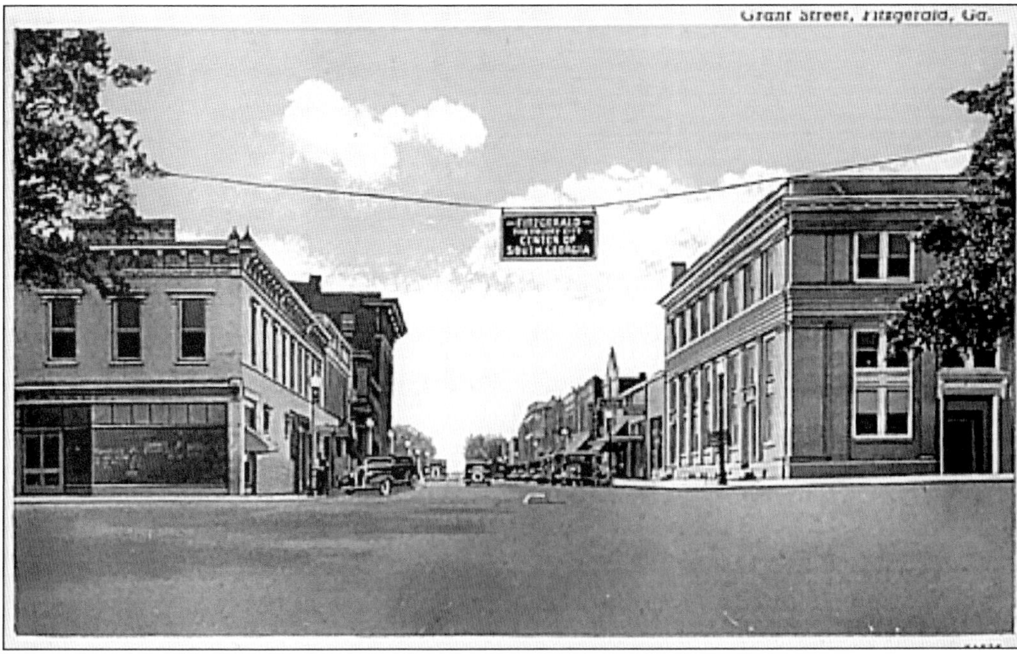

Grant Street, Fitzgerald. This sign hung over Grant Street, or U.S. 129, for many years and proclaimed "Fitzgerald, The Colony City, Center of South Georgia." Note the absence of traffic lights and parallel parking. The building on the right was the National Bank of Fitzgerald.

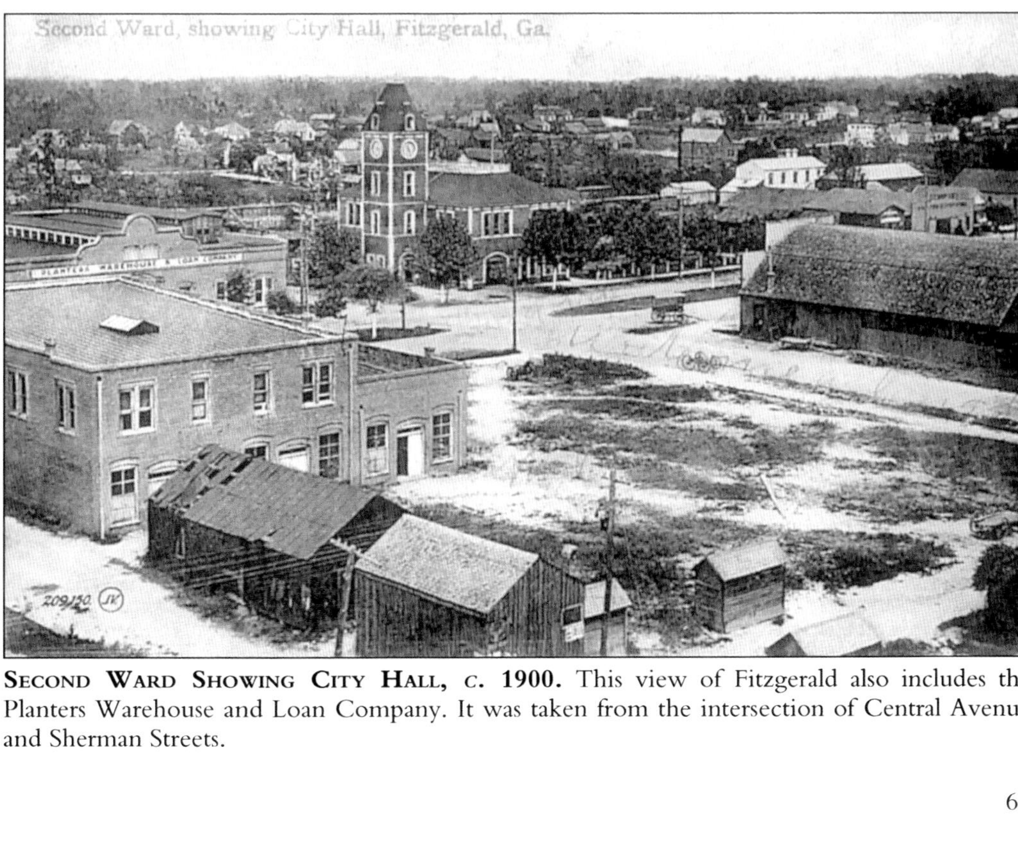

Second Ward Showing City Hall, *c.* 1900. This view of Fitzgerald also includes the Planters Warehouse and Loan Company. It was taken from the intersection of Central Avenue and Sherman Streets.

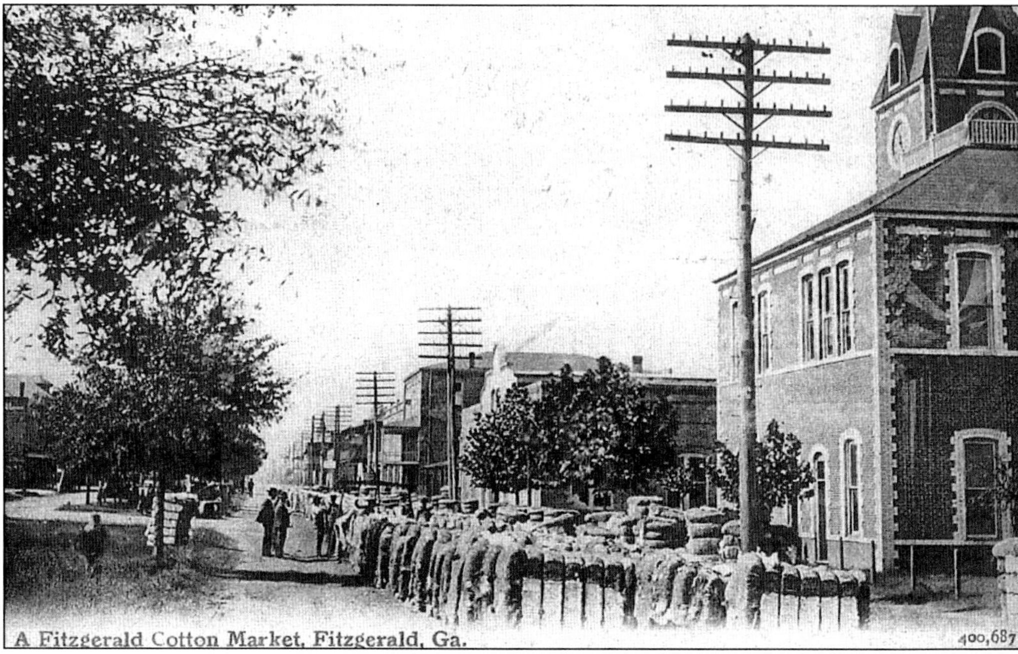

A FITZGERALD COTTON MARKET, c. 1905. The cotton is lined up along East Central Avenue; City Hall is on the right.

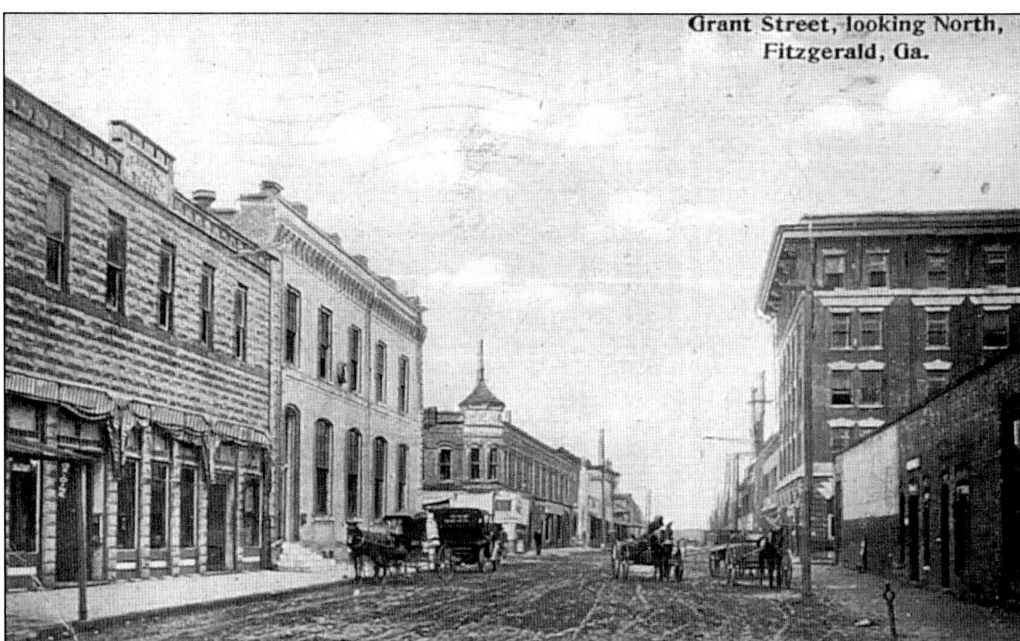

GRANT STREET LOOKING NORTH, c. 1908. In this view, made before the street was paved, readers see one Model T Ford and several horse-drawn carriages. The five-story building on the right was brand new.

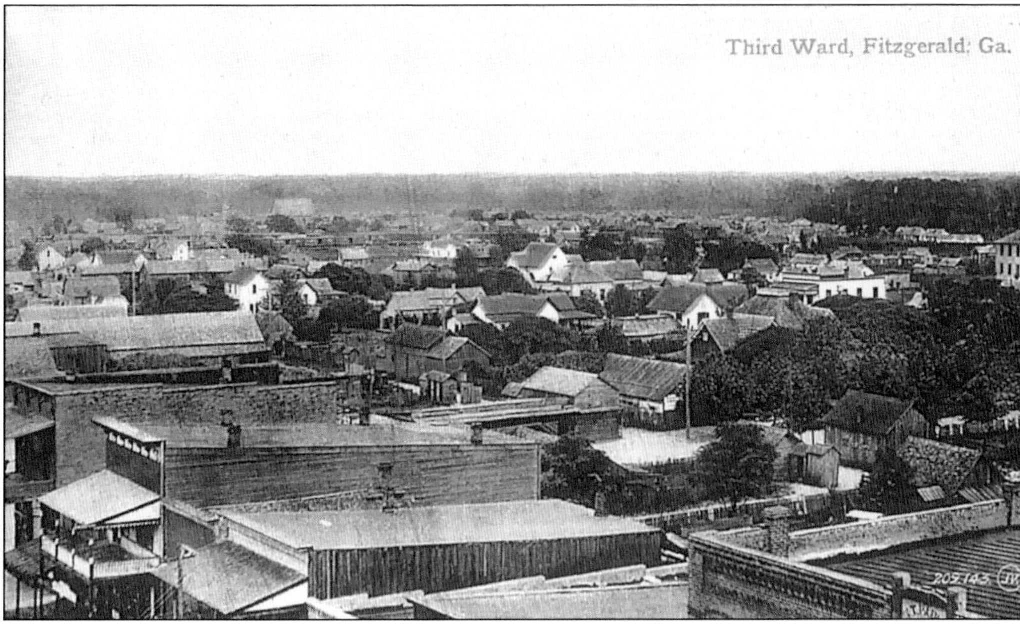

THIRD WARD, FITZGERALD. A birds-eye view was taken from atop the town's five-story building, looking southeast.

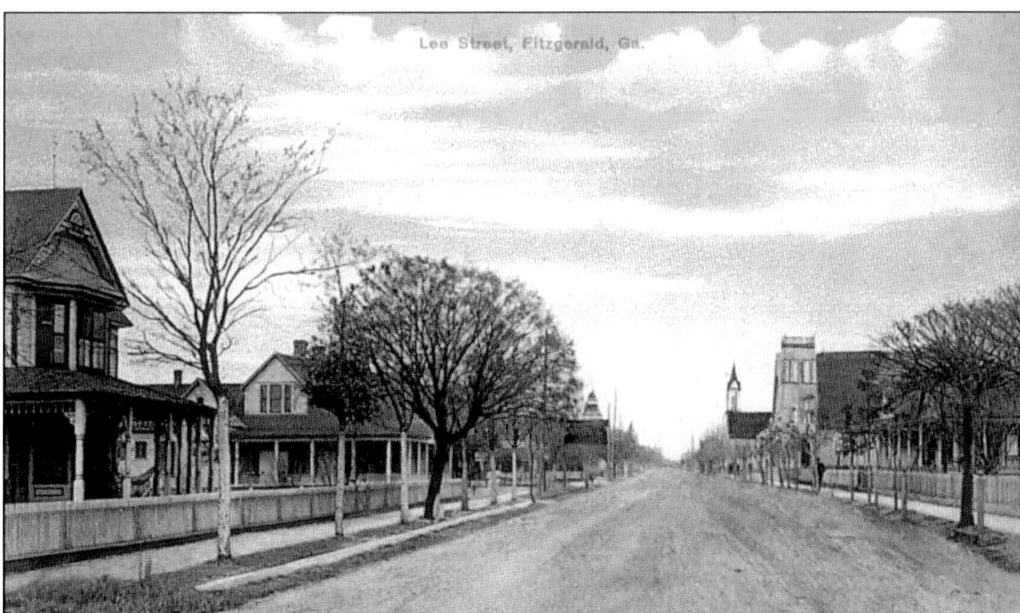

LEE STREET. This card was published by Simon's Brothers and Company and was printed in Germany.

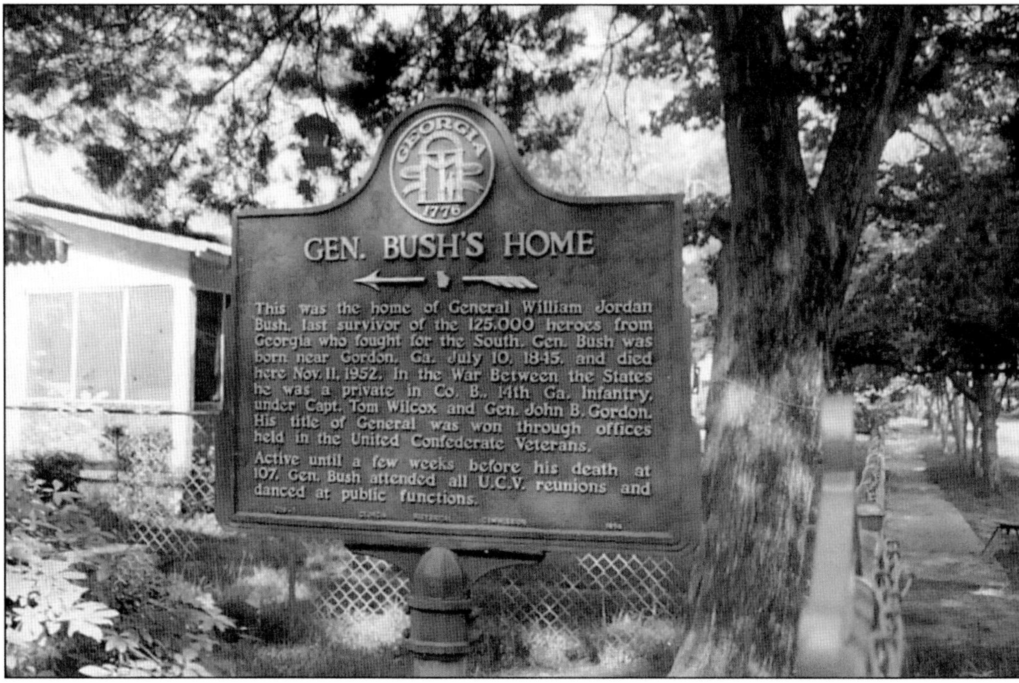

GEN. WILLIAM JORDAN BUSH. This marker points to the home of General Bush, who at 107 was the last survivor among Confederate soldiers to have fought in the War Between the States. The home is located on West Suwanee Street in Fitzgerald. General Bush died November 11, 1952.

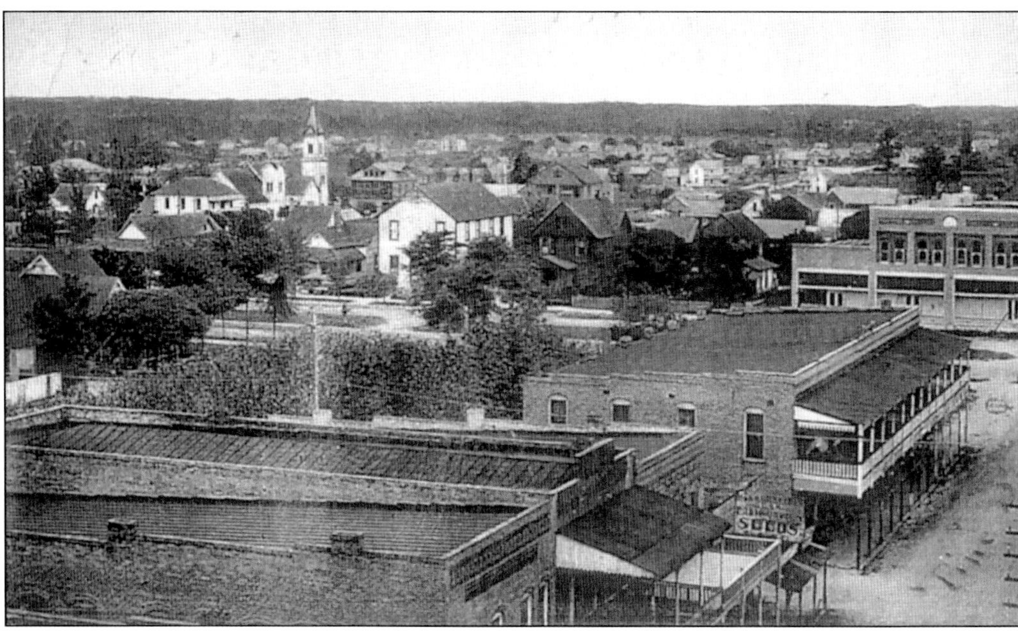

PINE STREET LOOKING SOUTHWEST. Visible in this postcard are the Odd Fellows building on the far right and the Women's Relief Corp building, the white two-story building just to the left on Main Street.

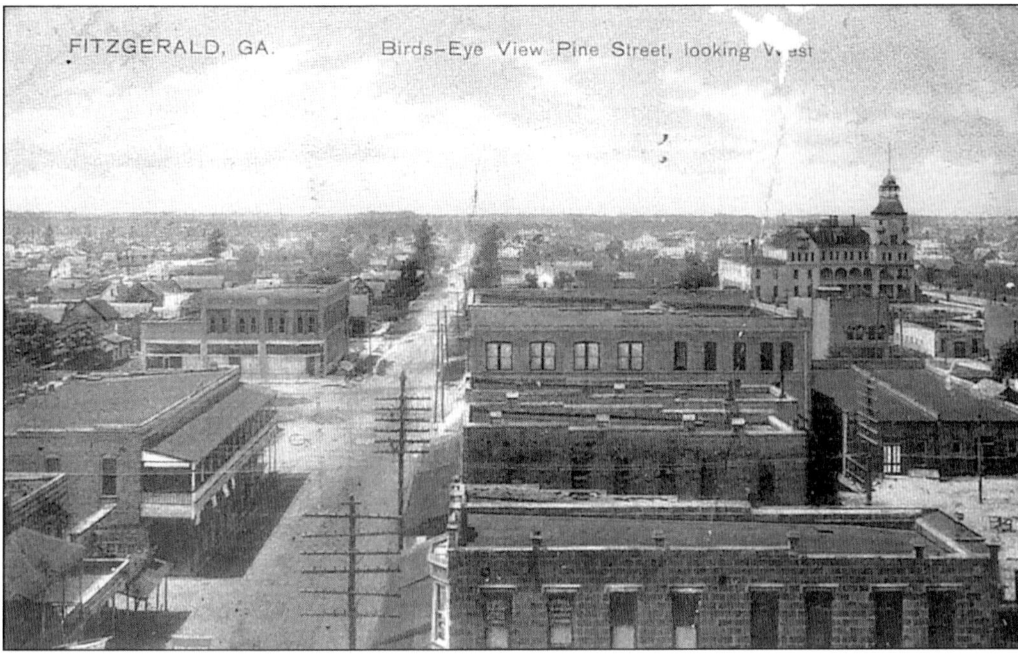

Pine Street Looking West. The Odd Fellows building is at far left and the towers of the Lee-Grant hotel can be seen at far right.

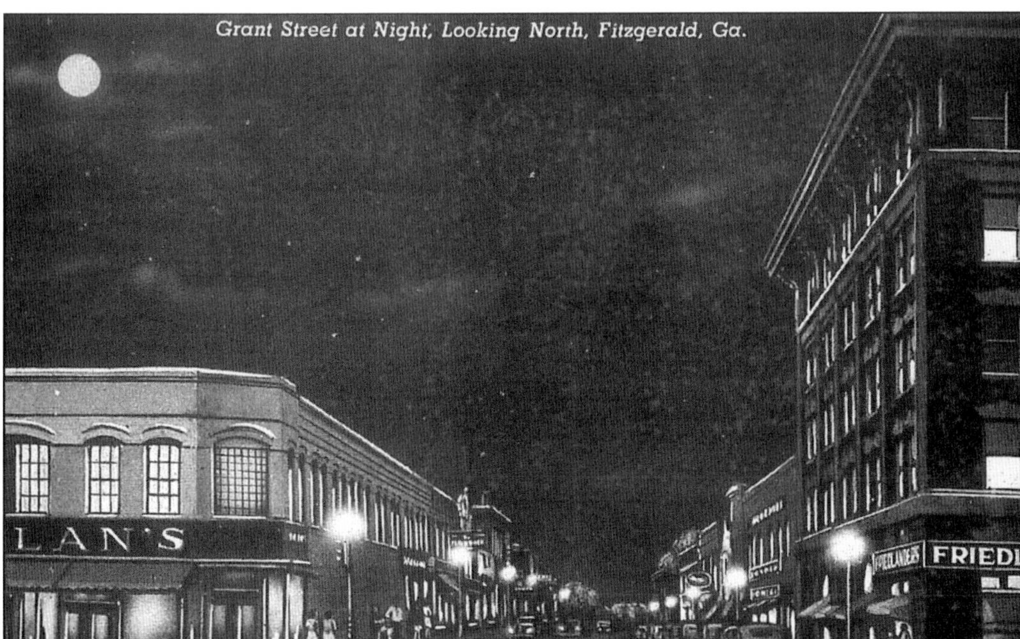

Grant Street at Night. McClellan's, a five-and-dime chain store, occupied the first building on the left for many years. Friedlanders, a clothing store, occupies the ground floor of the five-story building on the right.

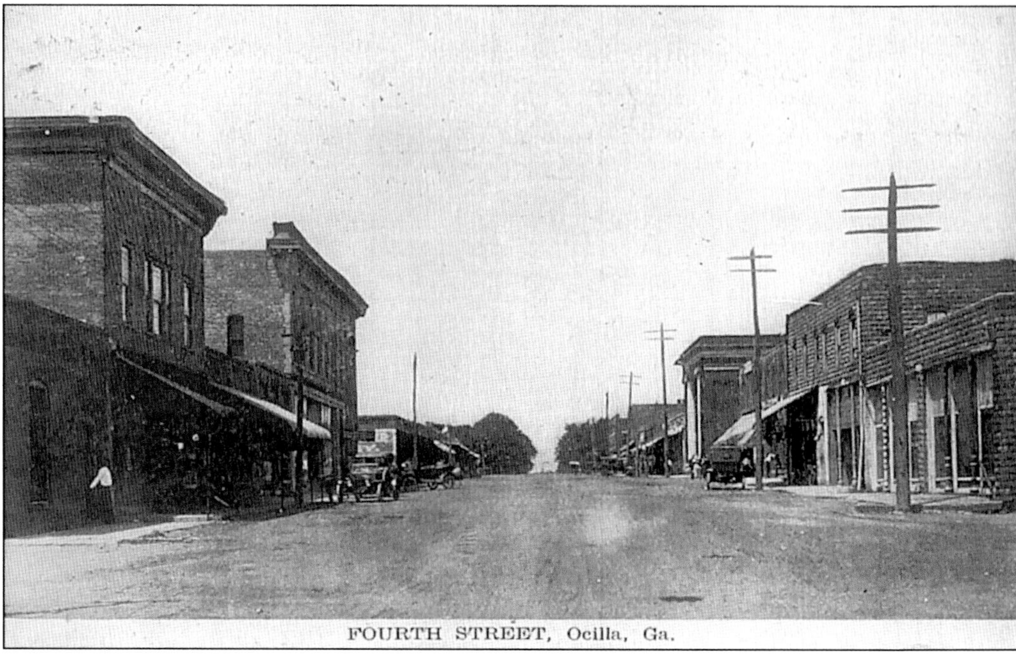

FOURTH STREET, OCILLA. Looking west, Fourth Street is captured around 1900.

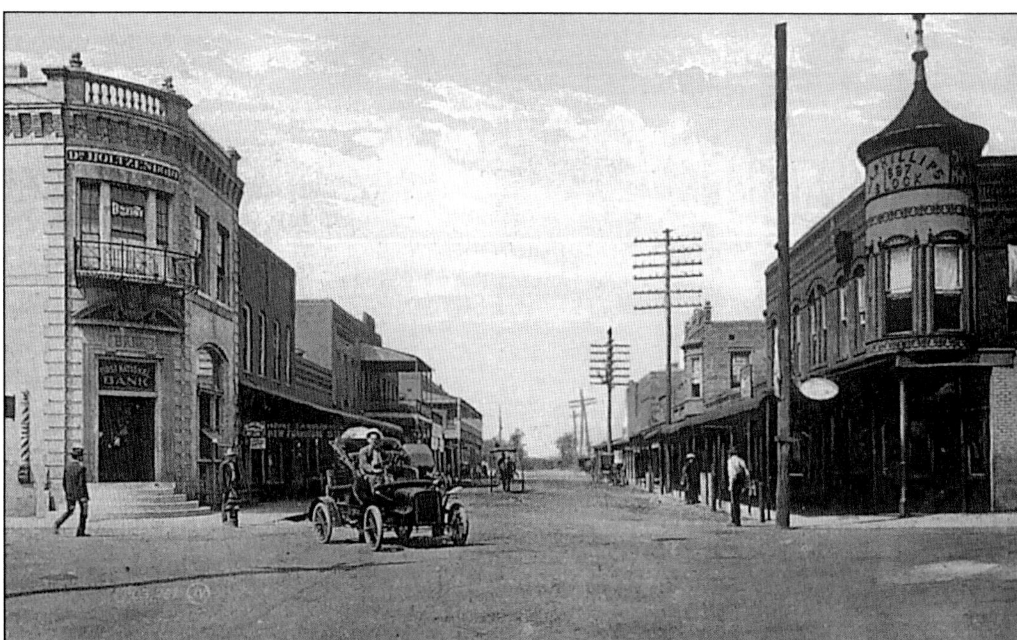

PINE STREET AND FIRST NATIONAL BANK. The top floor of the bank housed the office of Dr. Holzendorf, a dentist.

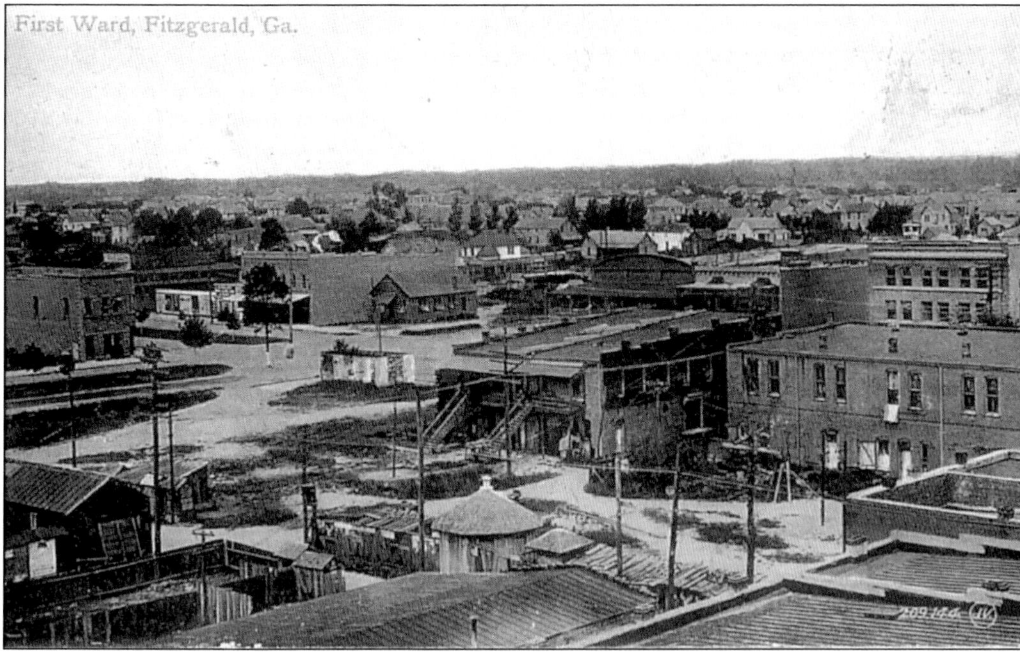

First Ward, Fitzgerald. This *c.* 1907 view of Fitzgerald was taken from the top of the five-story building.

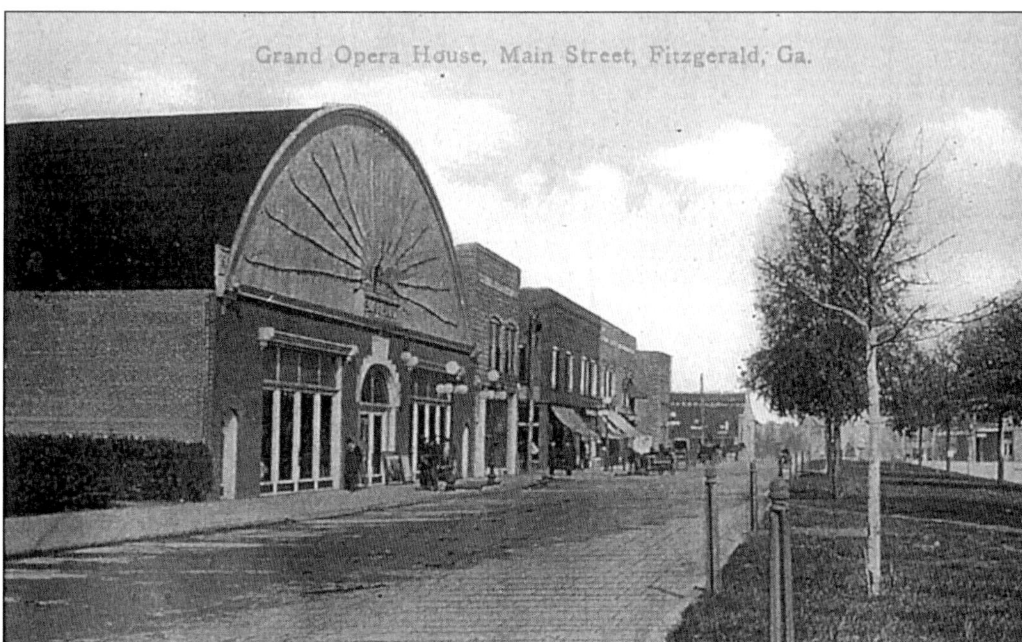

Grand Opera House. The opera house was located on Main Street in Fitzgerald. Note the horse- or mule-hitching posts in the picture.

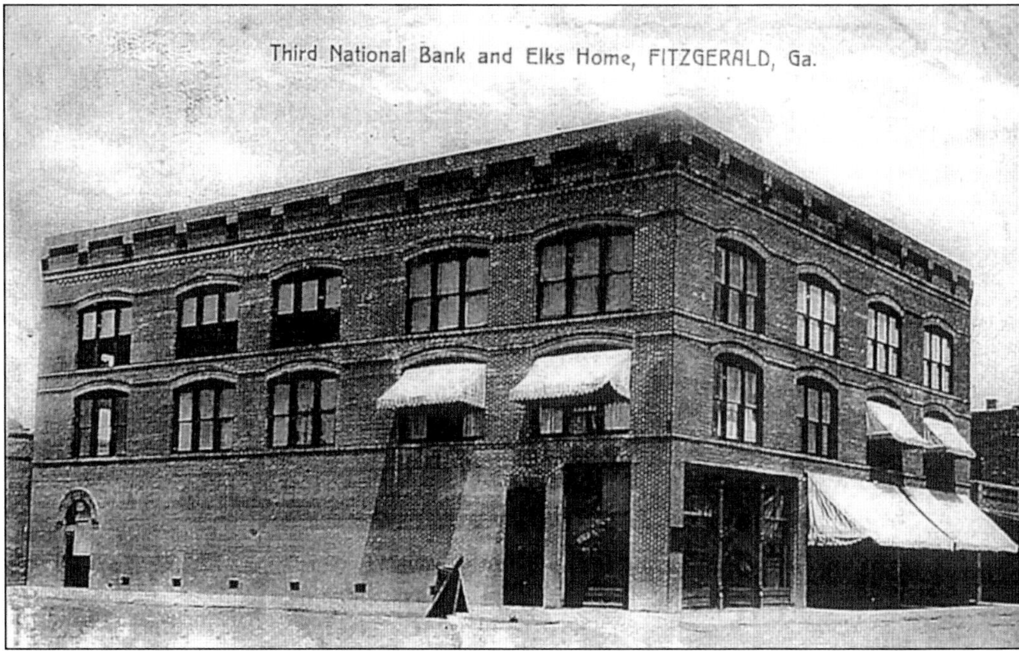

THIRD NATIONAL BANK AND ELKS HOME. This was the view at the corner of Main and Pine Streets. The building was demolished in 2001. (Courtesy of Louis Harper.)

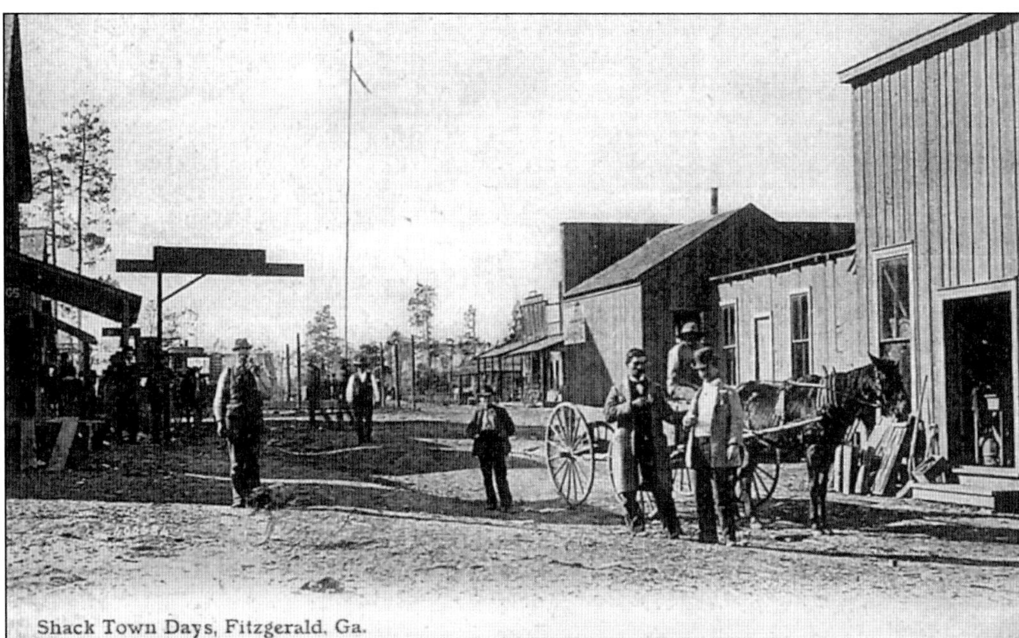

SHACK TOWN DAYS, FITZGERALD. The flagpole in the picture was probably located at the intersection of Main Street and Central Avenue.

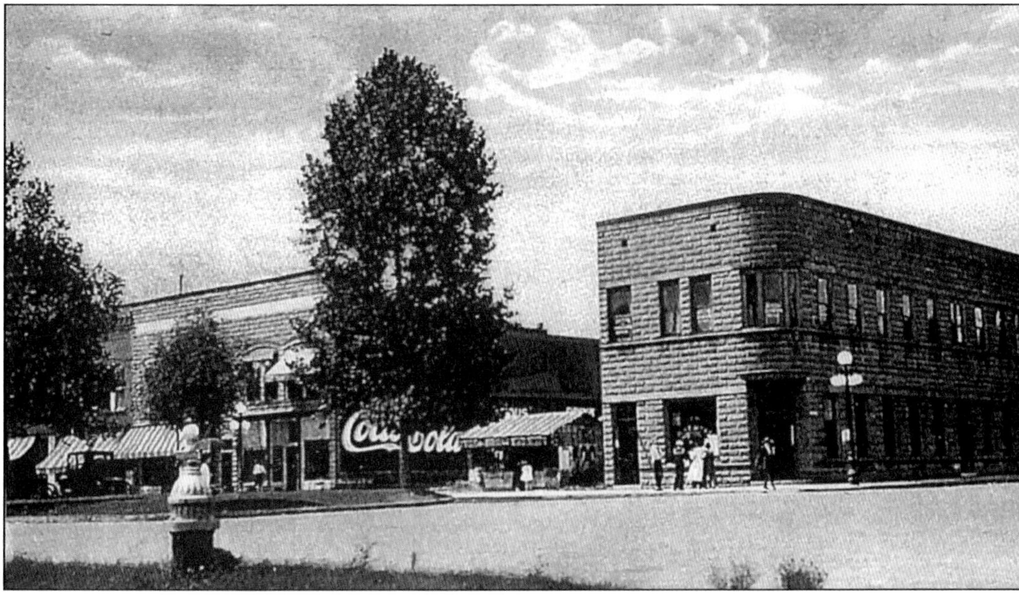

Corner of South Main and Central Avenue. Fitzgerald is depicted here around 1902. Note the prominent advertisement for Coca-Cola.

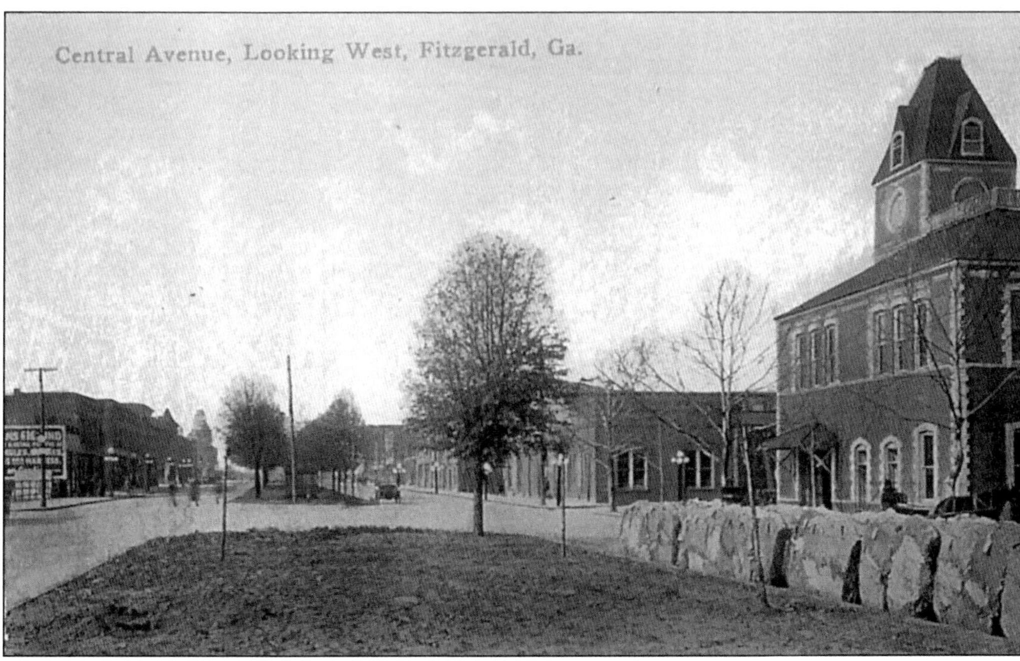

Central Avenue, Looking West. Cotton bales can be seen in front of the fire station and city hall. The cotton overflow leaves room for only one-way traffic. Bales averaged 500 pounds and were moved by one man with a two-wheel dolly.

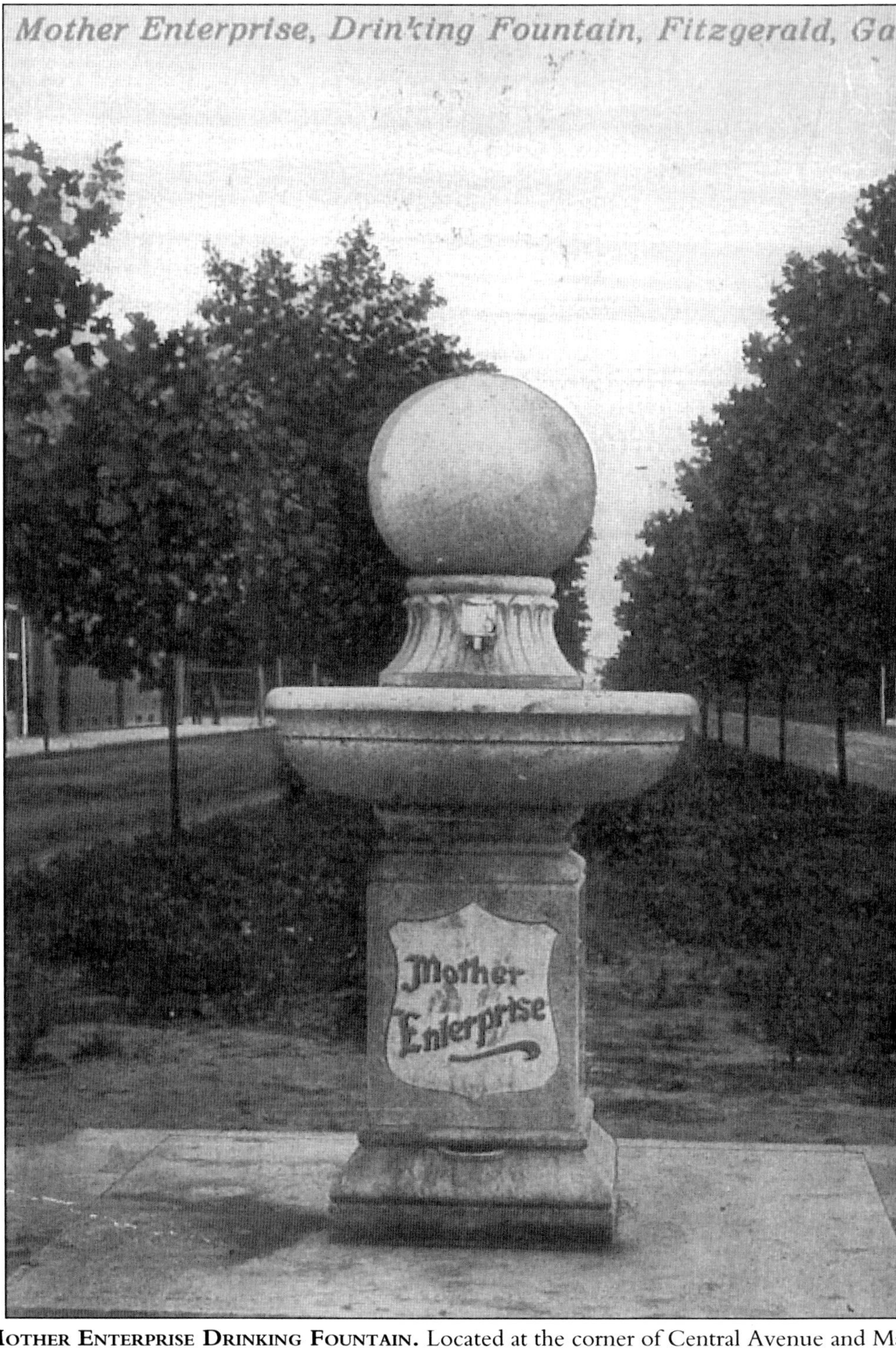

MOTHER ENTERPRISE DRINKING FOUNTAIN. Located at the corner of Central Avenue and Main Street in the center of Fitzgerald, the fountain still operates in 2001 and the water is used to sprinkle the surrounding park.

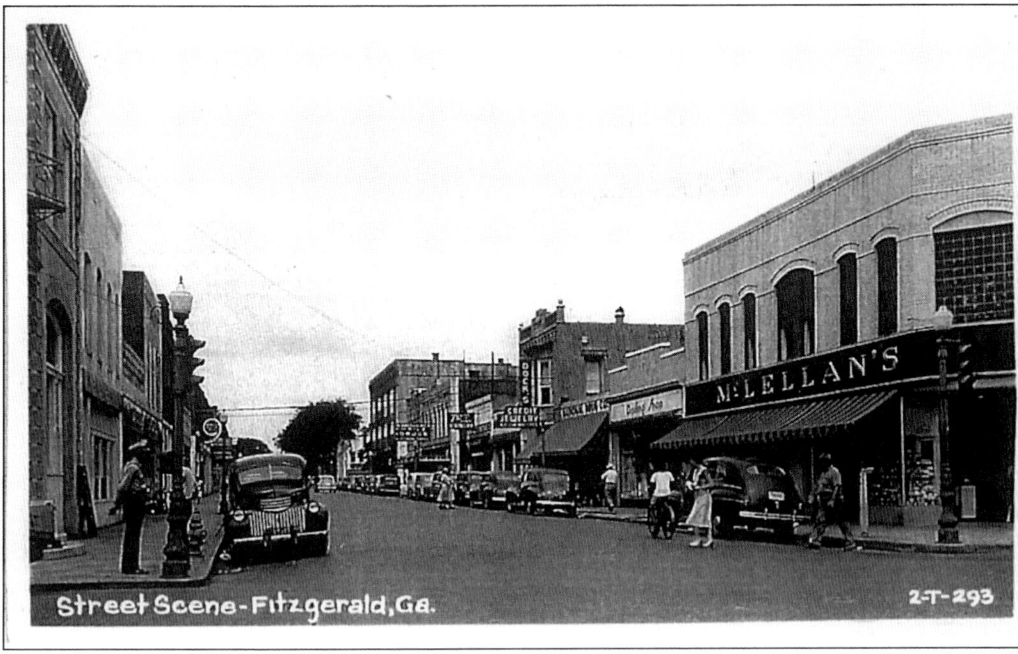

Pine Street, 1940s. In this view looking west, Police Chief Findlay is seen on the left street corner.

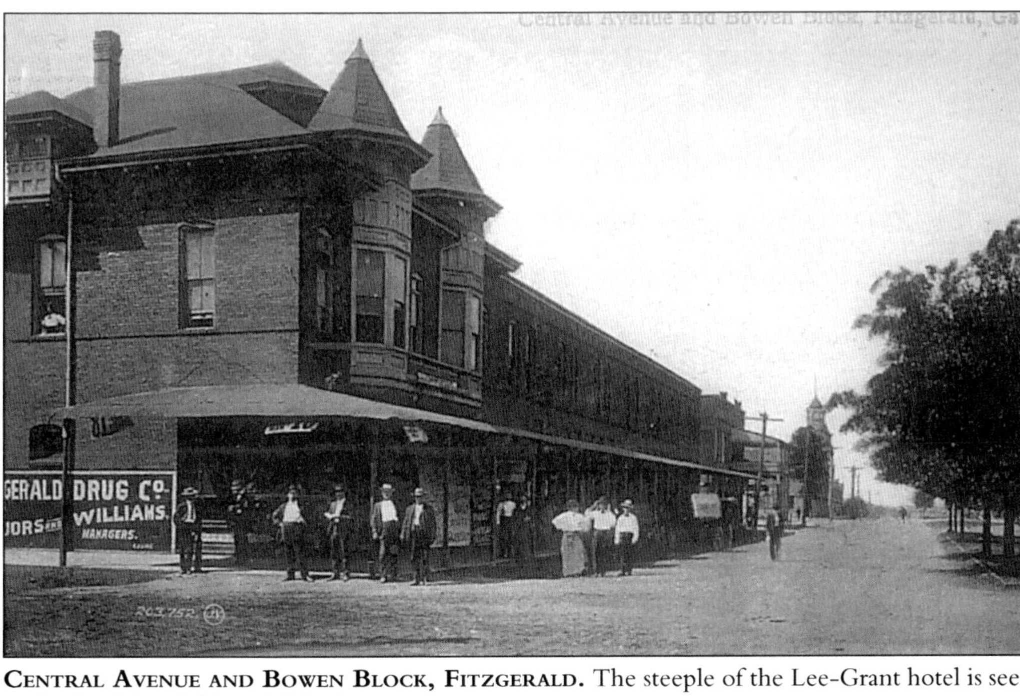

Central Avenue and Bowen Block, Fitzgerald. The steeple of the Lee-Grant hotel is seen at the far right of this *c.* 1900 view.

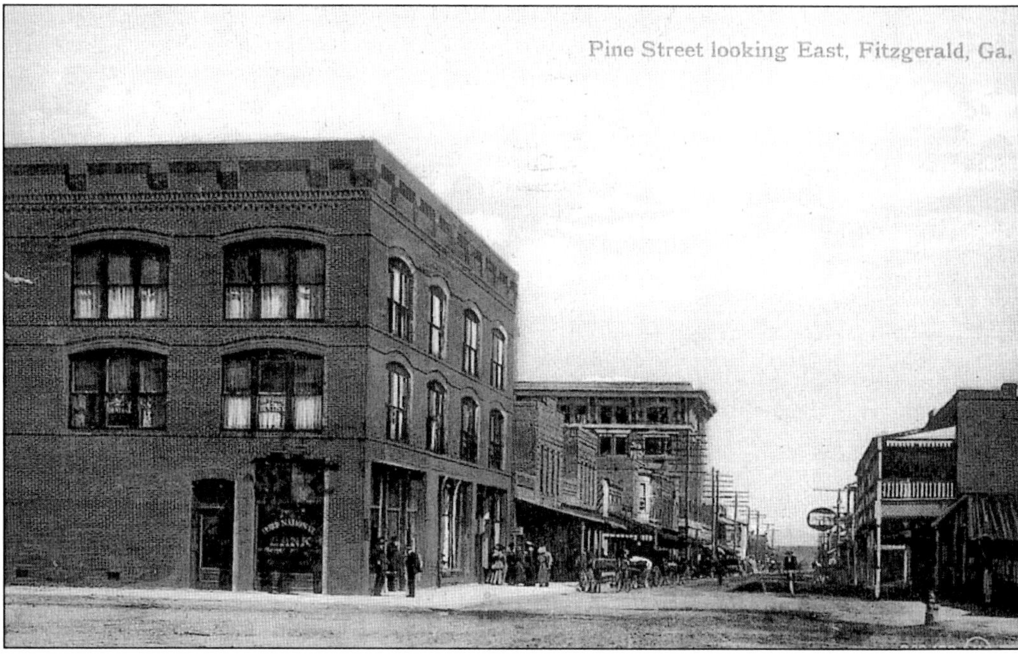

PINE STREET LOOKING EAST, FITZGERALD. On the left side of the street the three-story building was the Third National Bank, a hotel, and an A&P store. The building was leveled in 2001.

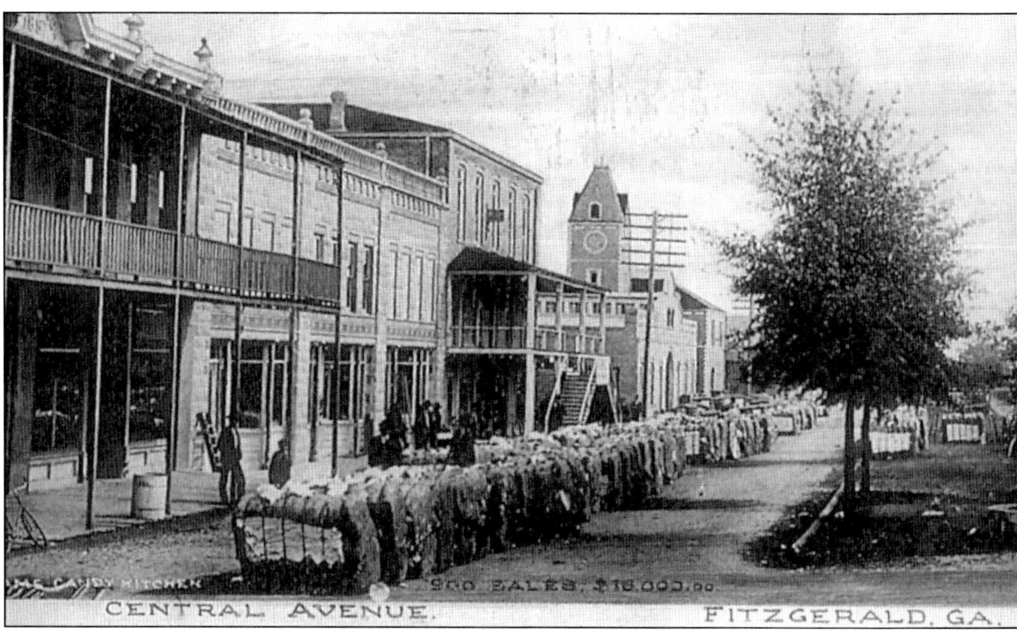

CENTRAL AVENUE c. 1897. The card reads "900 bales, $16,000." The cotton is piled in front of the Planters Warehouse and Loan Company where it must have been ginned. The tower of City Hall can be seen at left in this card published by Adams Candy Kitchen.

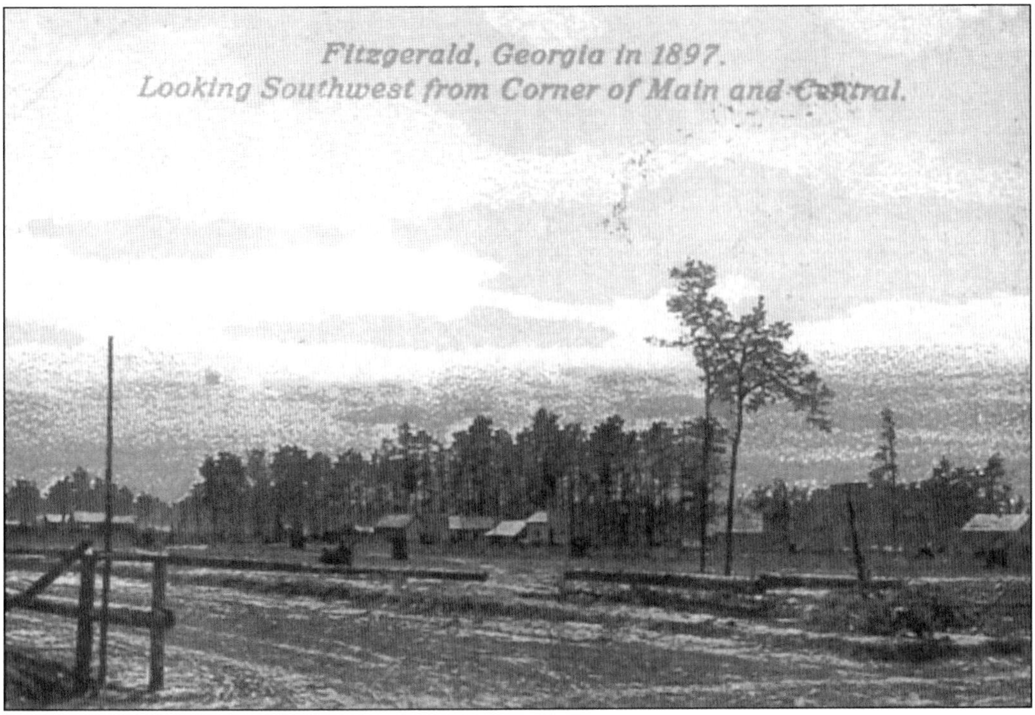

Looking Southwest from Corner of Main and Central. Two views captured from the same location are separated by 15 years—the top is from 1897 and the bottom is from 1912.

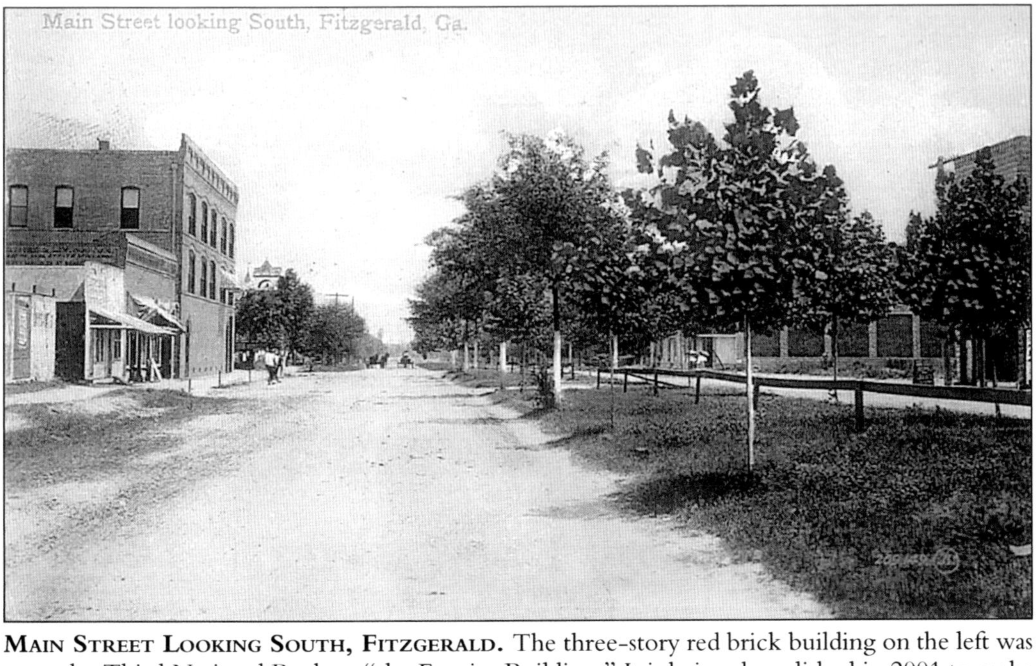

Main Street Looking South, Fitzgerald. The three-story red brick building on the left was once the Third National Bank or "the Empire Building." It is being demolished in 2001 to make way for a parking lot.

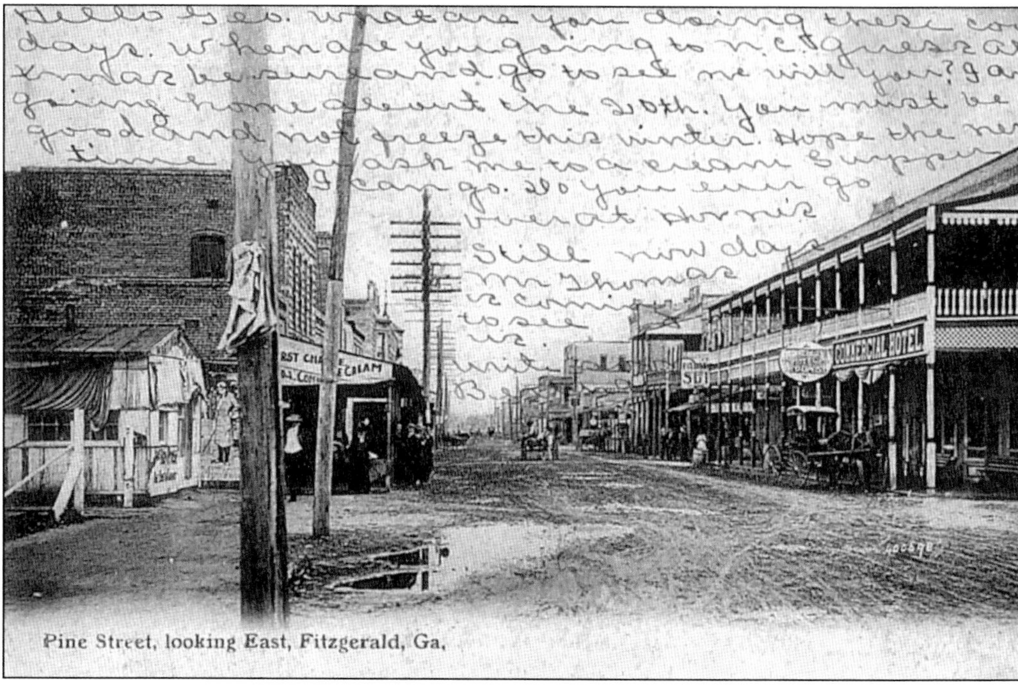

Pine Street Looking East, Fitzgerald. First Chance Ice Cream is on the left side of the street and the Commercial Hotel on the right. From the puddles on the street it appears there has been a recent rain.

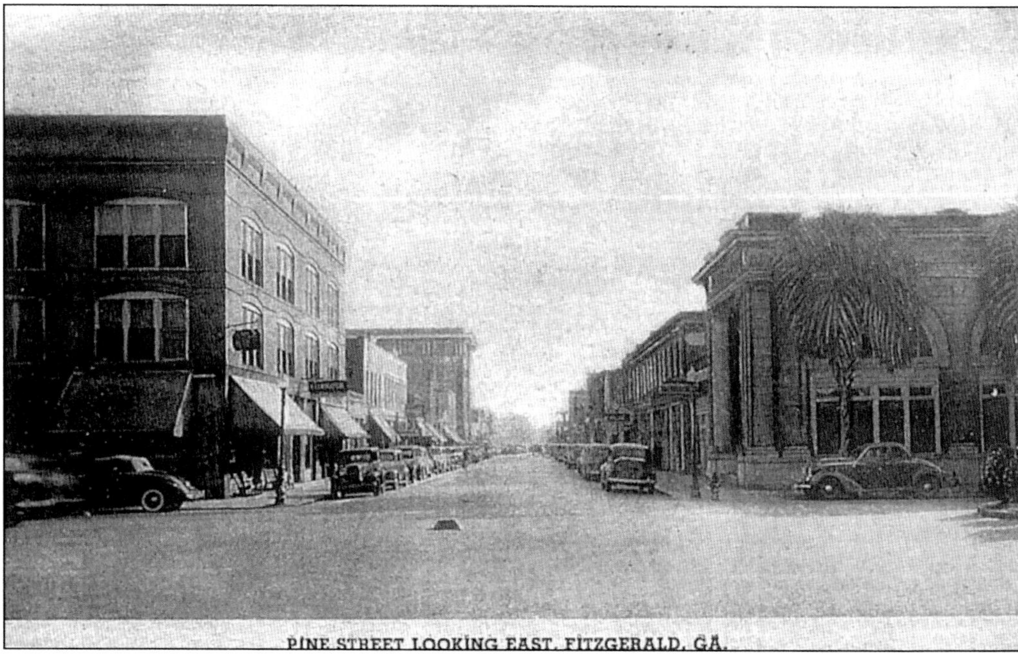

Pine Street Looking East. A 1930s view shows the street lined with automobiles.

Six

PEOPLE

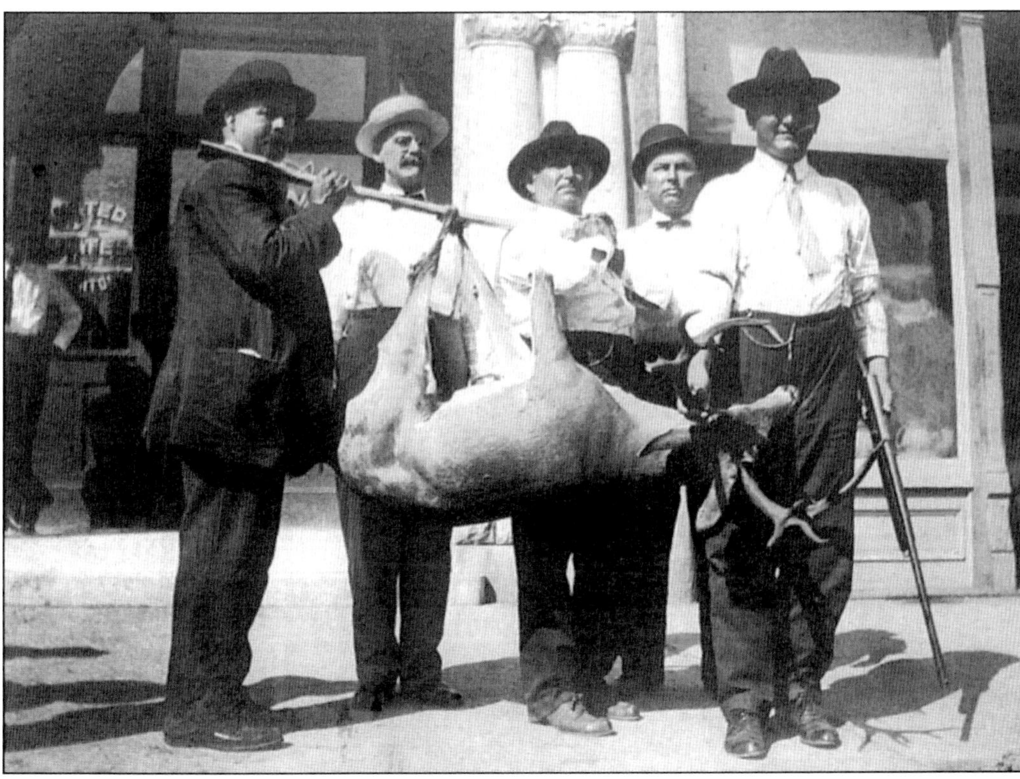

LOCAL HUNTERS. Dr. E.J. Dorminy, holding a Belgian automatic, stands proudly displaying a trophy buck. This photo was probably made around the time of World War I. Some locals hunted in Paulk's pasture near Brunswick. The buck appears to be an eight- or ten-pointer.

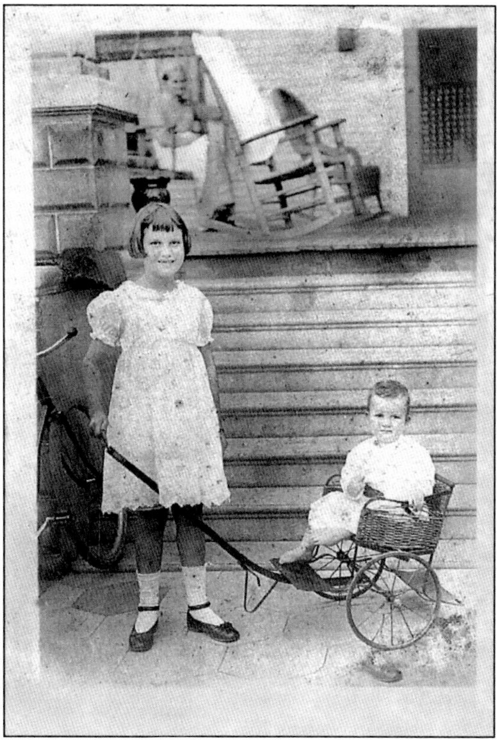

Isabell and Edna Jack Paulk, c. 1910. This real-photo postcard was made in Fitzgerald.

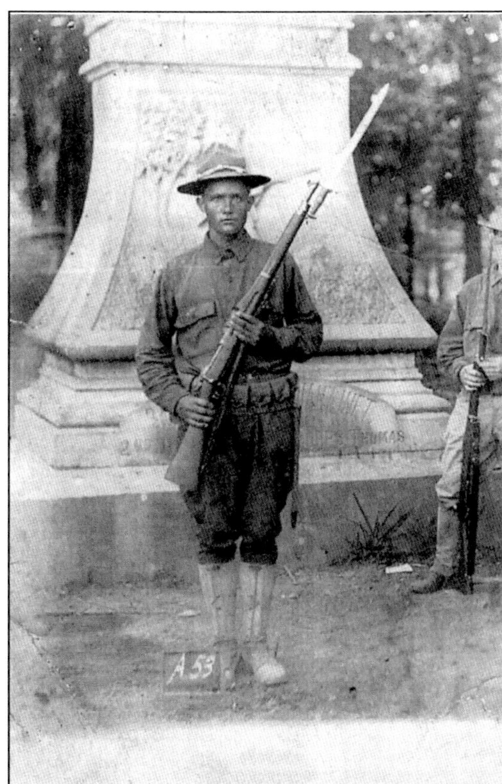

George David Davis, Ocilla, 1917. Davis stands with his firearm in front of a Confederate monument. (Courtesy of Mildred D. Cook.)

DAVIS BROTHERS, *c*. 1917. James Watson Davis and Tom Davis posed for this real-photo postcard in Ocilla. (Courtesy of Mildred D. Cook.)

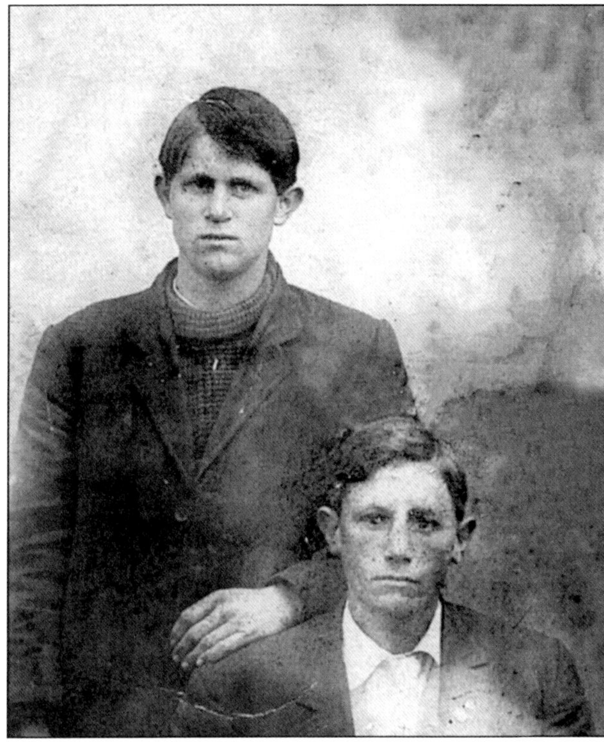

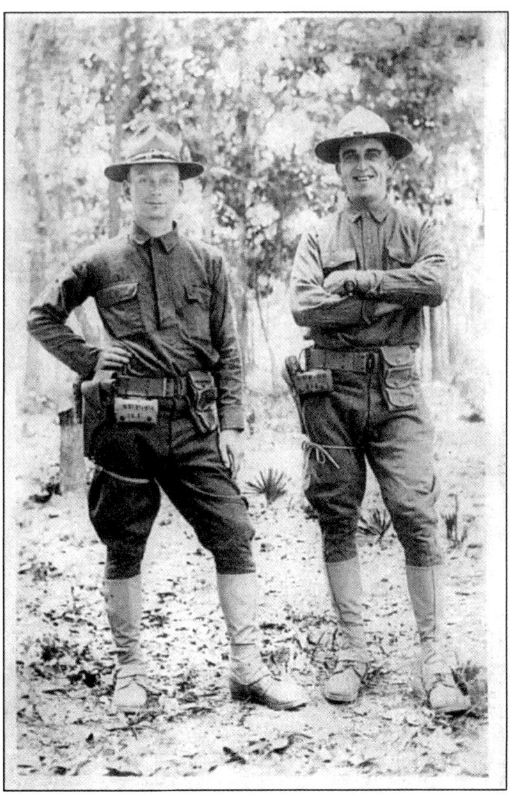

WORLD WAR I. These unidentified soldiers pose on a bivouac for a real-photo postcard ***c***. 1918.

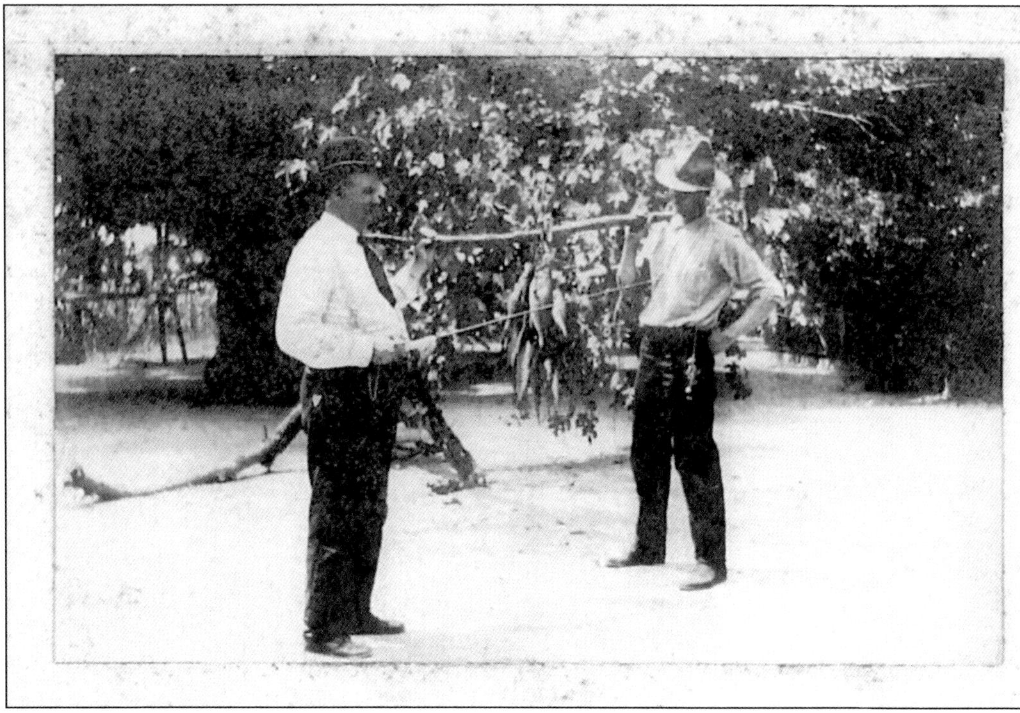

A Nice Catch, c. 1914. Dr. E.D. Dorminy and a friend display their catch. Notice Dorminy's short rod and reel. The big fish are "Southern trout" or large mouth black bass.

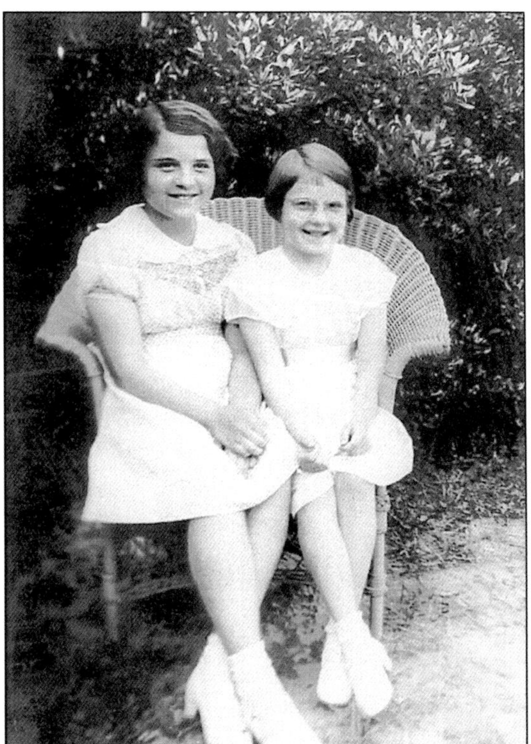

McElroy Sisters. Caroline McElroy and Mary McElroy are pictured around 1935 in Fitzgerald. The photograph was then made into a real-photo postcard.

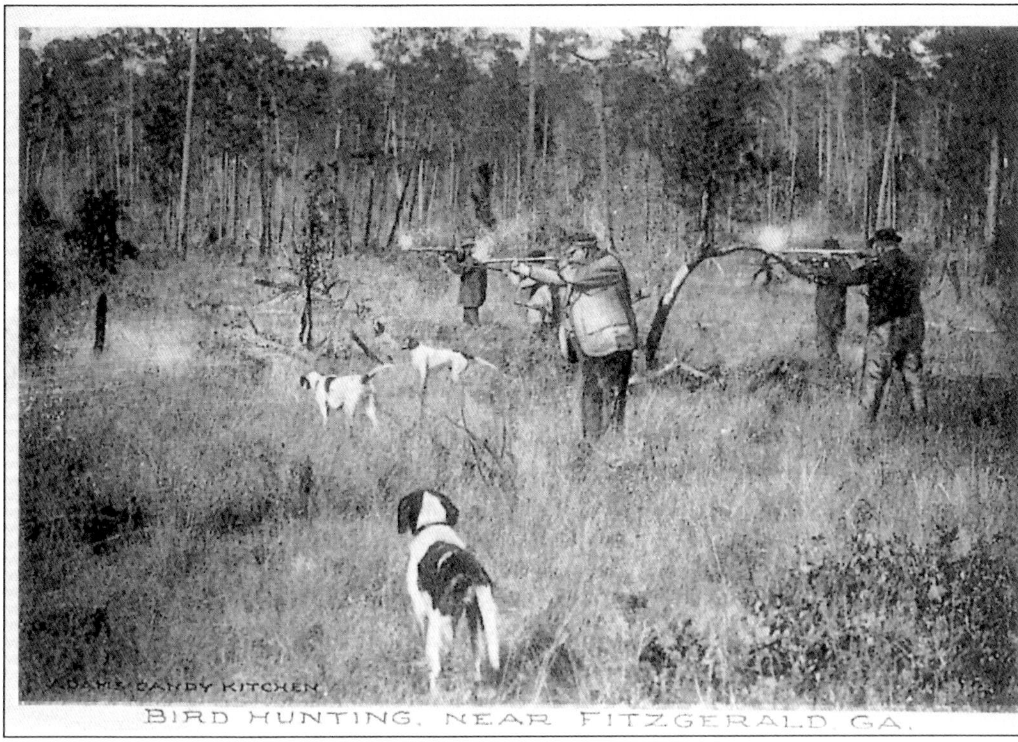

BIRD HUNTING NEAR FITZGERALD, C. 1907. The bird being hunted was known as a bob white, quail, or partridge—all terms referring to the same bird. Five hunters fire at once into a covey rise in this real-photo postcard. The dogs are liver-spotted pointers. This card was sold by Adams Candy Kitchen.

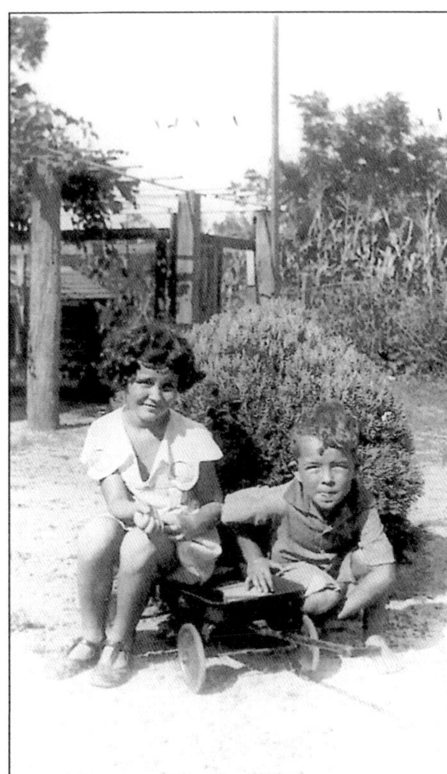

ANN HOPKINS AND MILTON HOPKINS JR. The siblings are pictured *c.* 1930 in Fitzgerald.

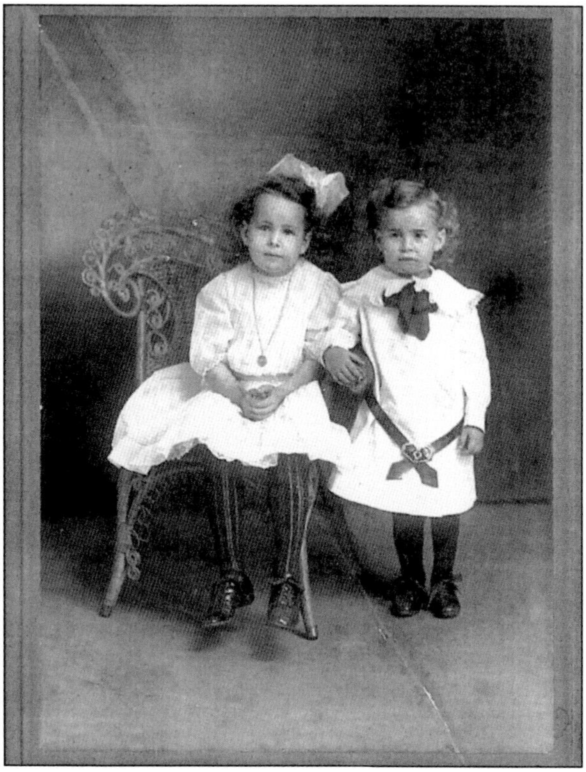

Hattie Lee Walker and Lewis Neighbors Walker. The Walker children posed for this photograph around 1906 in Fitzgerald.

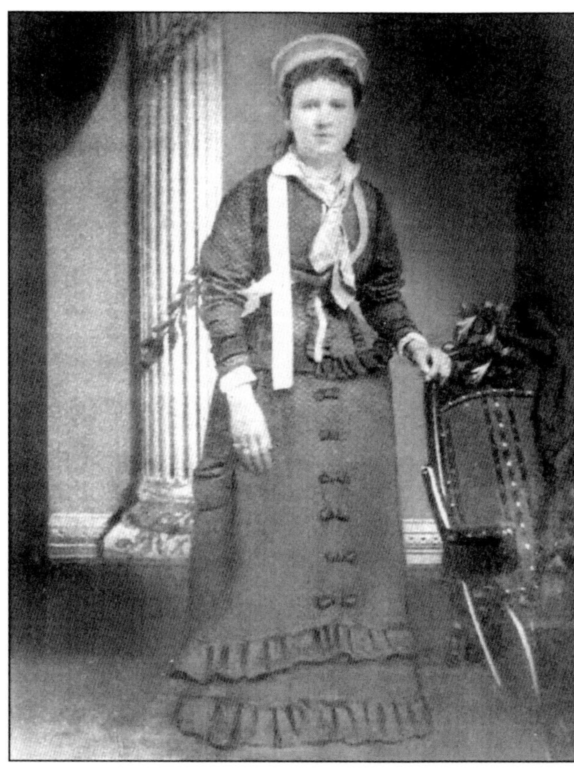

Caroline McElroy. Pictured *c*. 1900, Caroline was the mother of Dr. John Walter McElroy.

W.C. Bryan, 1909. Bryan served as an agent for the A. B. & A. Railroad as well as the Georgia and Florida Railroad. He is pictured touting Douglas and Coffee County Georgia as the "Livest Town" and "Best County."

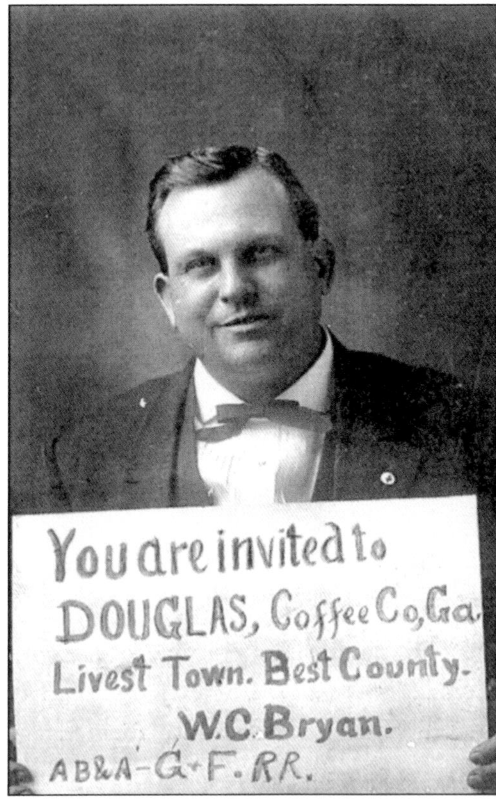

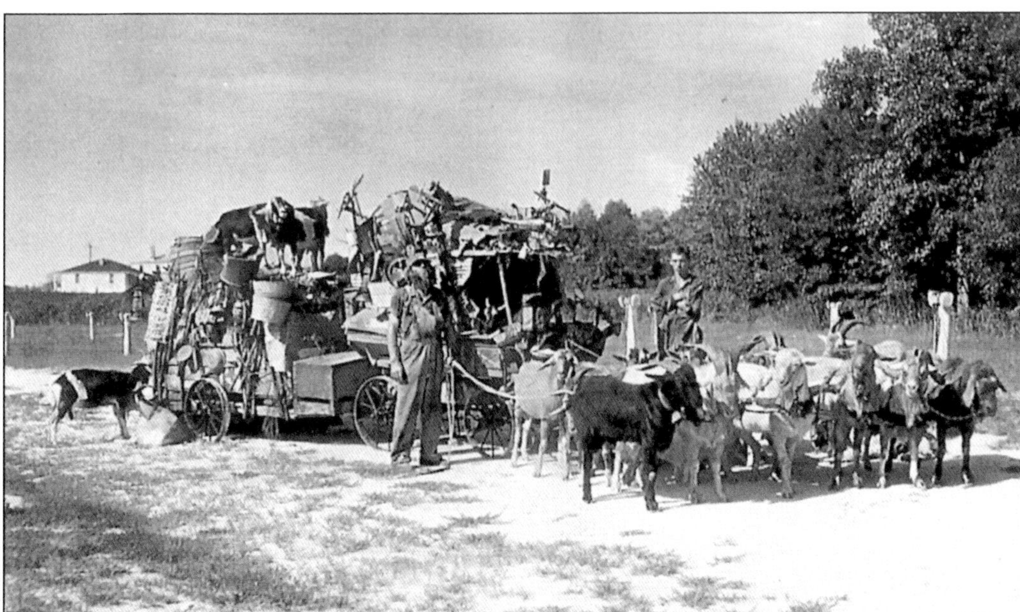

Ches McCartney, the Goat Man. McCartney traveled the area for over 40 years on his way to and from Florida. At one time he had 32 goats and slept with them at night. The author met him several times and remembers cars being backed up for miles behind him.

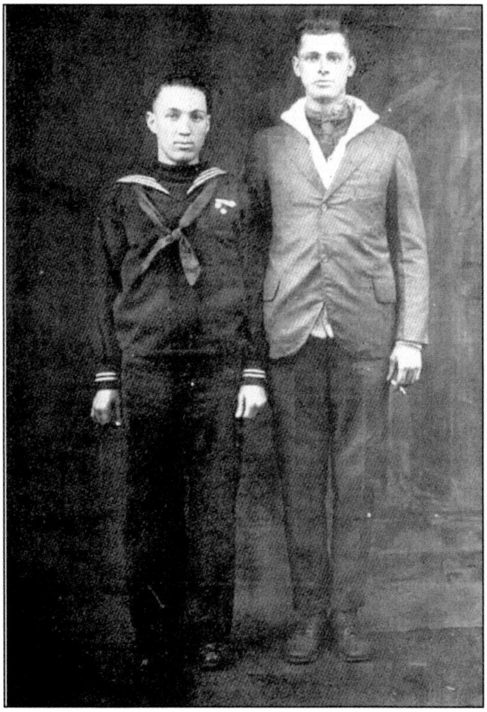

World War I. The man on the left is unidentified; the man on the right is Dean Hopkins.

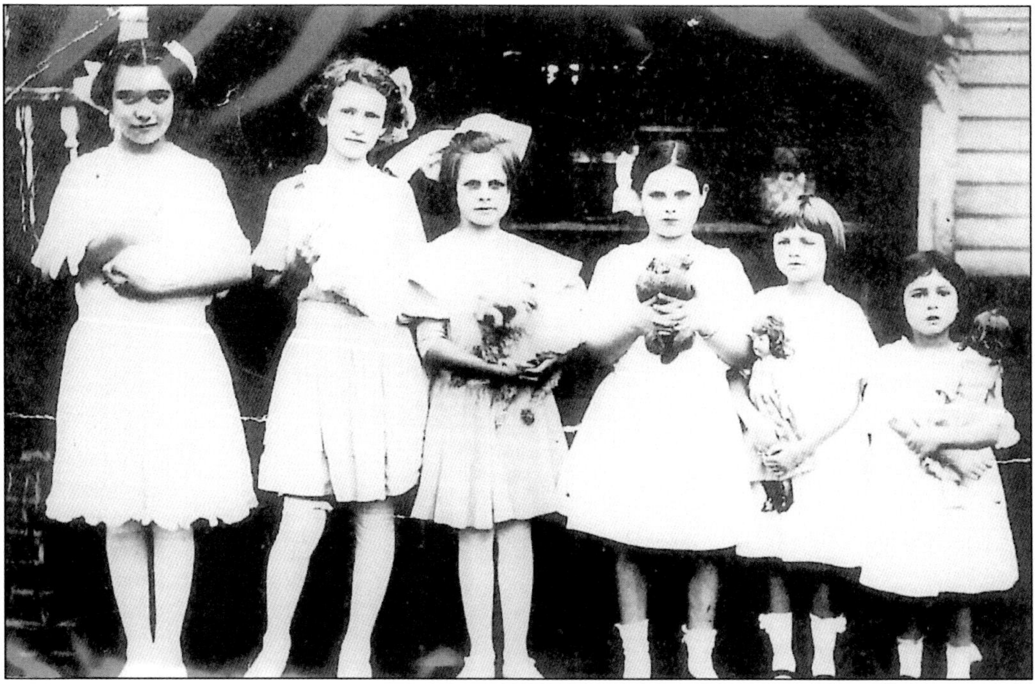

Hands Full. In this c. 1912 real-photo card, from left to right, two unidentified girls hold a live rabbit and a live duck, Eulalie Dorminy (1904–1995) holds a live puppy, Thelma Louise Dorminy (1903–1979) holds a live chicken, Annie Elizabeth Dorminy (1906–1986) holds a doll, and Frances Rebecca Dorminy (1908–1915) holds a doll.

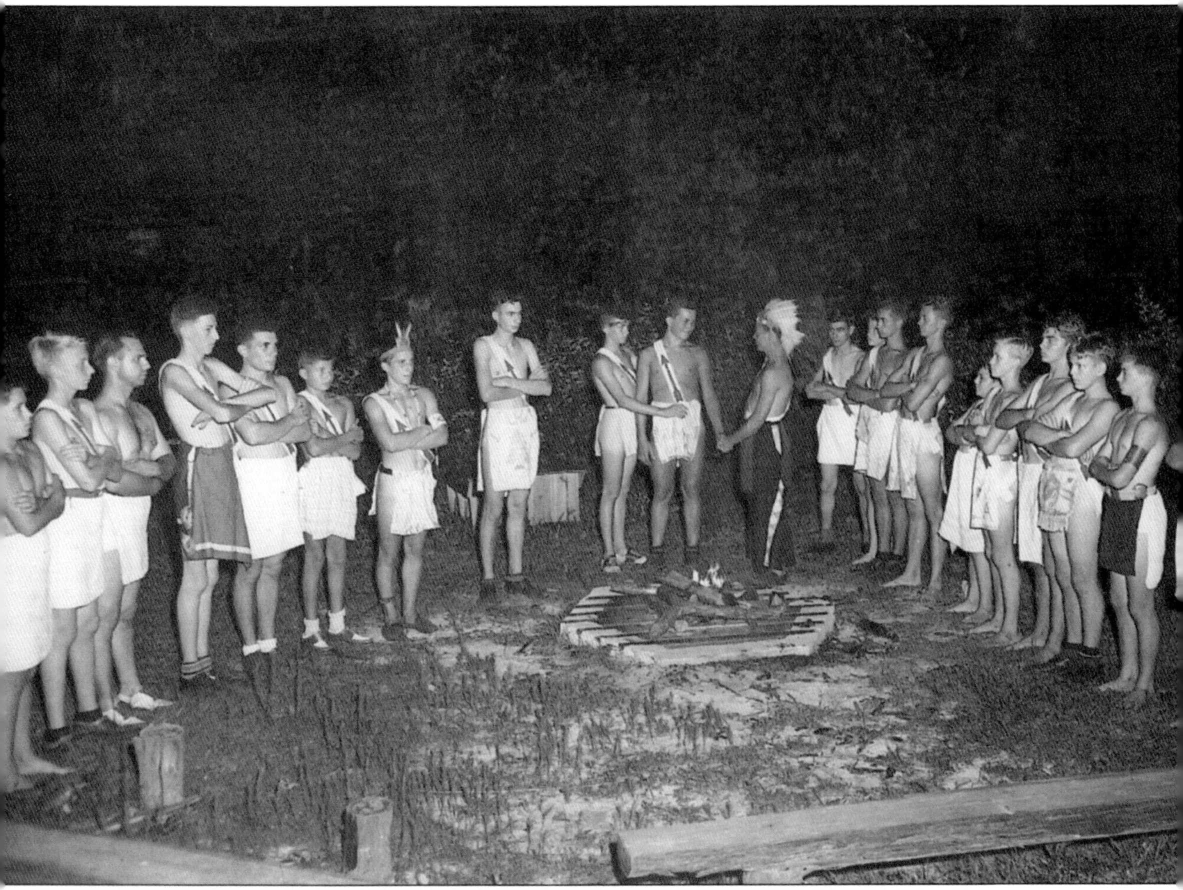

Order of the Arrow Boy Scouts of America. The Okefenokee Area Council met at the Laura Walker State Park in Waycross, Georgia, in 1942. Fitzgerald, Ocilla, and Valdosta scouts are pictured.

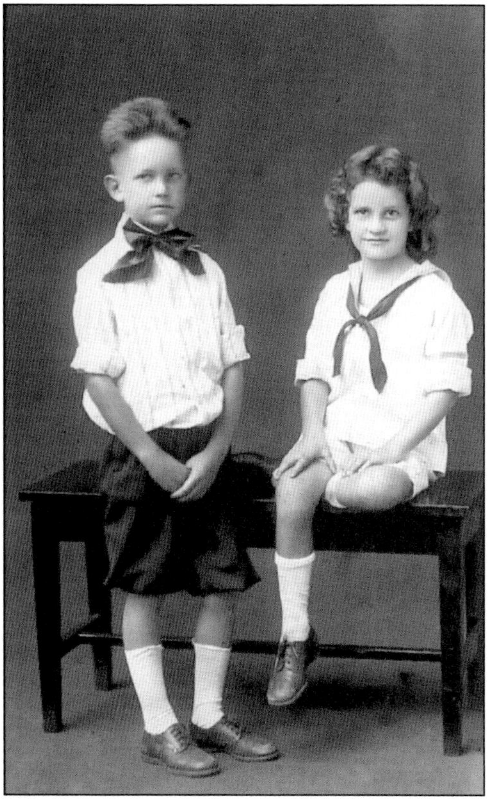

The Paulk Children. These siblings posed for a photograph in the early 20th century.

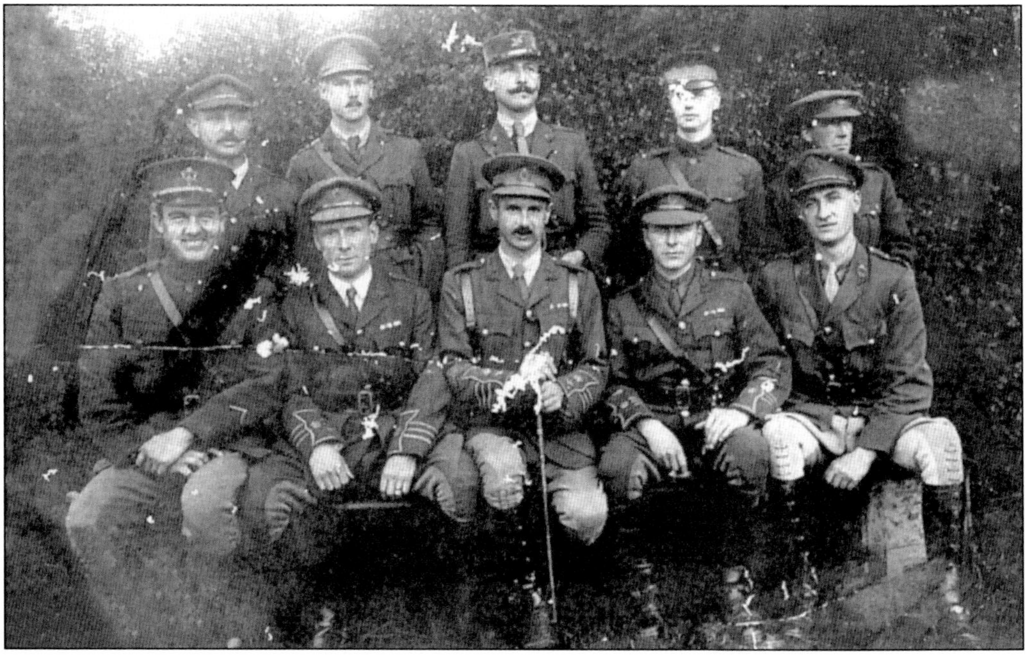

Dr. J. W. McElroy in France. Pictured on the first row, far left, Dr. McElroy is surrounded by French and British compatriots during World War I.

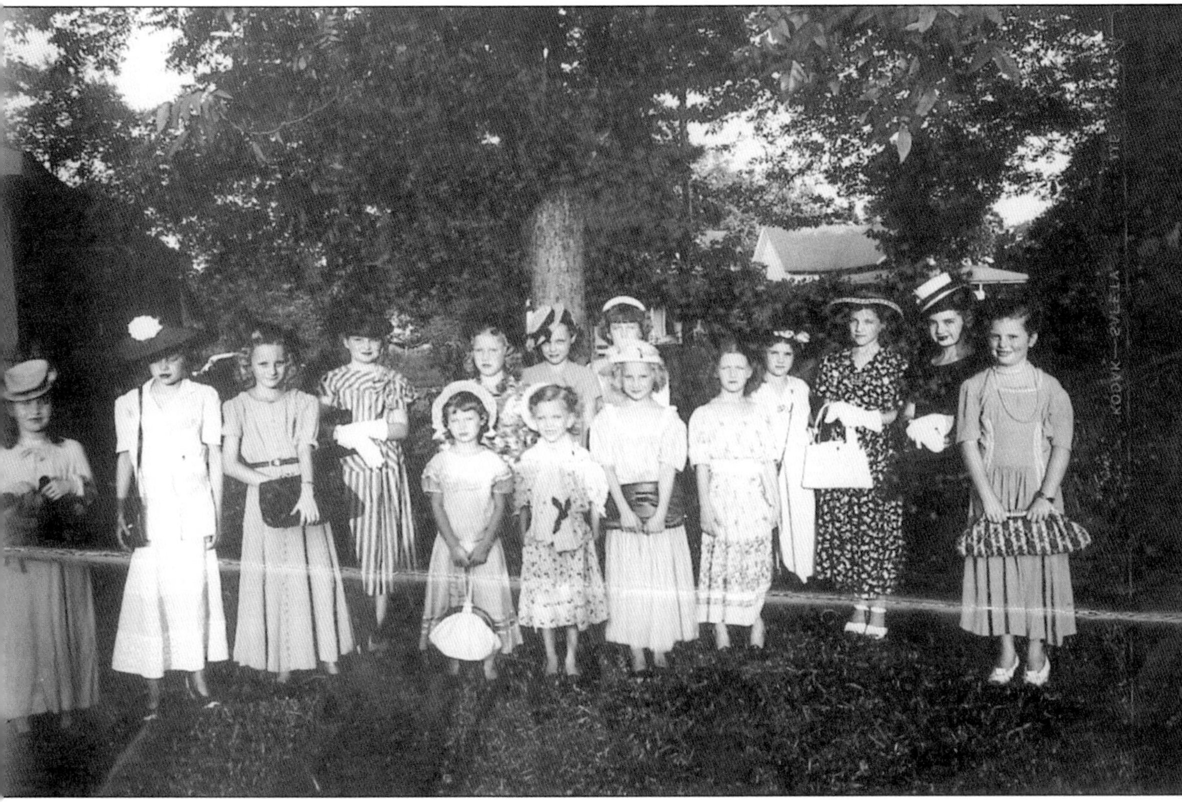

Dress-up Party. A 1940s photograph depicts a group of young girls in Fitzgerald playing "dress-up." Note the oversized clothes, hats, and purses.

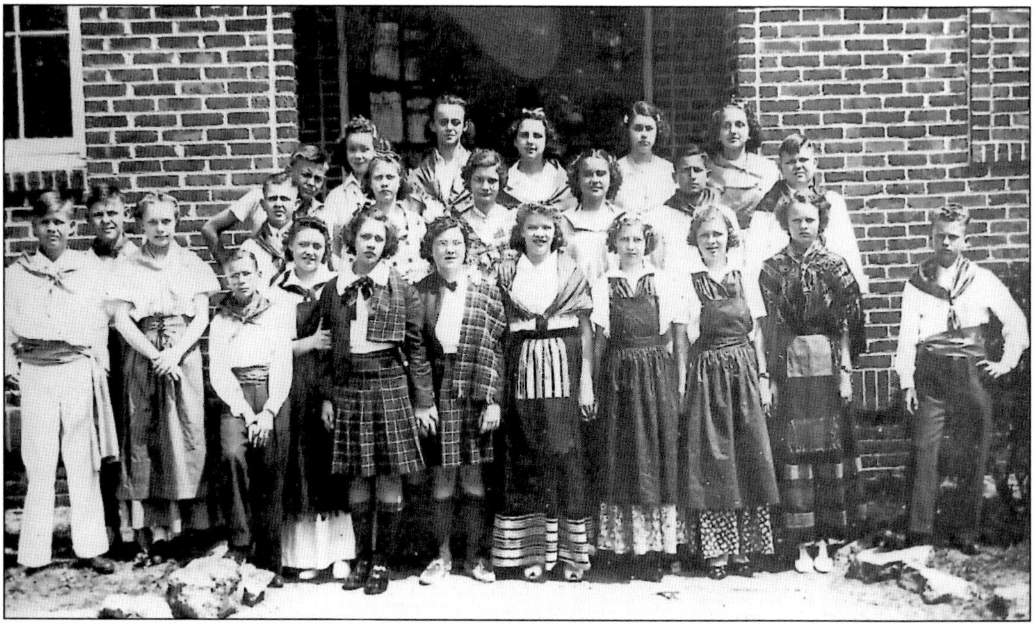

First Ward School, Fitzgerald. The seventh-grade students, pictured from left to right, include the following: (front row) Ollie Baker, two unidentified, Clyde Bailey, Maxine Faulk, Elaine Mann, Mary McElroy, Edna Tom Owens, Doris Goodwin, two unidentified, and Jack Gibbs; (middle row) Jack Courson, unidentified, Pauline House, unidentified, James Whittle, and Dewey Butler; (back row) Jack Cavanagh, Annibelle Cone, Florence Cross, Jeanette Norris, Lila Clark, and Melba Smith.

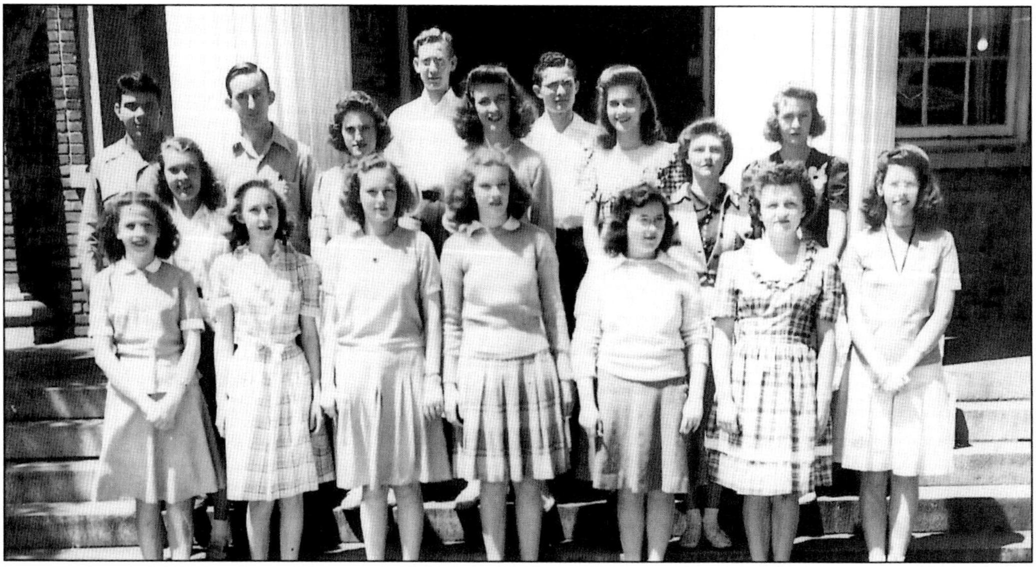

Fitzgerald High School, Class of 1945. From left to right are (front row) Martha Ann Sanders, Charlie Curtis Smith, Mildred Evans, Edna Tom Owens, Mary Edwin McElroy, Juanita Tomberlin, and Lila Clarke; (middle row) Jean Helton, LaNelle Bailey, Carolyn Mathis, Juliann McDaniel, Rosa Faye Spears, and Julia Francis Tucker; (back row) Donald Hobby, Henry Hitch, Leonard Hall, and Earl Troup.

Seven

Churches, Schools, and Public Buildings

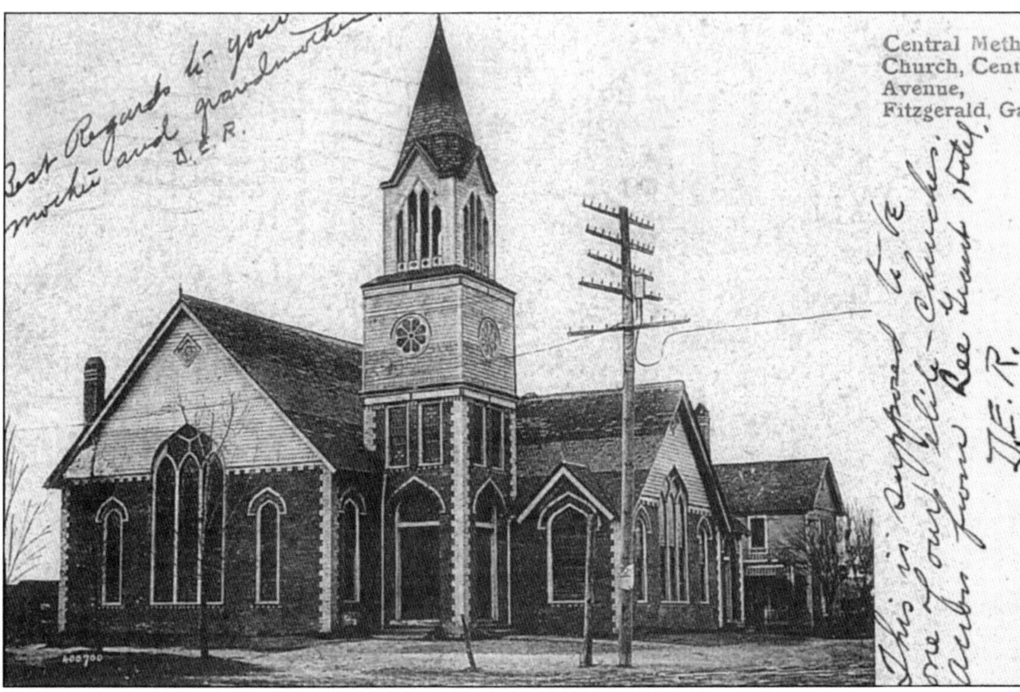

Central Methodist Church, Fitzgerald, Early 1900s. This church is located on Central Avenue across from the Lee-Grant Hotel. The sender wrote on the card "this is supposed to be one of our elite churches."

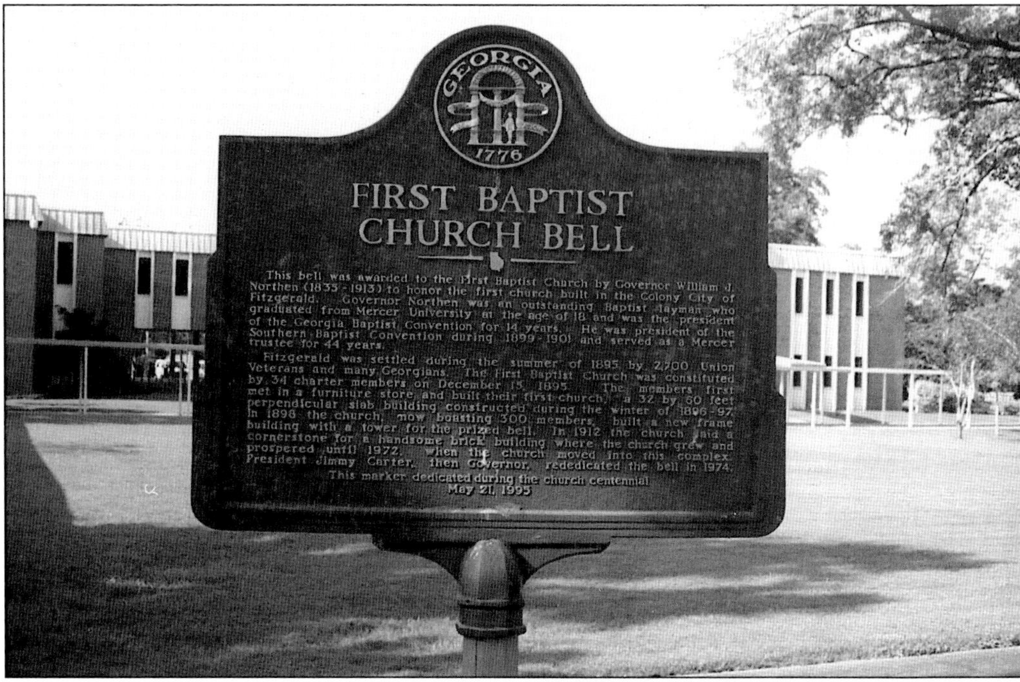

FIRST BAPTIST CHURCH BELL MARKER. In 1898 First Baptist Church built another building and belfry to house the prized bell. It was again moved to a new building in 1912 on South Main Street. This building was razed in 1972. The newest First Baptist Church is located on South Merrimac Drive where the bell is displayed. It was rededicated by President Jimmy Carter in 1974.

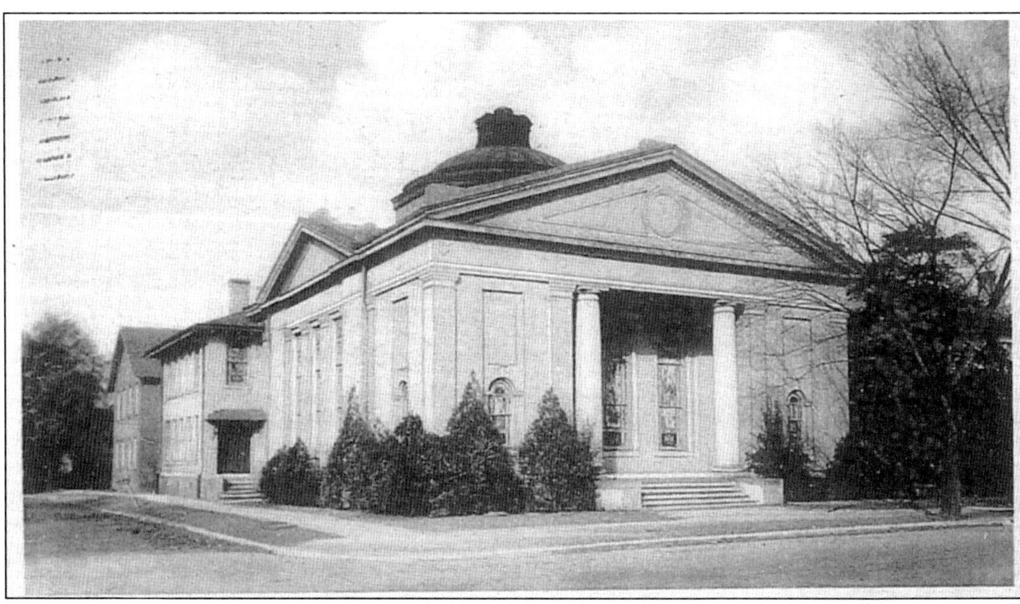

FIRST BAPTIST CHURCH, FITZGERALD. This church was built in 1912 on South Main Street. The postcard was mailed in 1942. The author was baptized here in the mid-1930s by Rev. James F. Singleton.

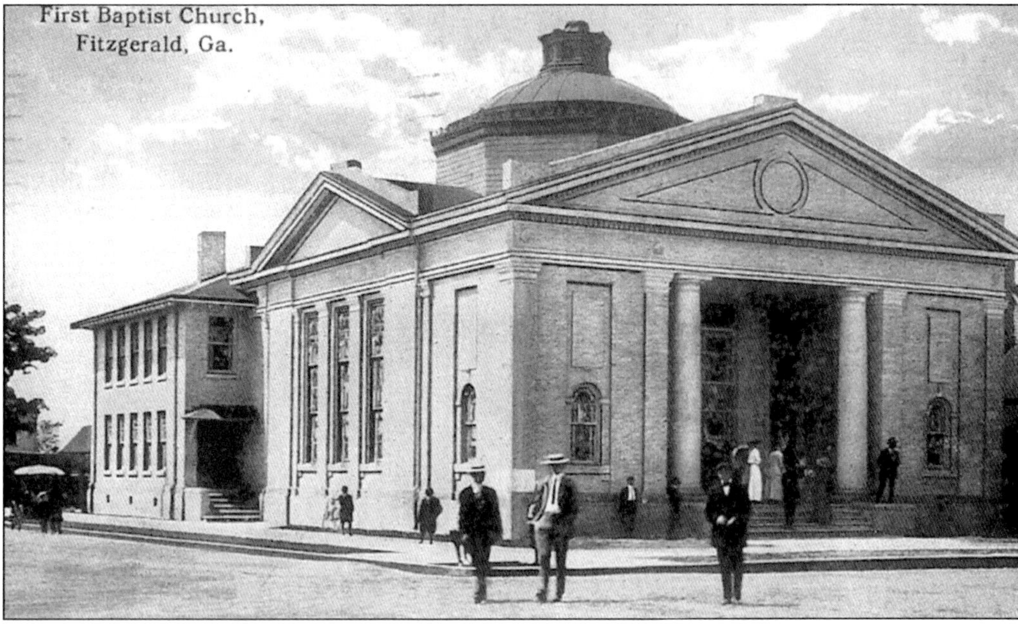

FIRST BAPTIST CHURCH, CORNER OF MAIN AND MAGNOLIA STREETS. In later years the dome was removed from the church. The whole building was razed in the 1980s and turned into a parking lot for Paulk Funeral Home.

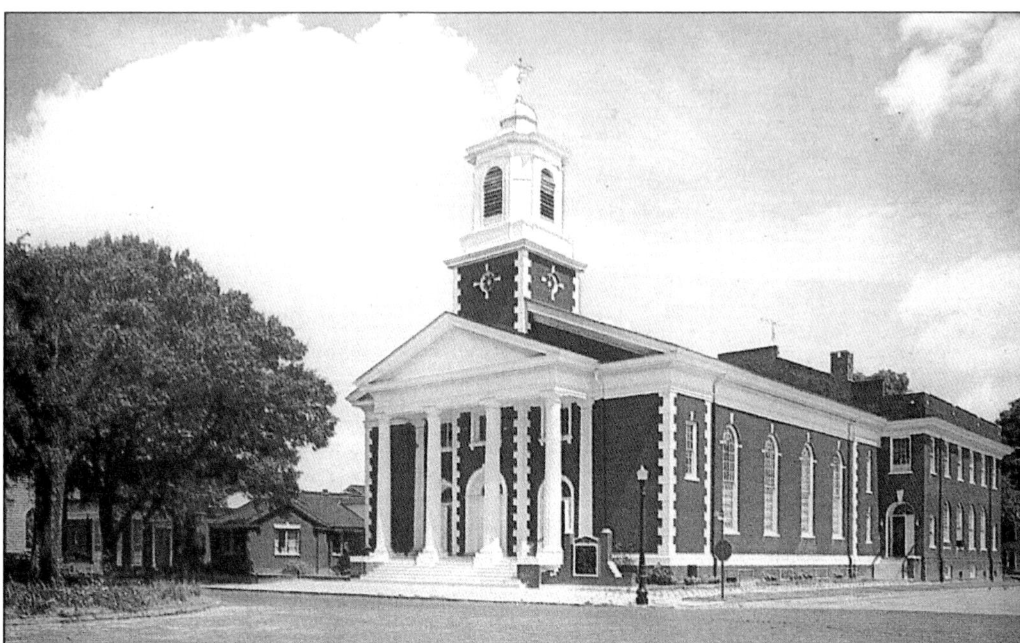

CENTRAL METHODIST CHURCH, FITZGERALD. The church is located on the corner of Lee Street and Central Avenue.

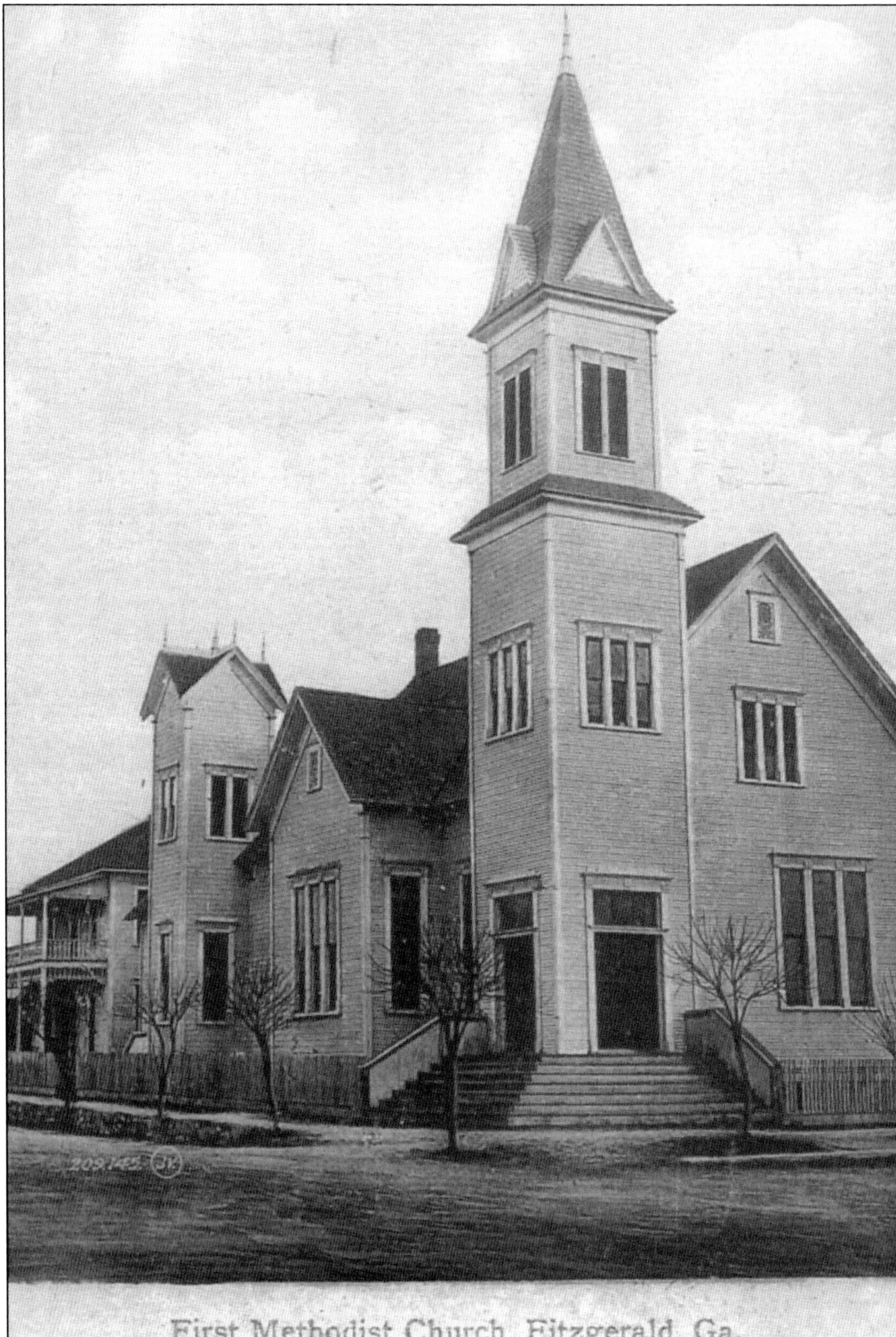

First Methodist Church. The church is pictured in Fitzgerald c. 1905.

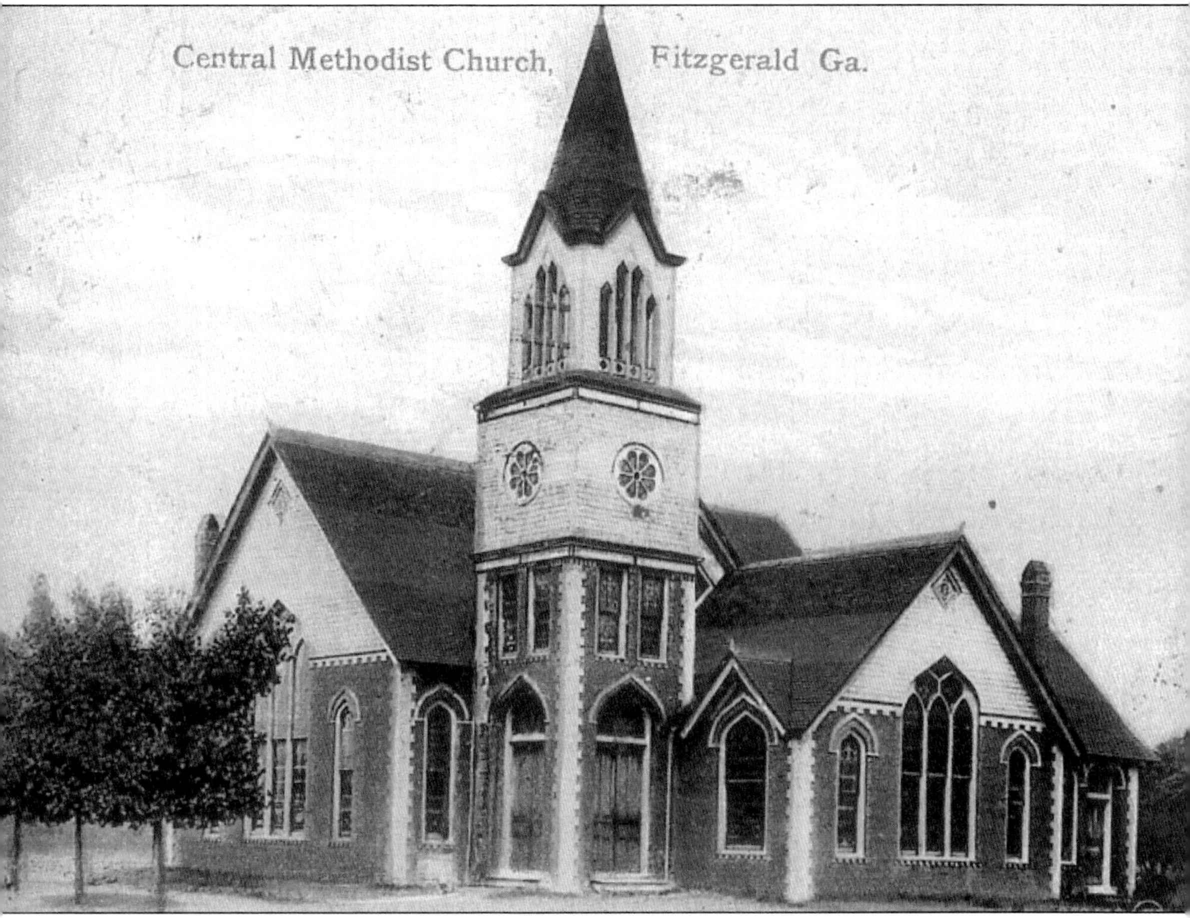

CENTRAL METHODIST CHURCH. Another postcard shows the church as it appeared in Fitzgerald in 1920.

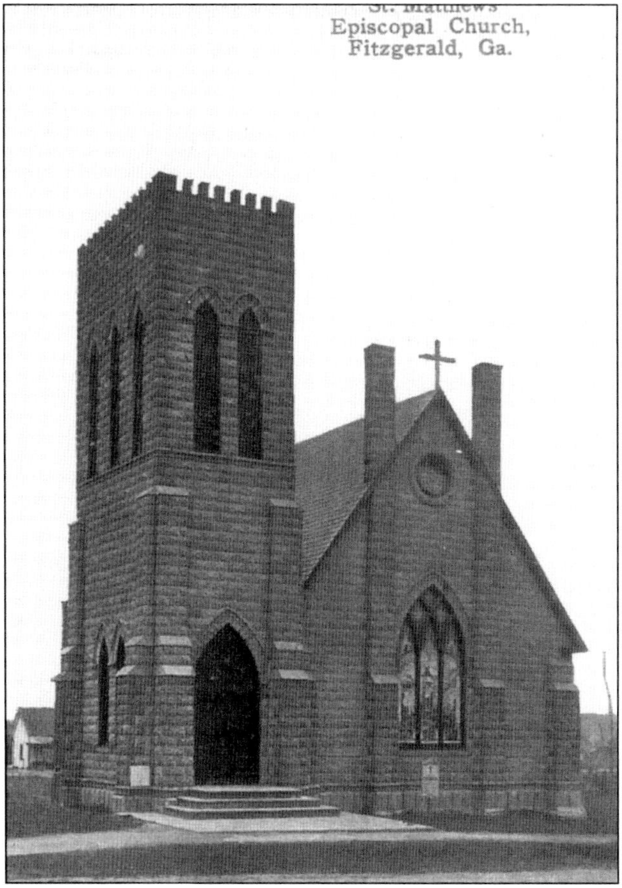

St. Matthews Episcopal Church. It was built in 1905 at 212 West Pine Street with granitoid block from the Fitzgerald Granitoid Company.

Central Christian Church. This church is located at 326 South Lee Street in Fitzgerald.

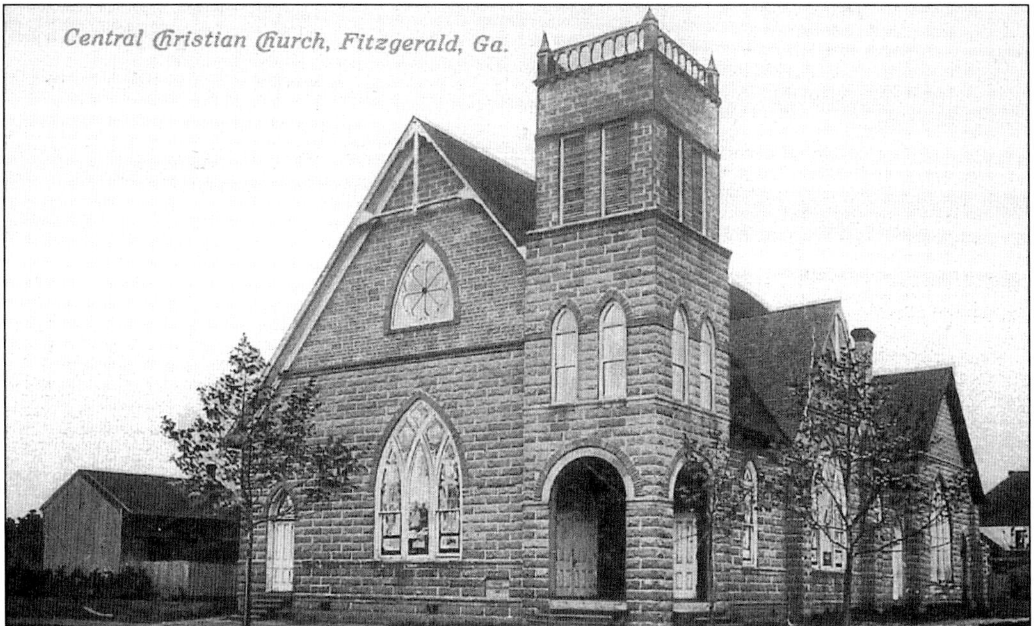

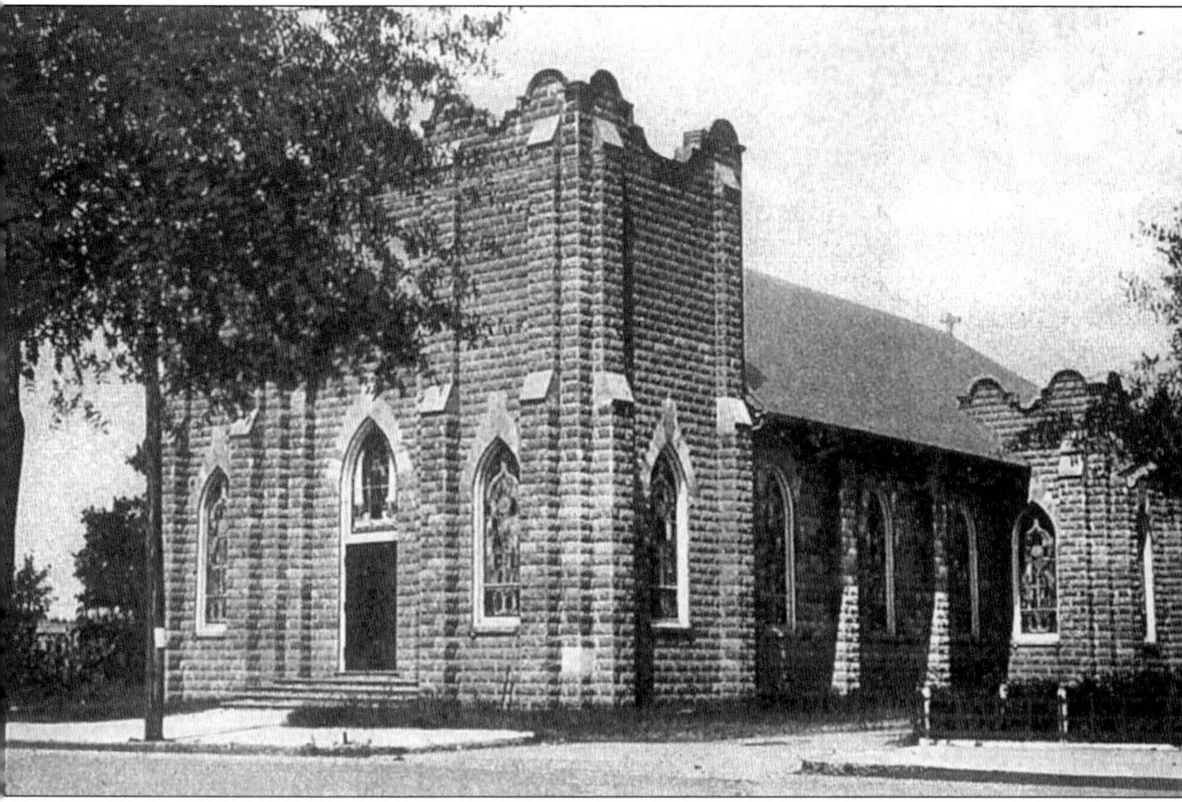

CATHOLIC CHURCH, FITZGERALD. Located on West Central Avenue, the church was demolished in the 1960s. (Courtesy of Louis Harper.)

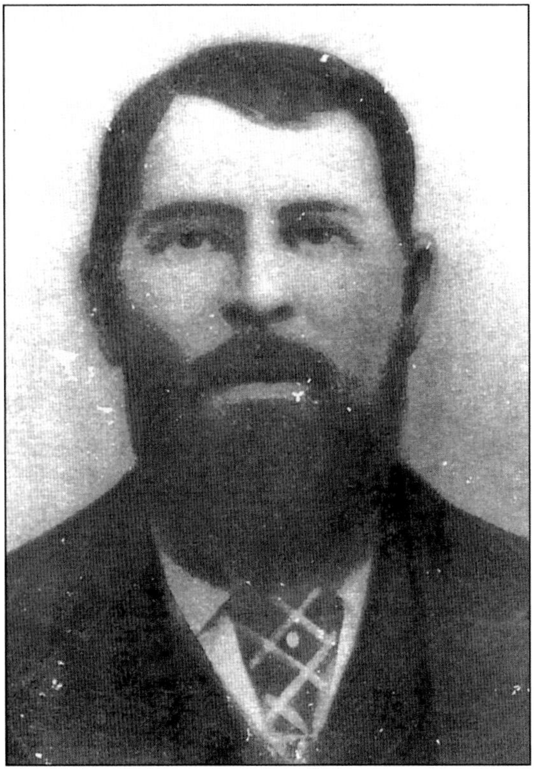

Joel Gaskin (1838–1904). Gaskin was the founder of Gaskin Springs Camp Meeting in Douglas, Georgia in 1895. He later gave the land to the Methodist church and camp meetings are held there each year. Methodist Bishop Arthur J. Moore delivered his first sermon as a "boy" preacher at Gaskin Springs. (Courtesy of Jim Cottingham.)

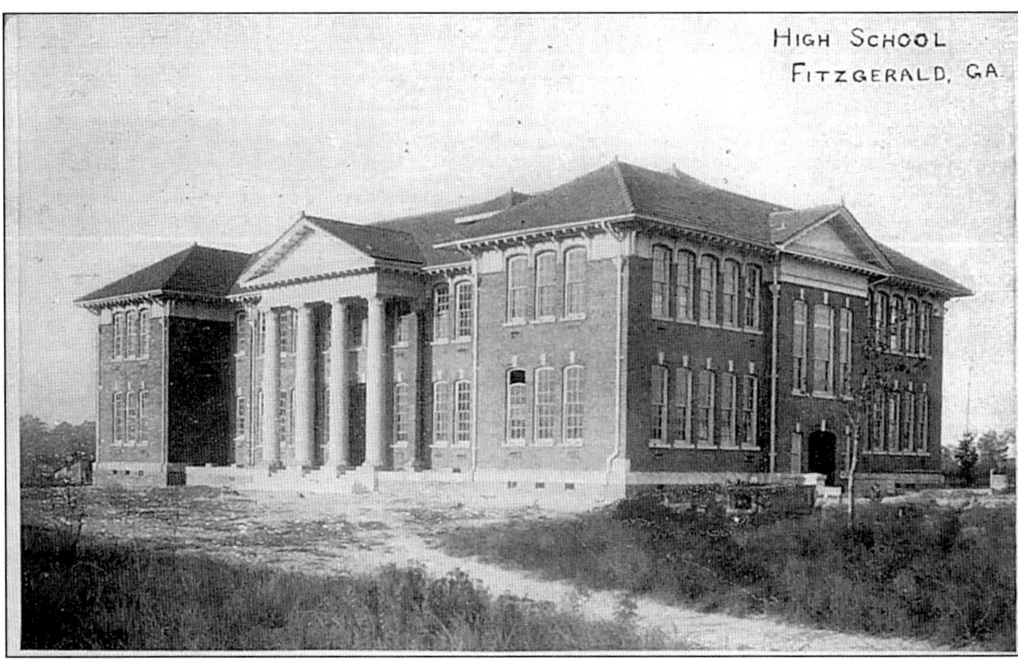

High School, Fitzgerald. The school was built in 1909 and this real-photo postcard is postmarked 1912.

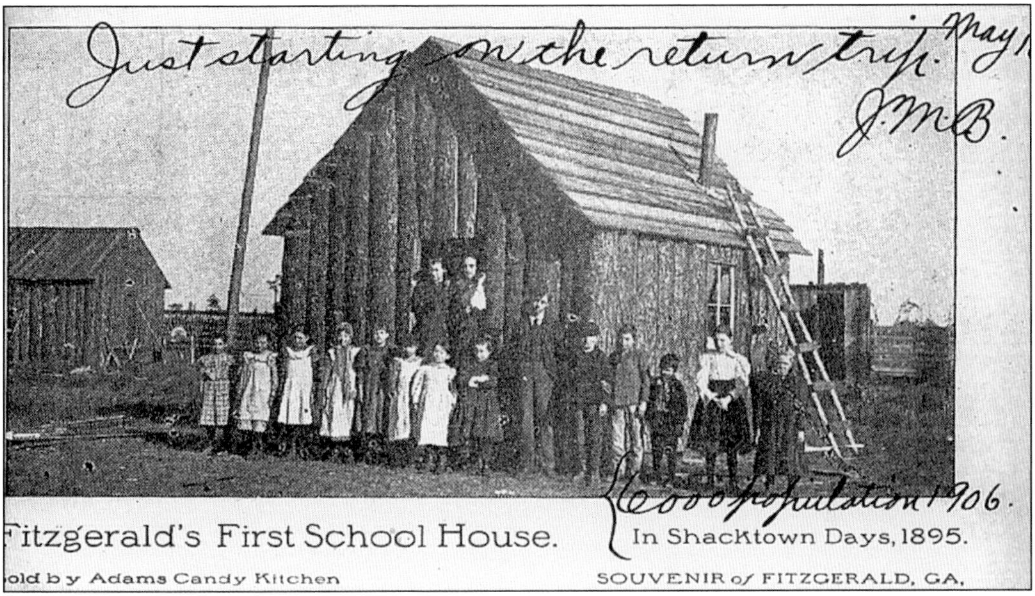

FITZGERALD'S FIRST SCHOOL HOUSE. A handwritten note on the card speculates "6,000 population 1906." The exterior sheeting on the school is sawmill throwaway pine slabs. The card was sold by Adams Candy Kitchen.

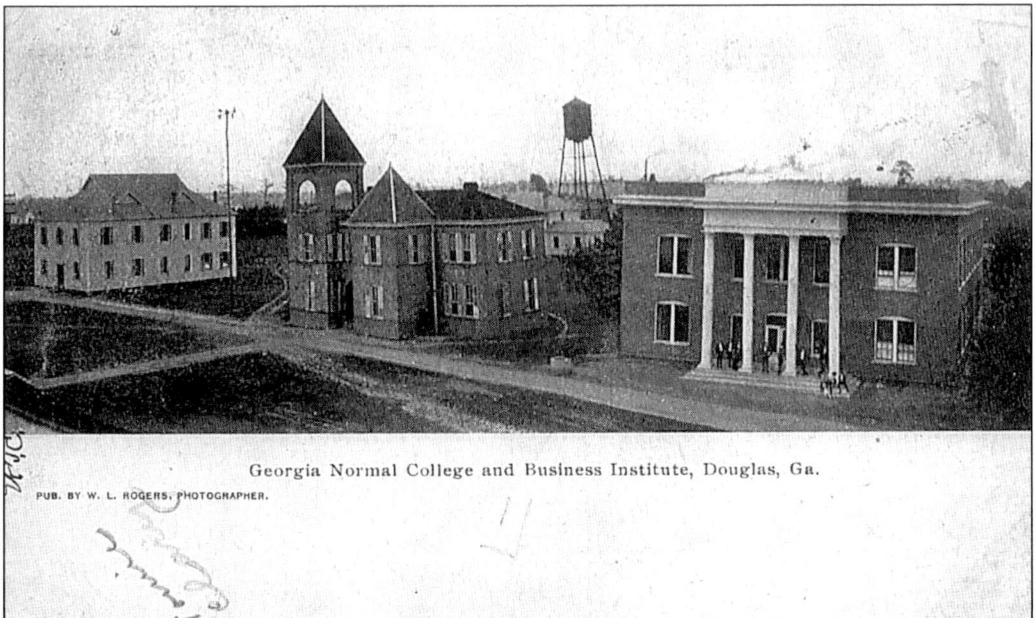

GEORGIA NORMAL COLLEGE AND BUSINESS INSTITUTE. This school was located in Douglas and is pictured here in 1914.

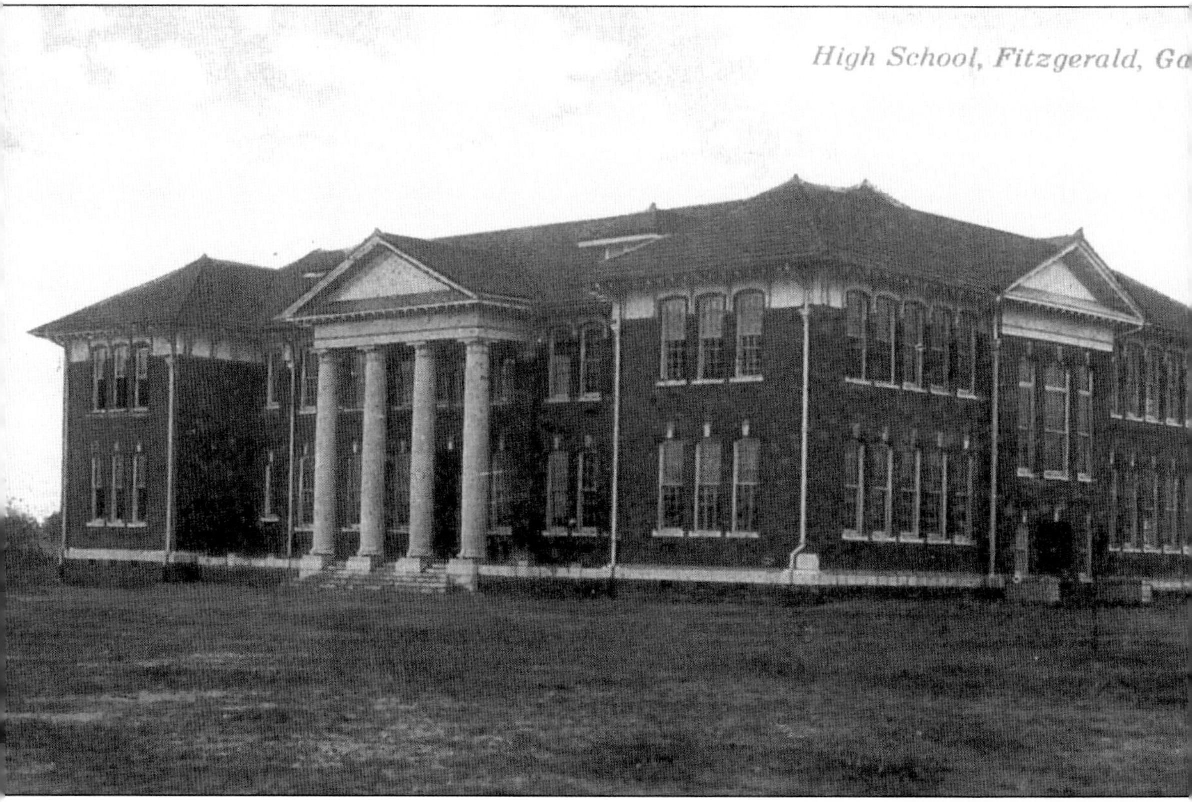

High School, Fitzgerald, Georgia. Built in 1909 on South Johnston Street, the school is being remodeled in 2001.

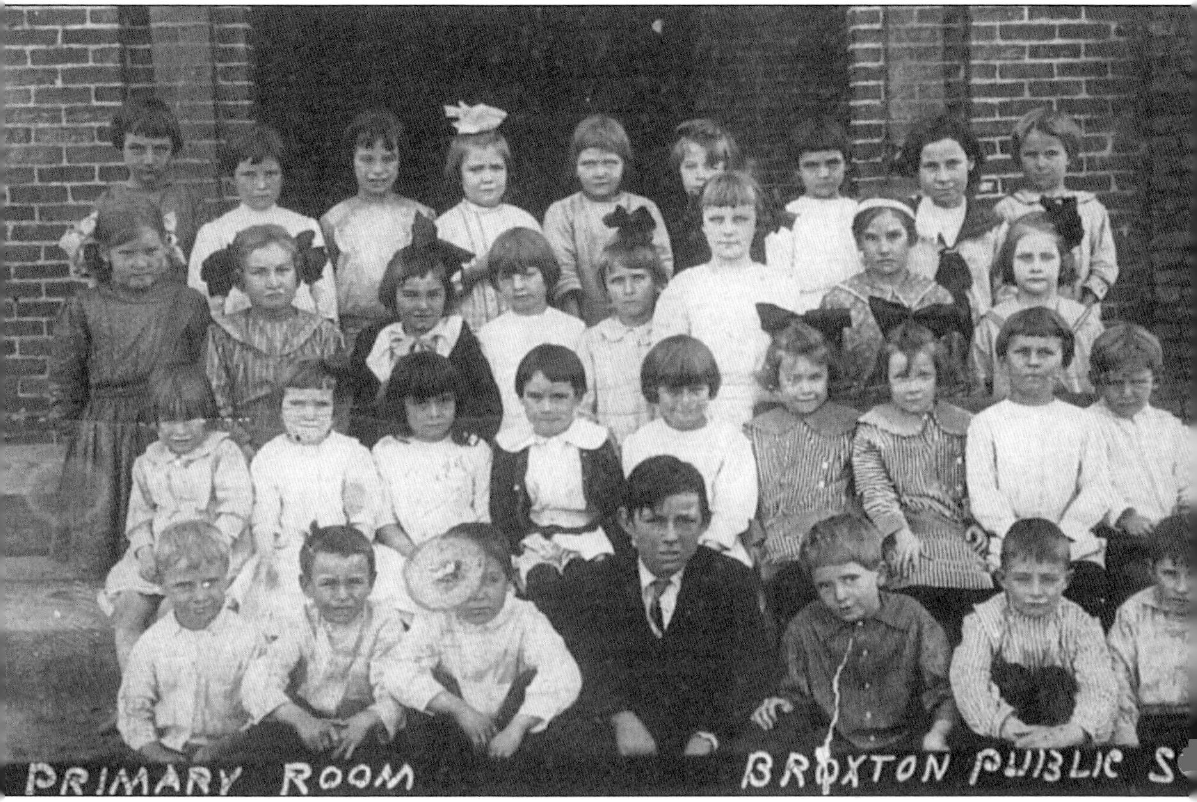

BROXTON PUBLIC SCHOOL, BROXTON, GEORGIA. Included in this early 1900s photo are Eulalie, Thelma, and Annie Elizabeth Dorminy.

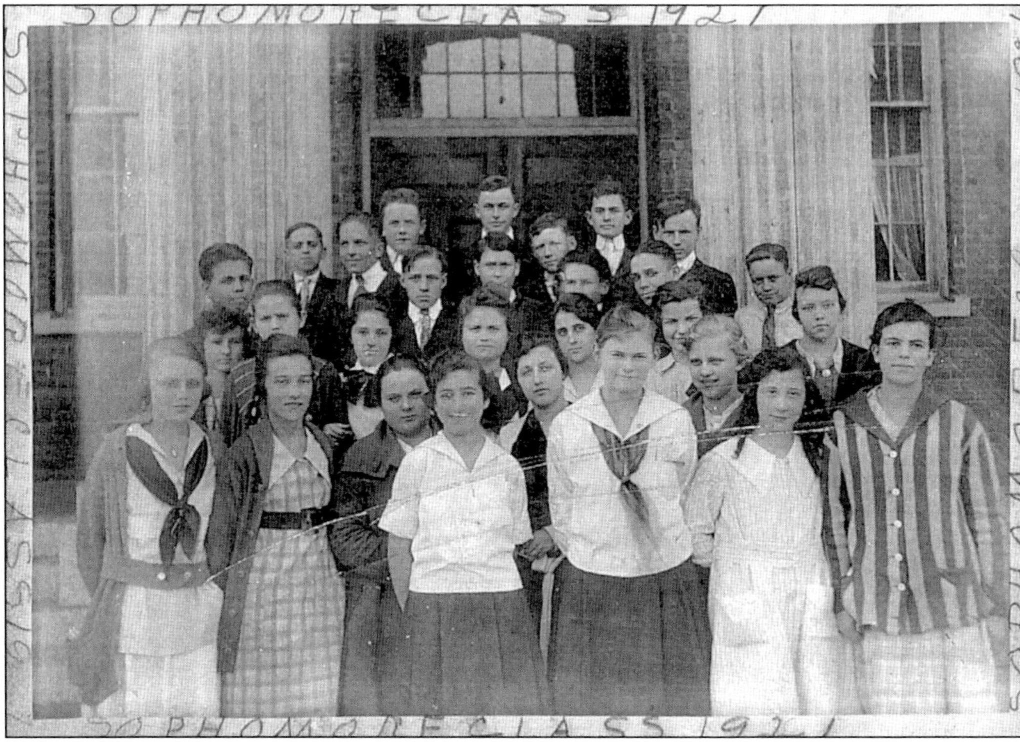

FITZGERALD HIGH SCHOOL SOPHOMORE CLASS, 1921. The author's mother-in-law, Thelma Dorminy, is pictured third from the left in the second row.

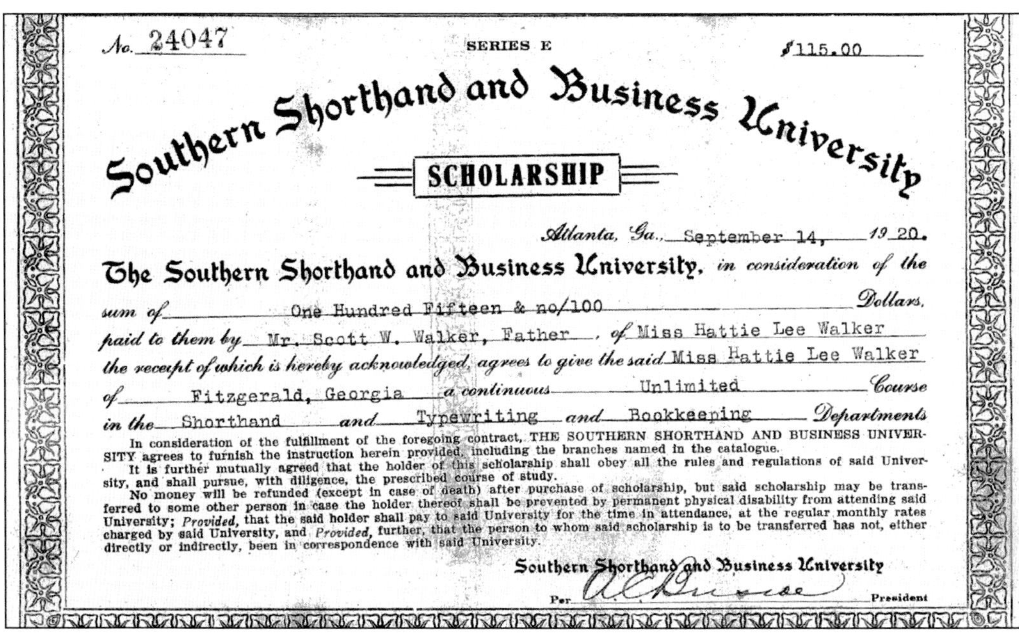

No. 24047 SERIES E $115.00

Southern Shorthand and Business University

SCHOLARSHIP

Atlanta, Ga., September 14, 1920.

The Southern Shorthand and Business University, in consideration of the sum of One Hundred Fifteen & no/100 Dollars, paid to them by Mr. Scott W. Walker, Father, of Miss Hattie Lee Walker the receipt of which is hereby acknowledged, agrees to give the said Miss Hattie Lee Walker of Fitzgerald, Georgia a continuous Unlimited Course in the Shorthand and Typewriting and Bookkeeping Departments

In consideration of the fulfillment of the foregoing contract, THE SOUTHERN SHORTHAND AND BUSINESS UNIVERSITY agrees to furnish the instruction herein provided, including the branches named in the catalogue.

It is further mutually agreed that the holder of this scholarship shall obey all the rules and regulations of said University, and shall pursue, with diligence, the prescribed course of study.

No money will be refunded (except in case of death) after purchase of scholarship, but said scholarship may be transferred to some other person in case the holder thereof shall be prevented by permanent physical disability from attending said University; *Provided*, that the said holder shall pay to said University for the time in attendance, at the regular monthly rates charged by said University, and *Provided*, further, that the person to whom said scholarship is to be transferred has not, either directly or indirectly, been in correspondence with said University.

Southern Shorthand and Business University

Per [signature] President

HATTIE LEE WALKER, SCHOLARSHIP RECIPIENT. Hattie Lee Walker, the author's mother, was the recipient of this scholarship in the amount of $115 to Southern Shorthand and Business University in Atlanta in September of 1920.

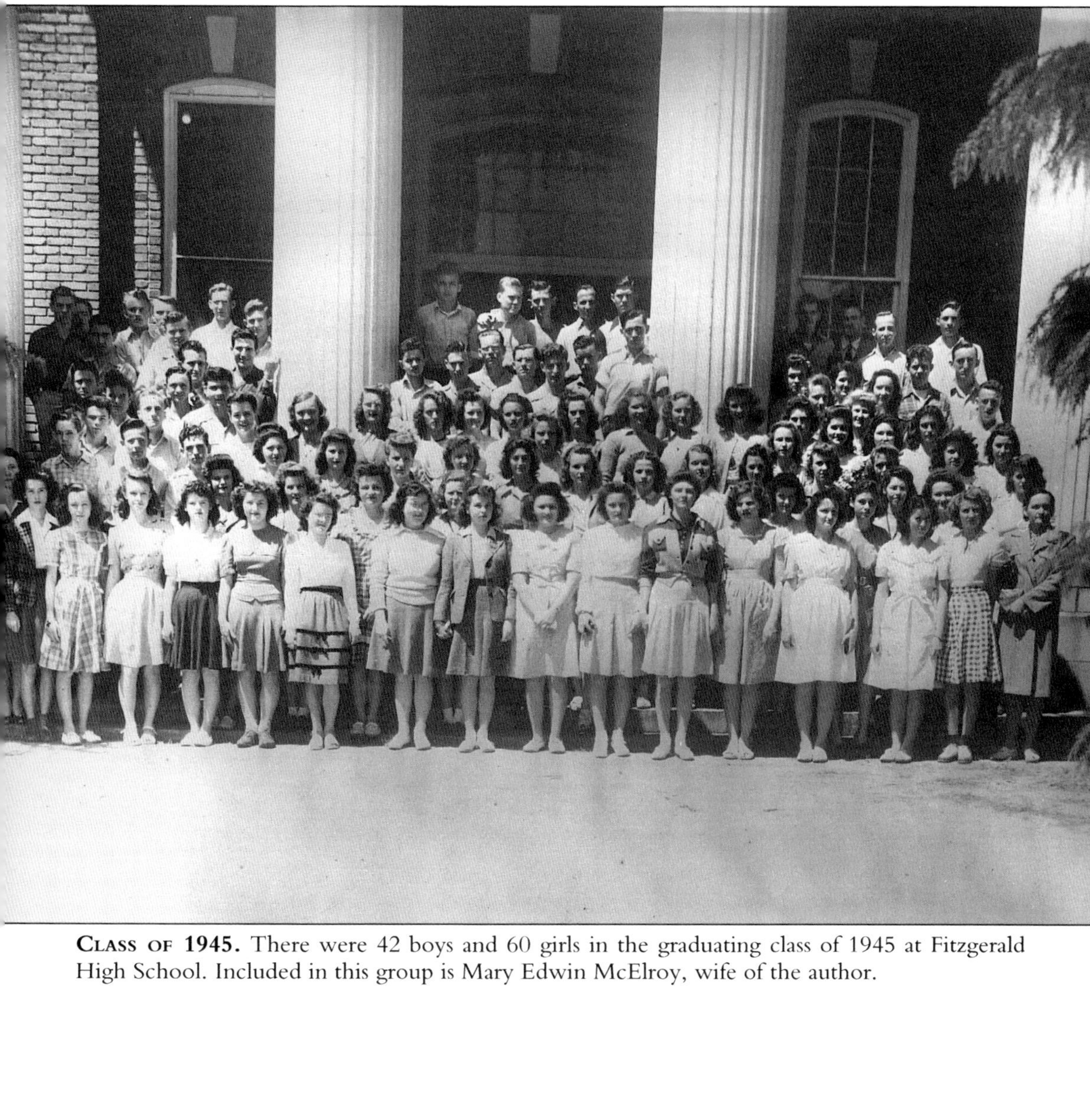

CLASS OF 1945. There were 42 boys and 60 girls in the graduating class of 1945 at Fitzgerald High School. Included in this group is Mary Edwin McElroy, wife of the author.

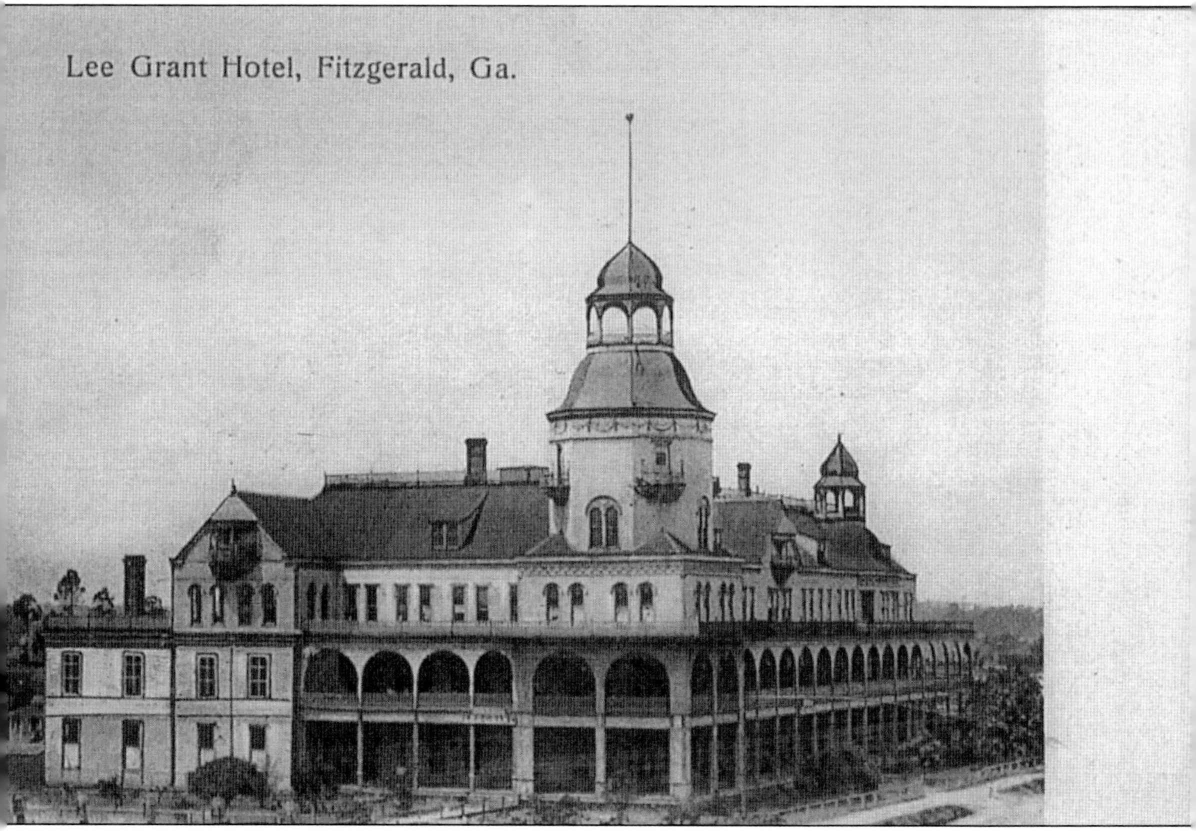

LEE-GRANT HOTEL, FITZGERALD, 1930S. It was said to be the largest wooden structure in the state of Georgia, and probably built as a work relief project to busy unemployed carpenters and artisans. Construction began in 1896 and was completed in 1898. This card was created by Paul E. Trouche of Charleston, South Carolina and published in Germany in the late 1890s. (Courtesy of Louis Harper.)

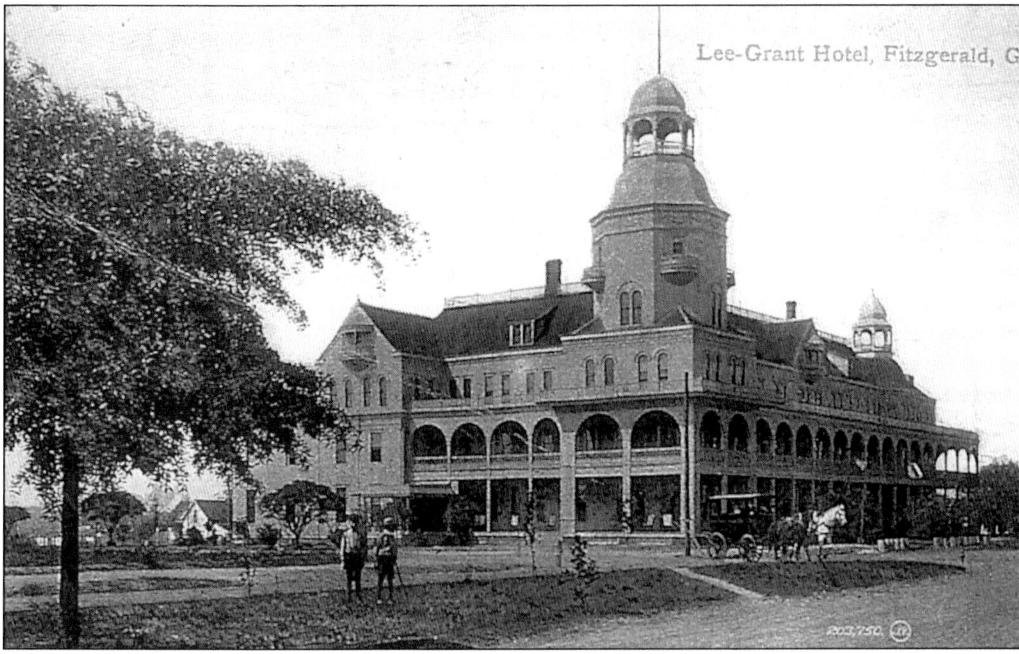

Lee-Grant Hotel, *c.* 1906. This view was taken from the corner of West Central Avenue and Lee Street.

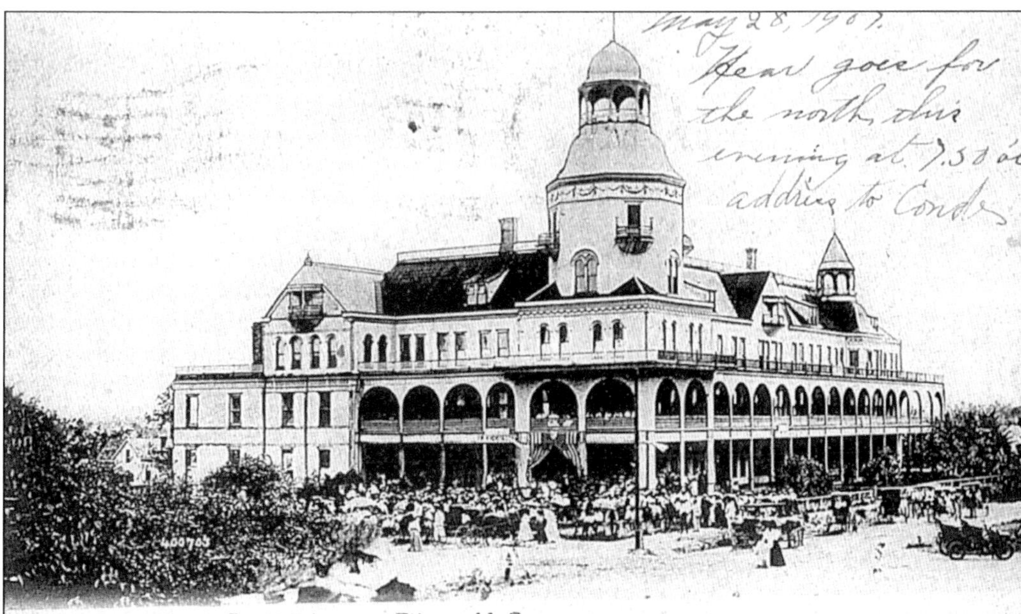

Lee-Grant Hotel, *c.* 1907. Horses and buggies outnumber automobiles in this view of the hotel.

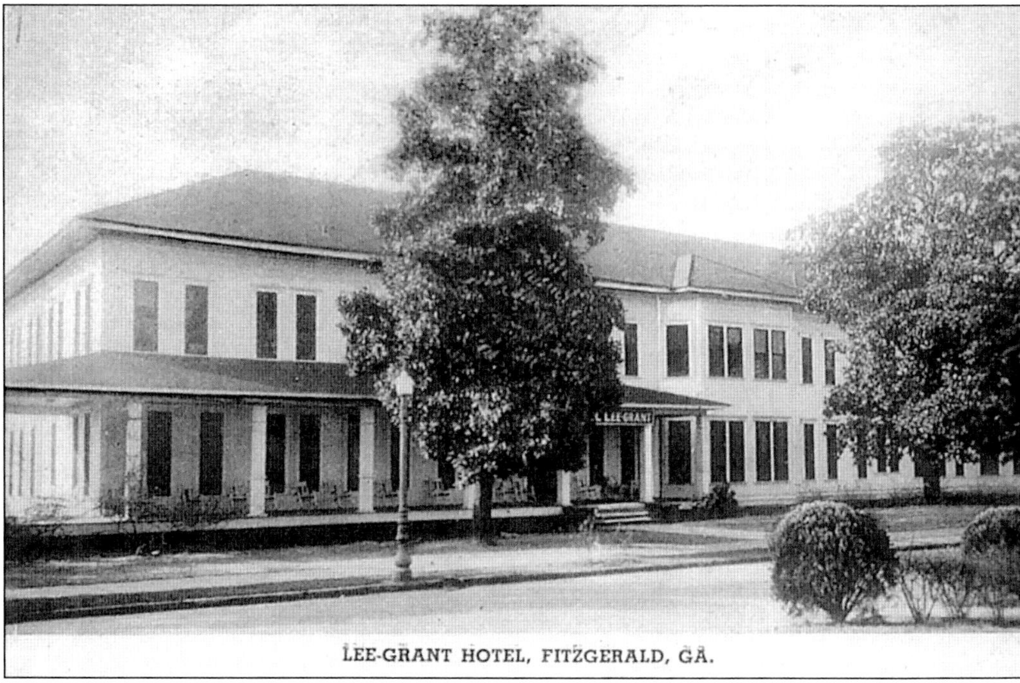

Lee-Grant Hotel, 1930s–1940s. All ornate "gingerbread" decorations have been removed by the time, as well as the third story. In its latter days several civic clubs met here weekly for a scrumptious, home-cooked meal. The building was razed in the 1960s–1970s and a Piggly Wiggly arose on the spot. Magnolia trees have been removed and paved over.

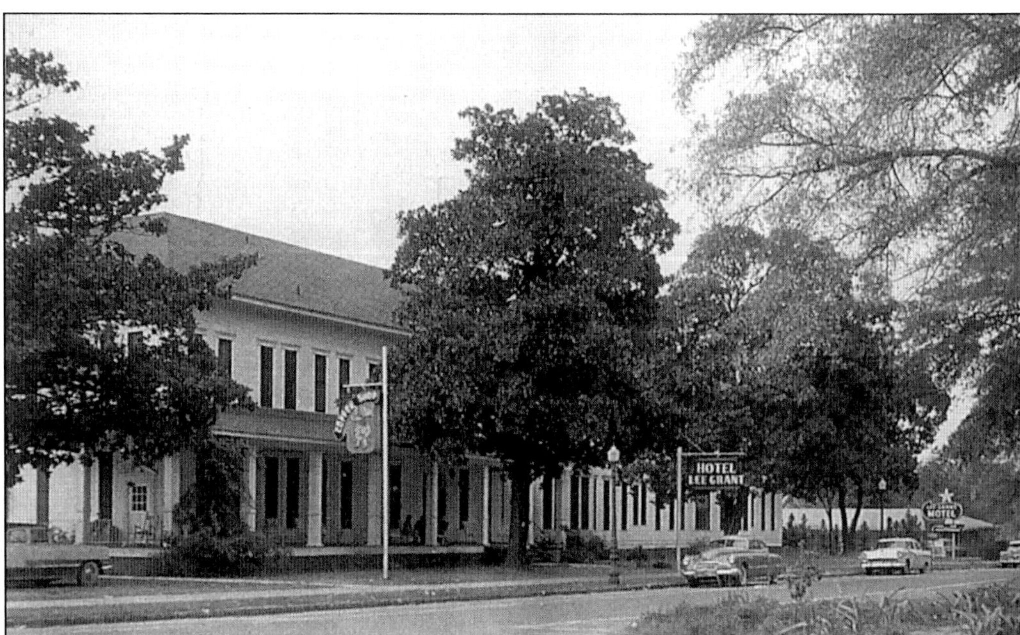

Lee-Grant Hotel, c. 1955. A five- or six-unit Lee Grant Motel was added to the west side of the main hotel, which advertises a coffee shop.

THE ALDINE HOTEL, FITZGERALD. This advertisement from the 1907 City Directory described the amenities of the hotel, located on East Pine Street. (Courtesy of Jack Paulk.)

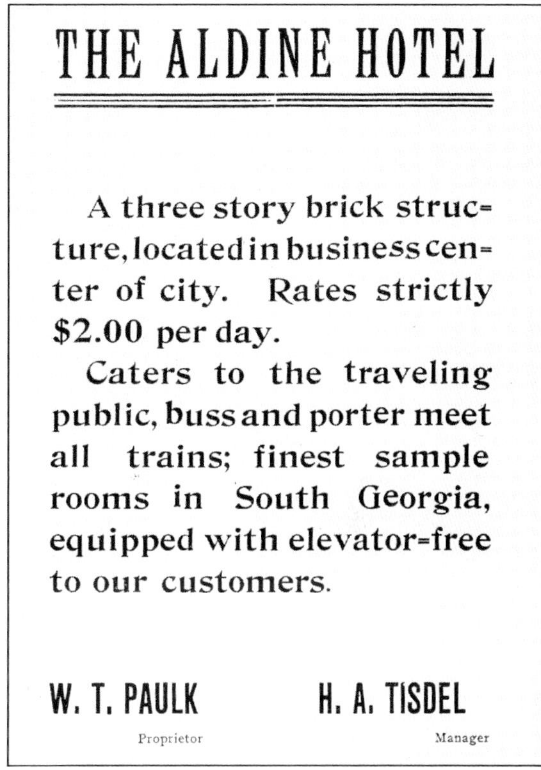

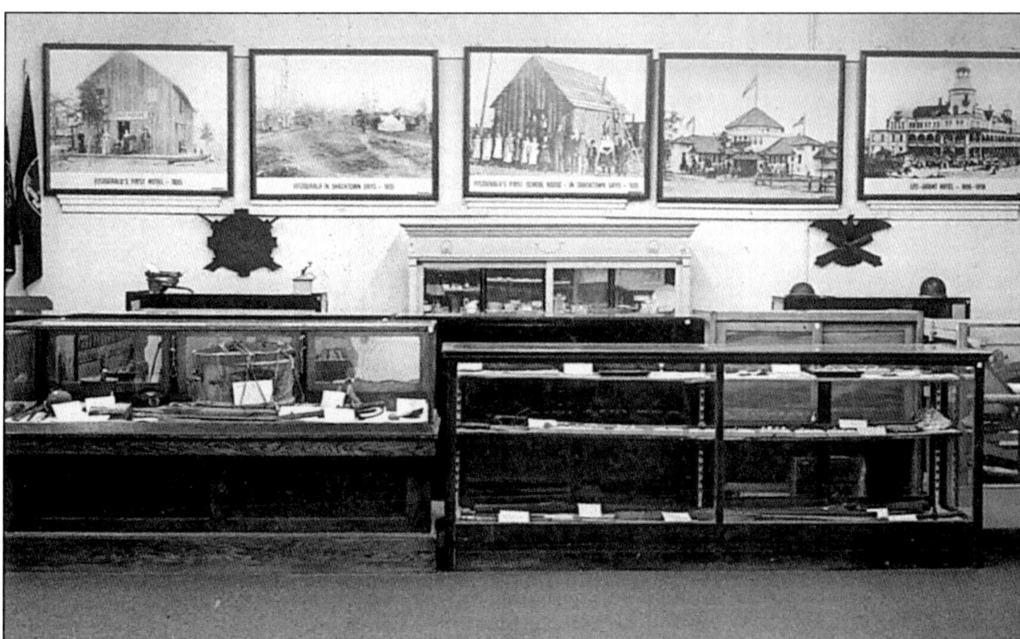

BLUE & GRAY MUSEUM, FITZGERALD, GEORGIA. The museum is housed in the freight section of the old A. B. & A. railroad depot built in 1909. The Fitzgerald City Offices are now located on North Johnston Street.

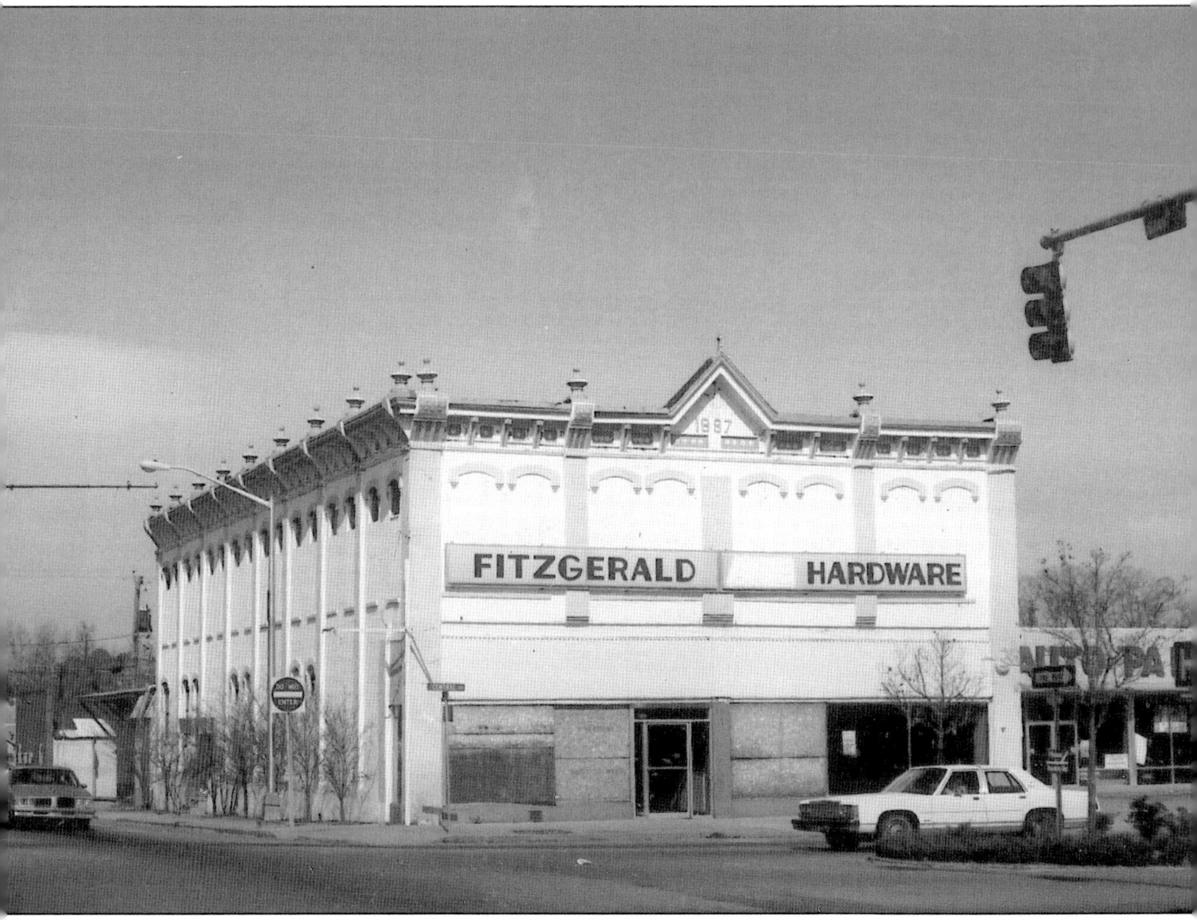

Fitzgerald Hardware, Corner of Grant Street and East Central Avenue. Built in 1897, this was one of the early businesses in the community. The building is now occupied by the *Fitzgerald Herald Leader,* the town's only newspaper.

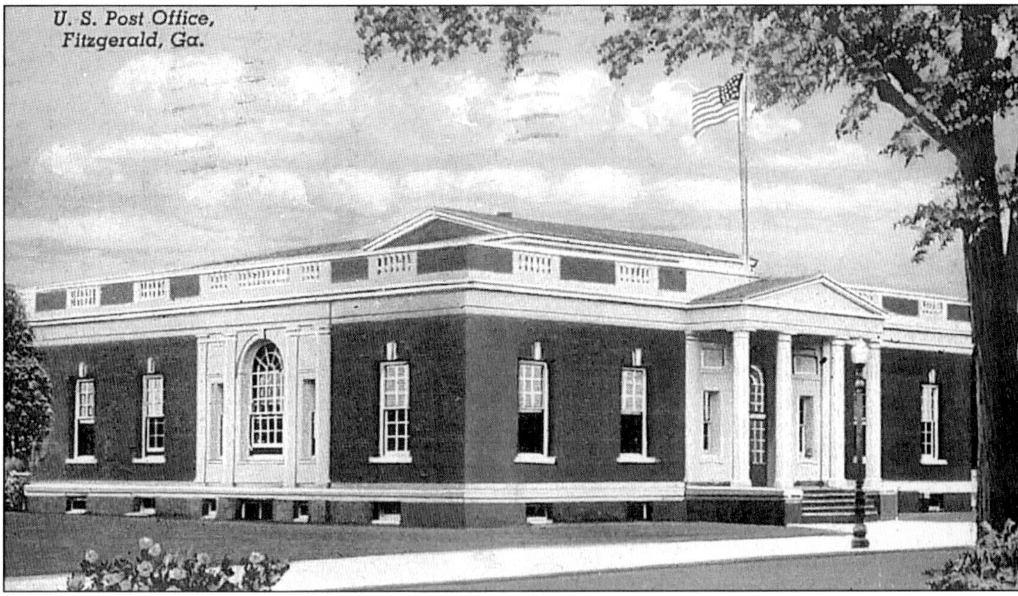

U.S. POST OFFICE, FITZGERALD, GEORGIA. Built in 1918, the building is extant and now known as the Federal Building.

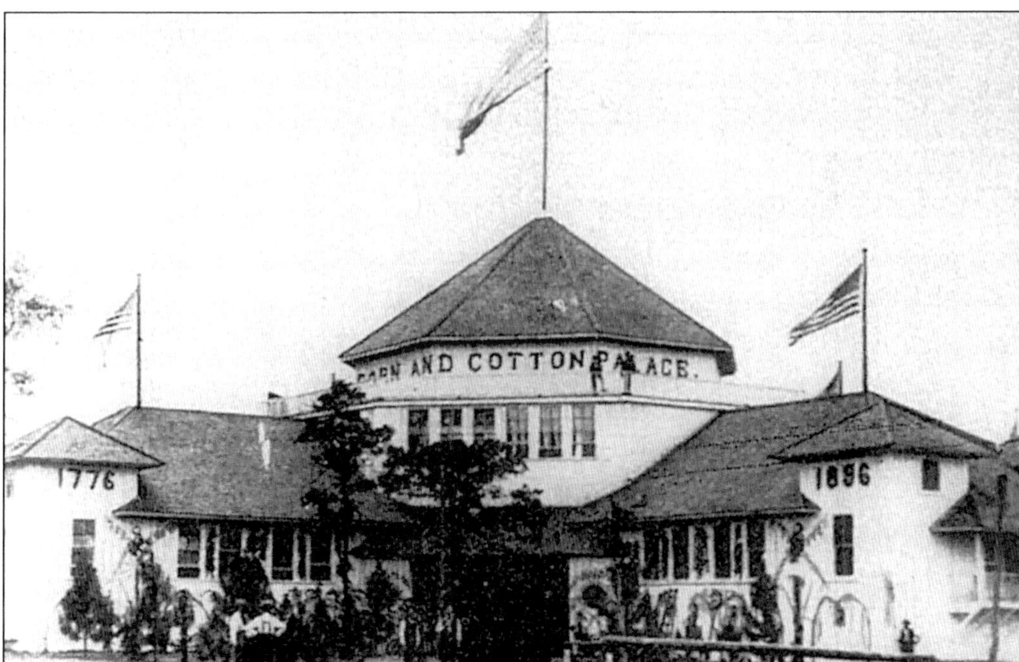

CORN AND COTTON PALACE, FITZGERALD, GEORGIA, 1896. This imposing structure was built on the west corner of Main Street and Central Avenue to celebrate the colonists' first harvest in 1896. It was used as a community center until destroyed by fire in 1897. The eyewitness story goes that an ambitious volunteer fireman torched the shake single roof to demonstrate how efficient their fire crew was. The fire got out of control and the heart pine building was leveled in short time.

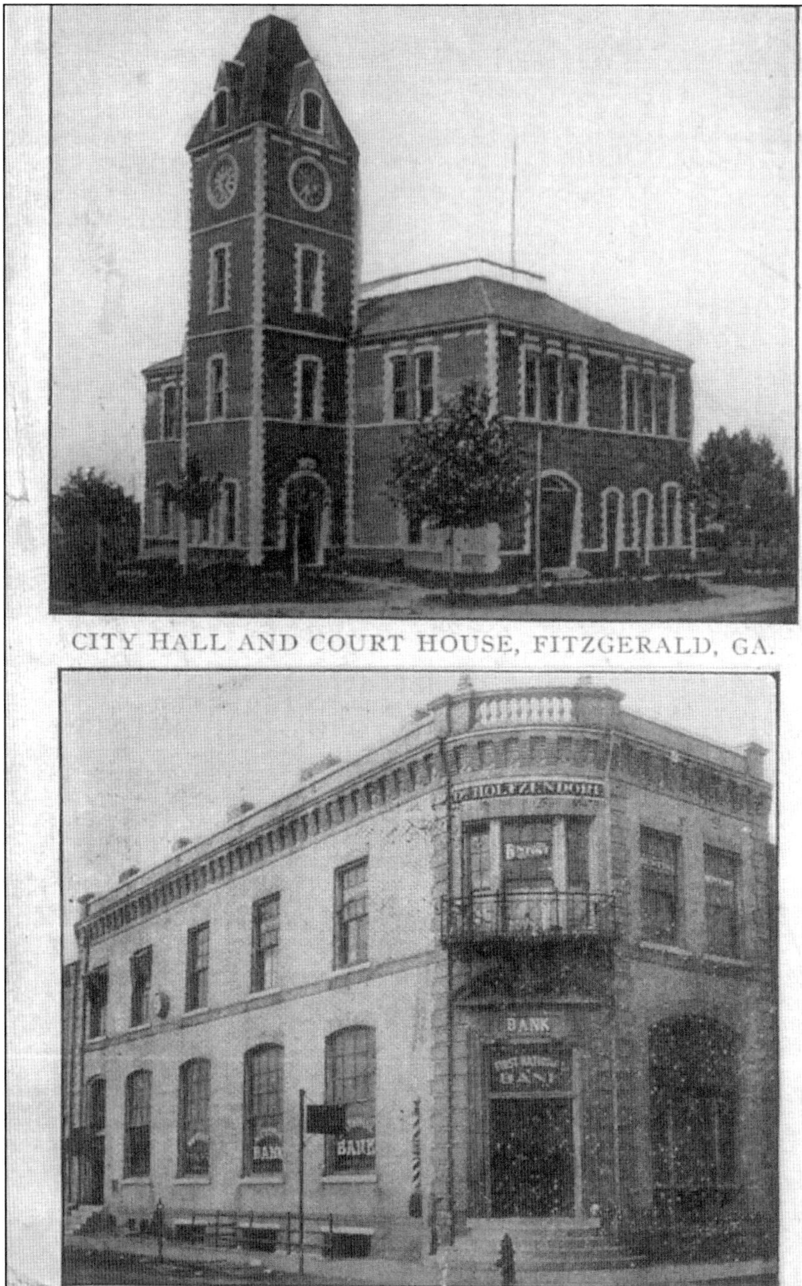

City Hall and Court House, First National Bank. These buildings were captured on a real-photo postcard c. 1908. "City Hall and Court House" should actually read "City Hall and Fire Station." The tower has since been removed.

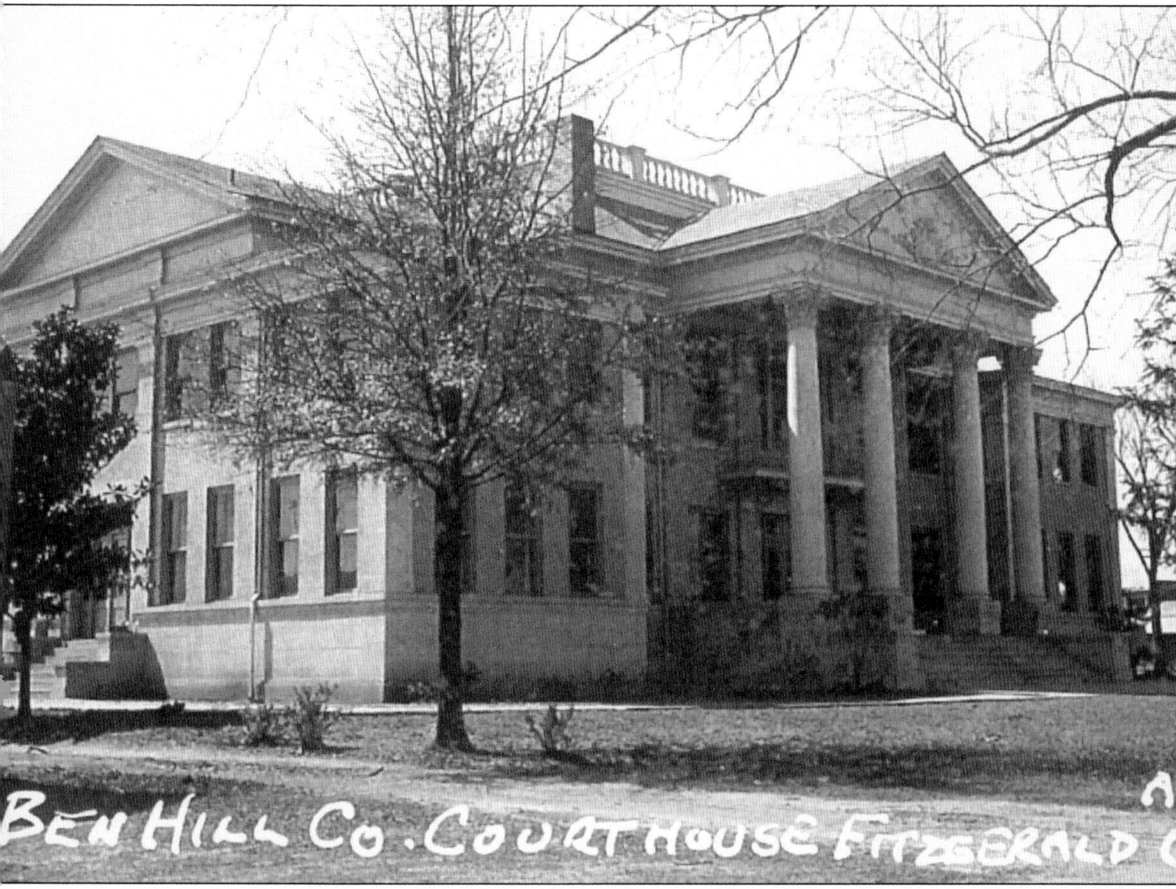

BEN HILL COUNTY COURTHOUSE. The county courthouse is located in Fitzgerald on East Central Avenue and was built in 1909.

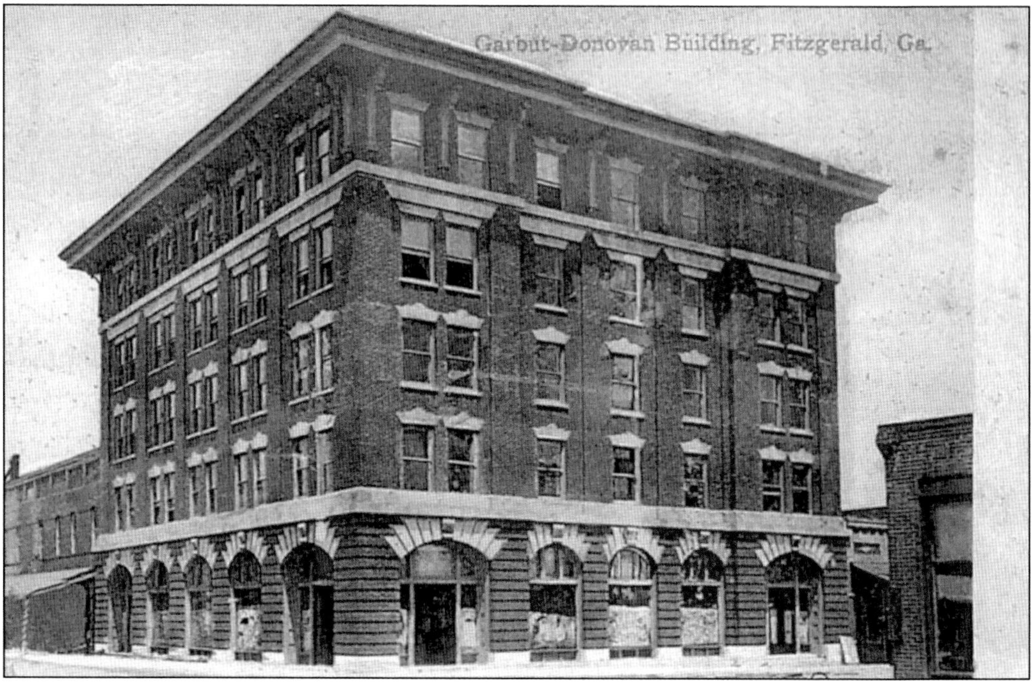

GARBUT-DONOVAN BUILDING, FITZGERALD, GEORGIA. Built in 1905, the building has recently been renovated. Most "birds-eye-view" photographs were taken from here.

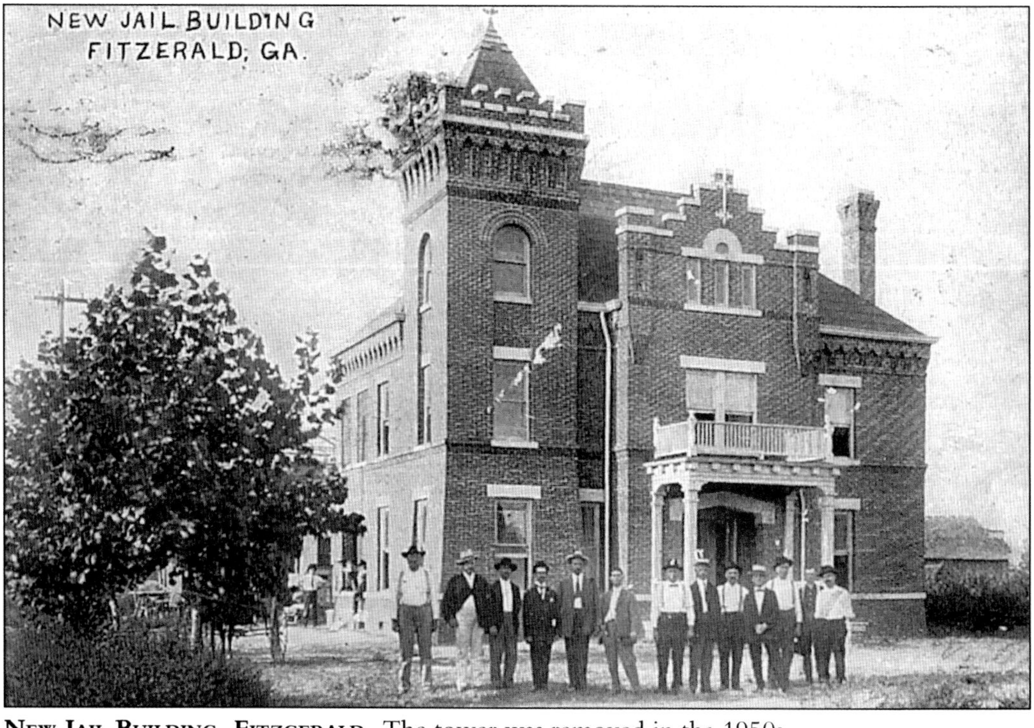

NEW JAIL BUILDING, FITZGERALD. The tower was removed in the 1950s.

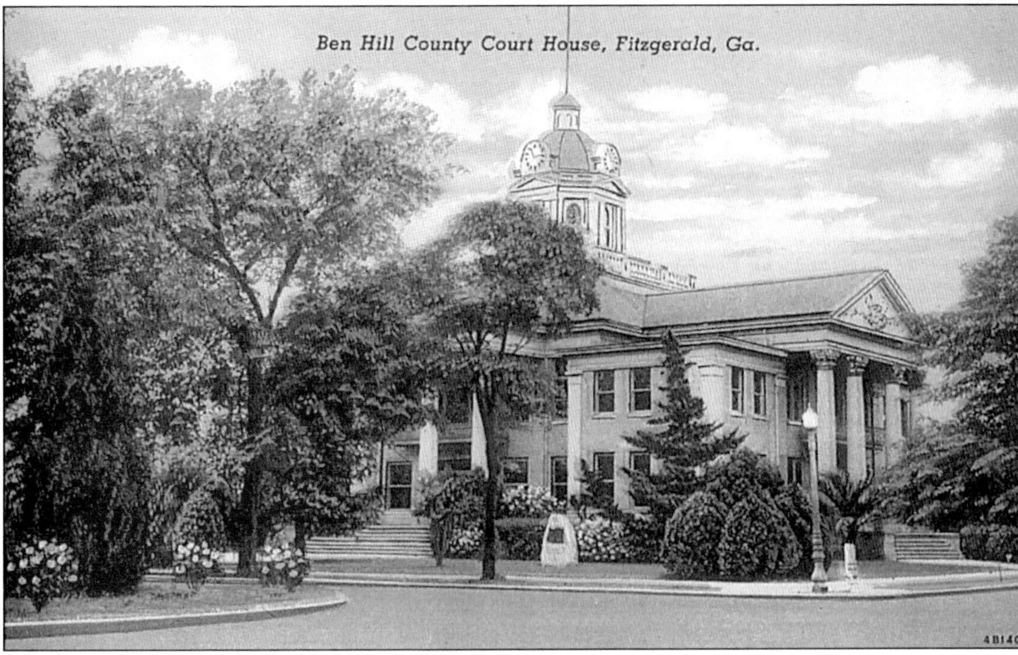

BEN HILL COUNTY COURTHOUSE. A granite marker on the lawn reads "In grateful appreciation of the boys of Ben Hill County who gave their service during the World War. Erected by Nathaniel Abney Chapter, Daughters of American Revolution, Dec. 28, 1928." The clock tower fell through to the ground floor and was never replaced.

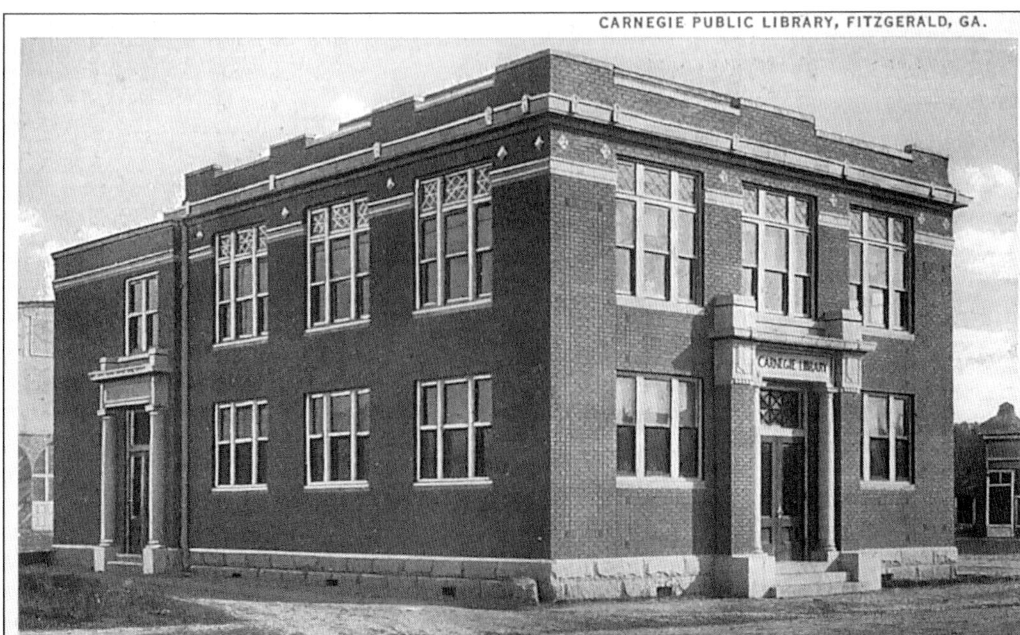

CARNEGIE PUBLIC LIBRARY, FITZGERALD. The library was built in 1915 on South Lee Street. It is extant in 2001 but abandoned.

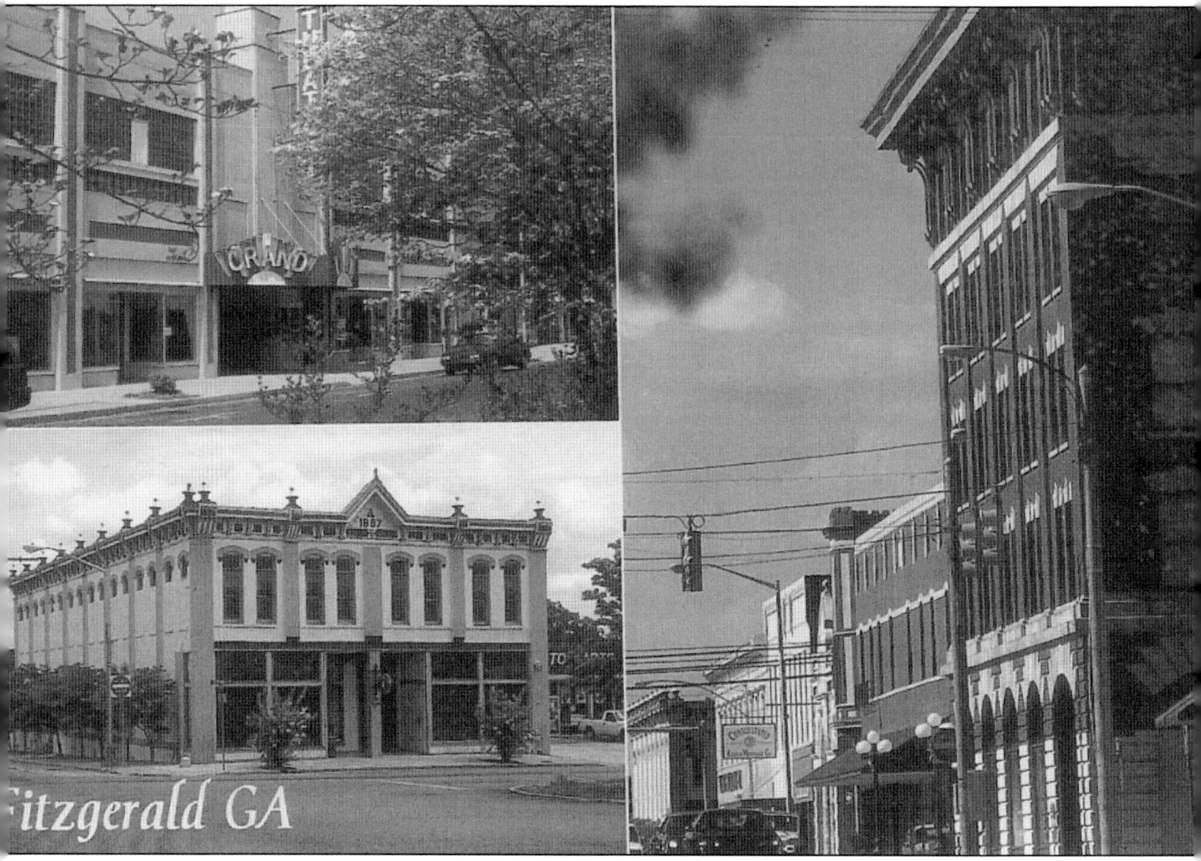

Modern-Day Fitzgerald. In the top left is the restored Grand Theatre; the bottom left shows the building that now houses the ***Fitzgerald Herald-Leader*** newspaper office. The right side of the postcard is a view of Grant Street showing the 1907 Gilbert-Donovan building.

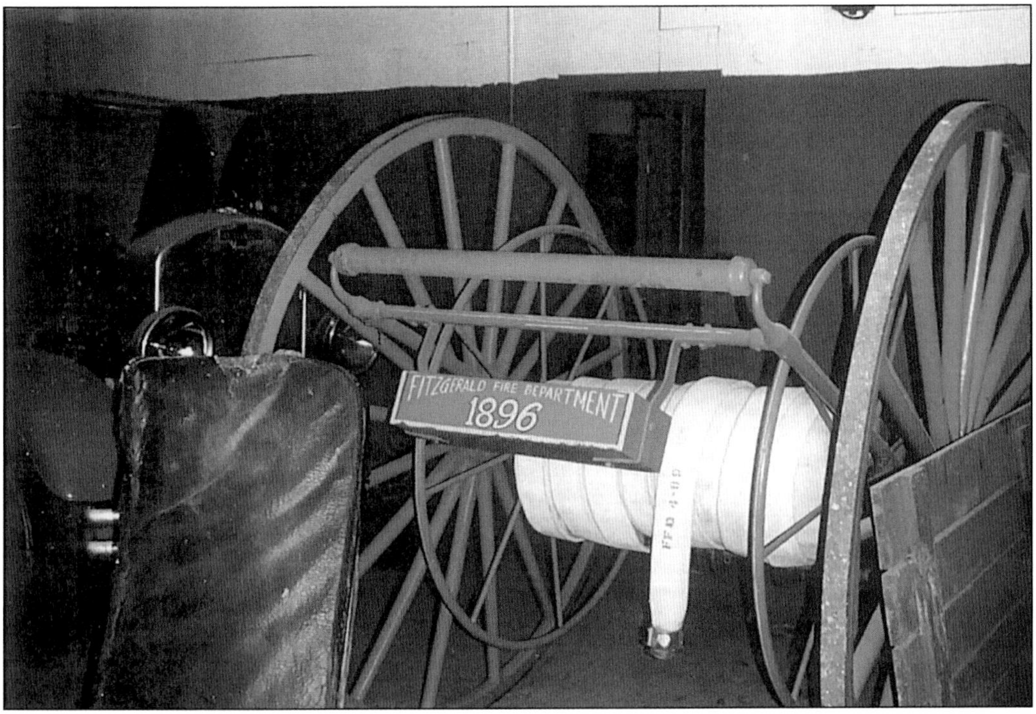

Fitzgerald Fire Department. This horse-drawn hose reel dates to 1896.

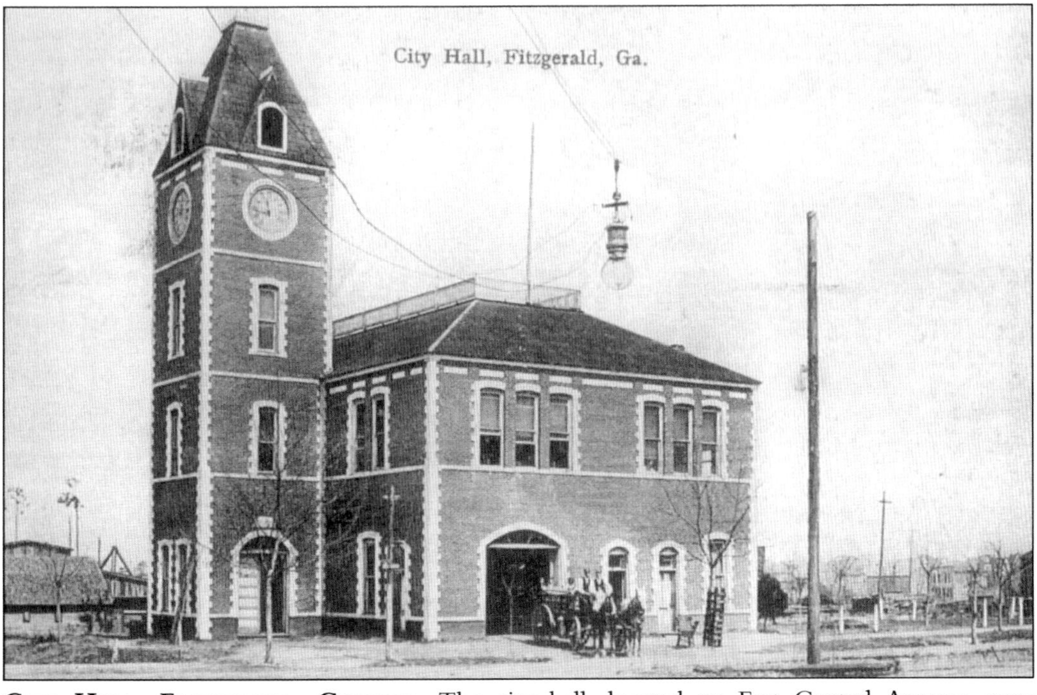

City Hall, Fitzgerald, Georgia. The city hall, located on East Central Avenue, now houses the fire department. The tall steeple has been removed. Note the horse-drawn wagon and the period streetlight.

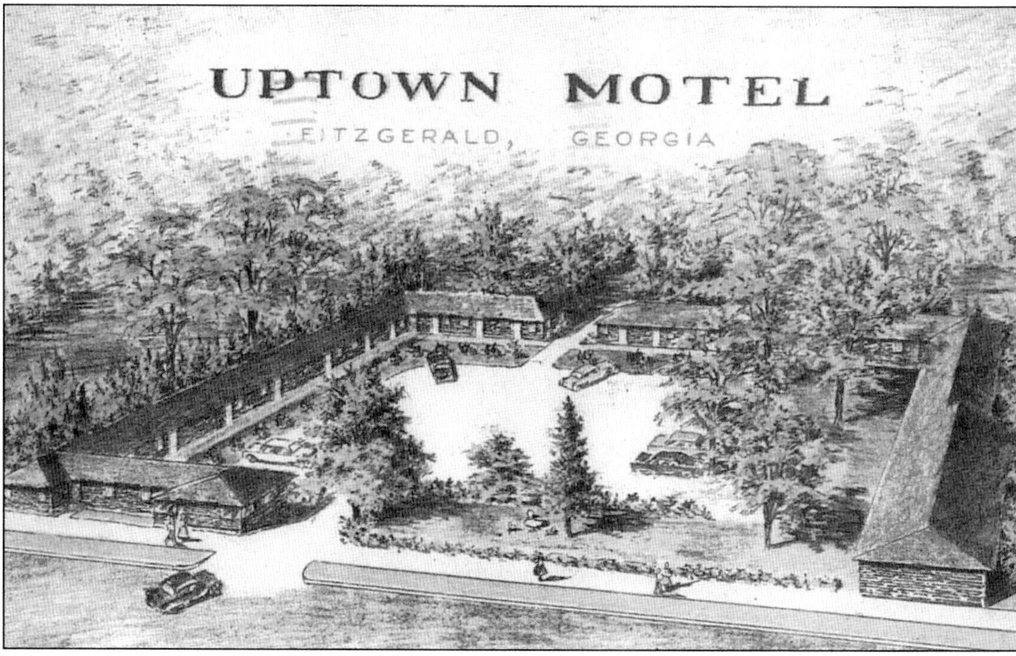

Uptown Motel. This Fitzgerald motel was advertised on a 1960s postcard.

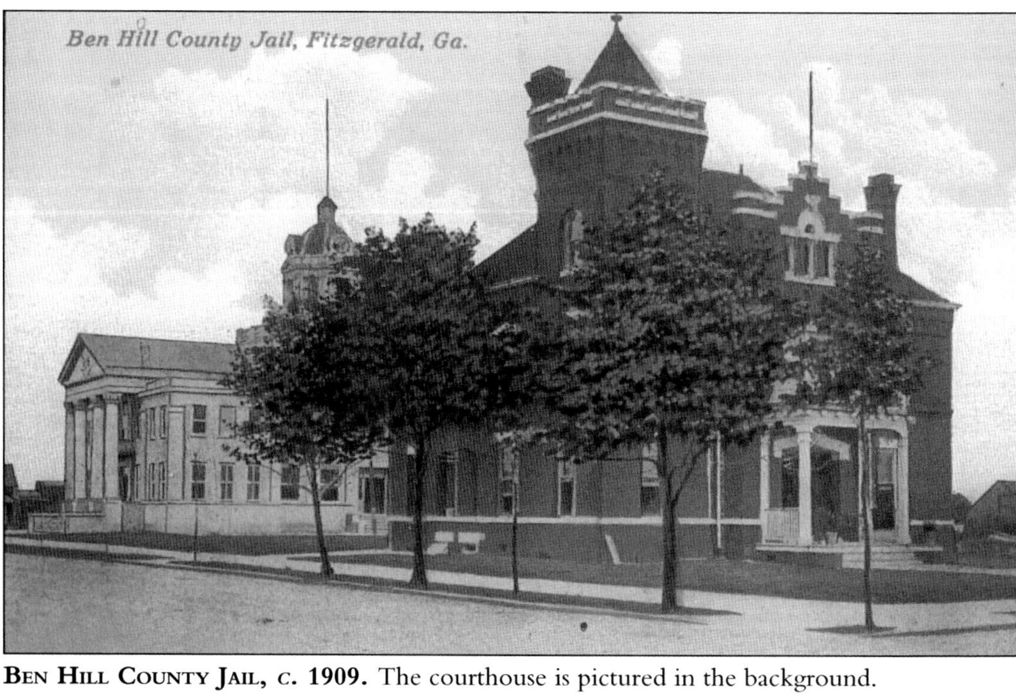

Ben Hill County Jail, c. 1909. The courthouse is pictured in the background.

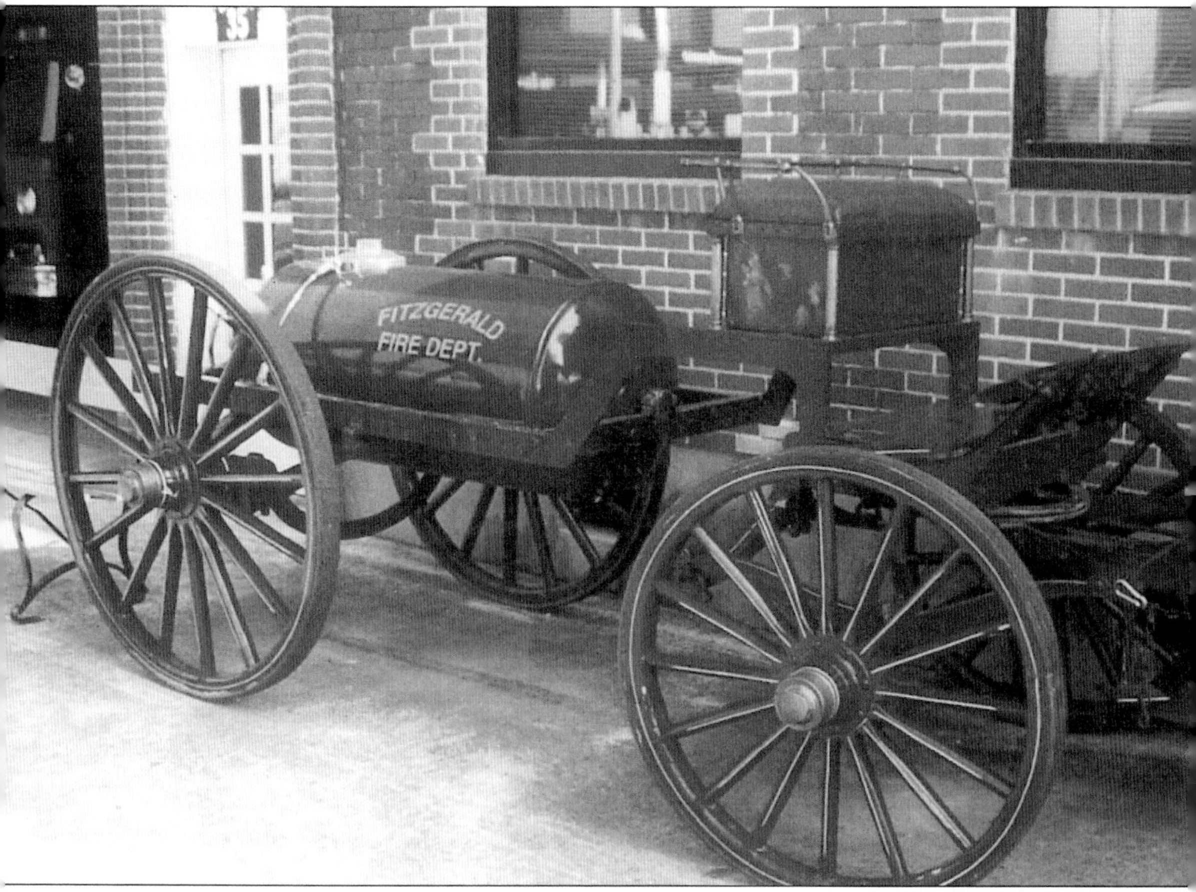

FITZGERALD FIRE DEPARTMENT. This horse-drawn fire wagon is really an oversized fire extinguisher. The 100-gallon tank can be turned on two bearings. The brass opening at the rear contained a bicarbonate of soda and sulfuric acid. When inverted the two mixed with water and produced hose pressure—for a short time anyway.

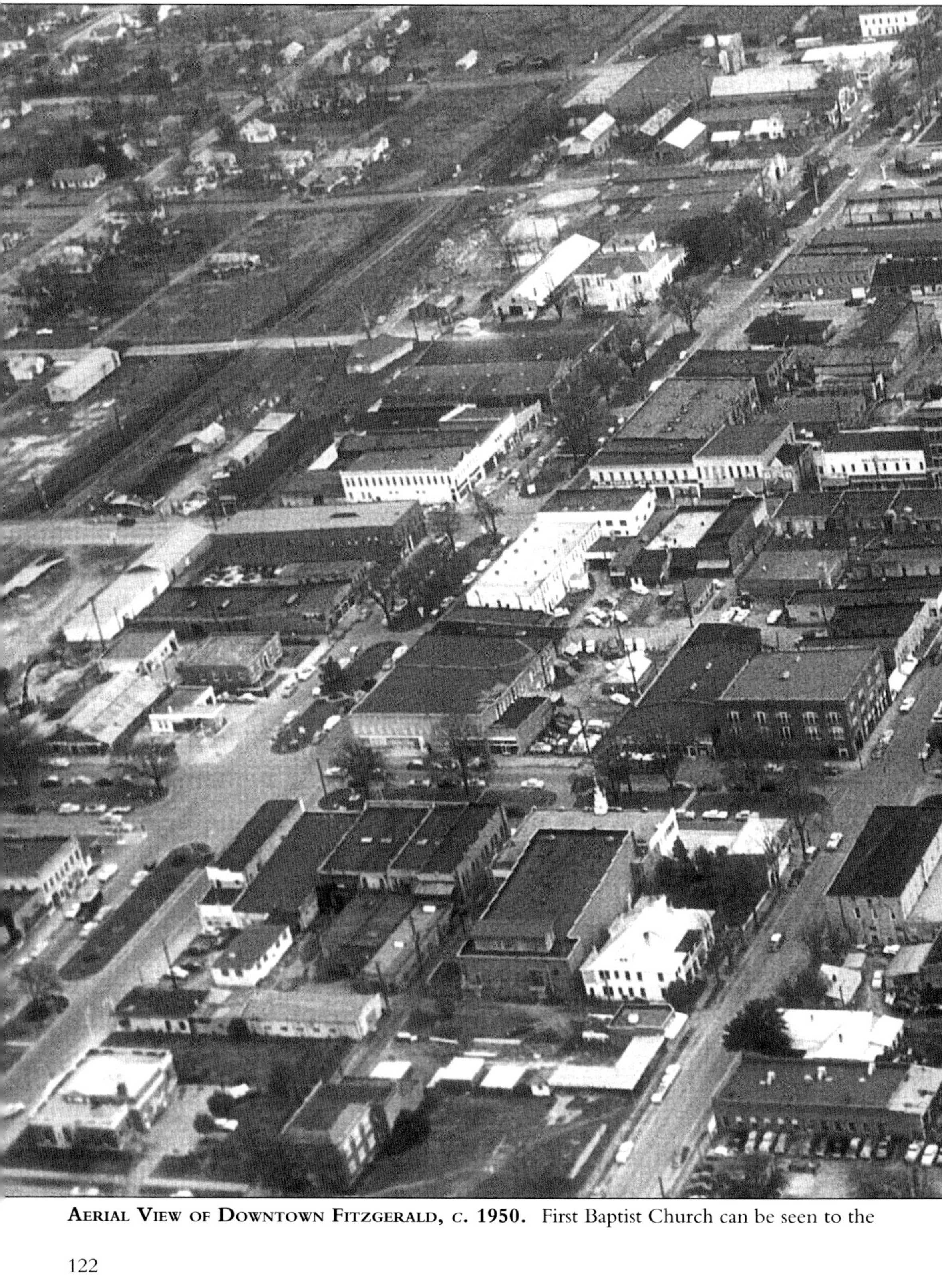

AERIAL VIEW OF DOWNTOWN FITZGERALD, C. 1950. First Baptist Church can be seen to the

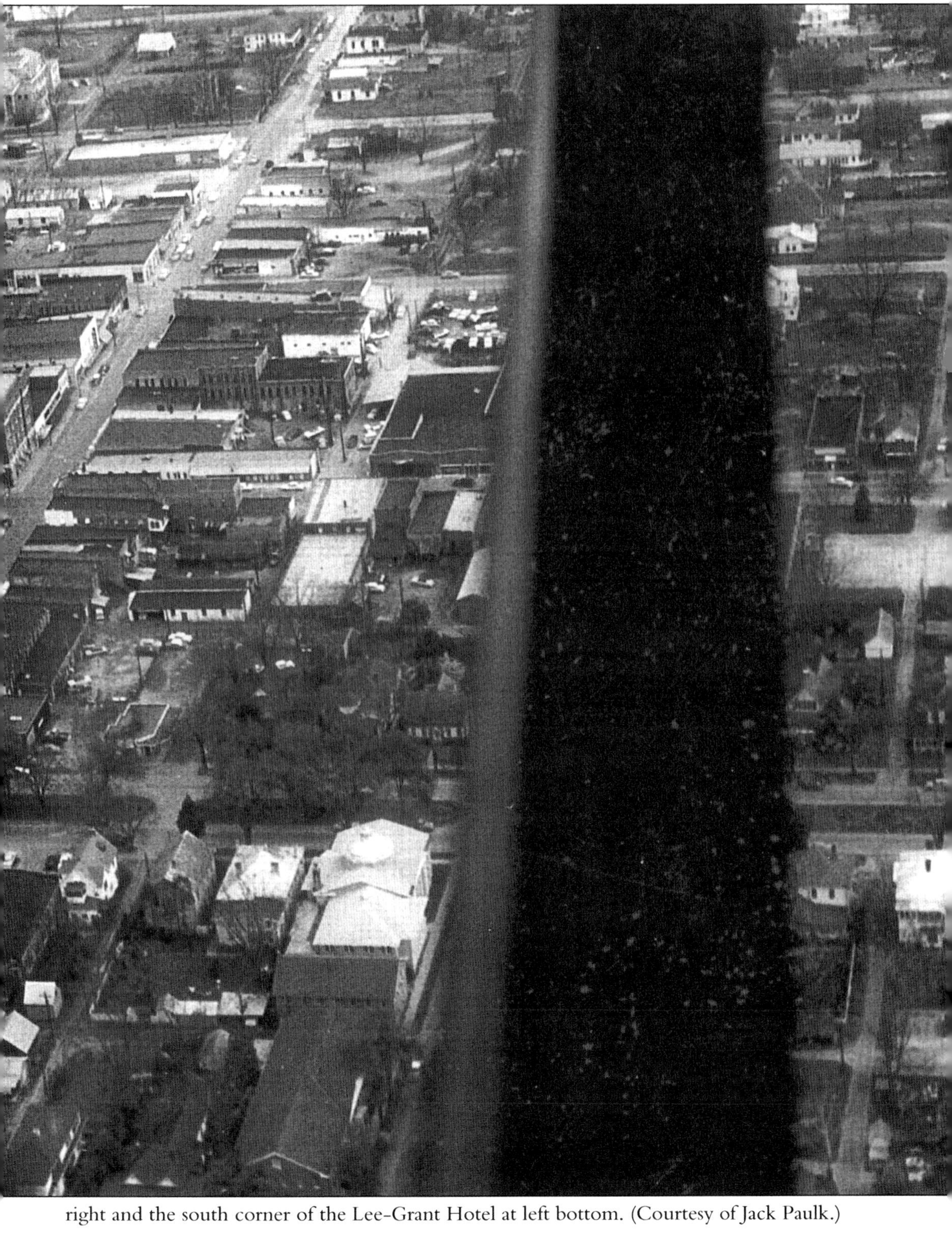

right and the south corner of the Lee-Grant Hotel at left bottom. (Courtesy of Jack Paulk.)

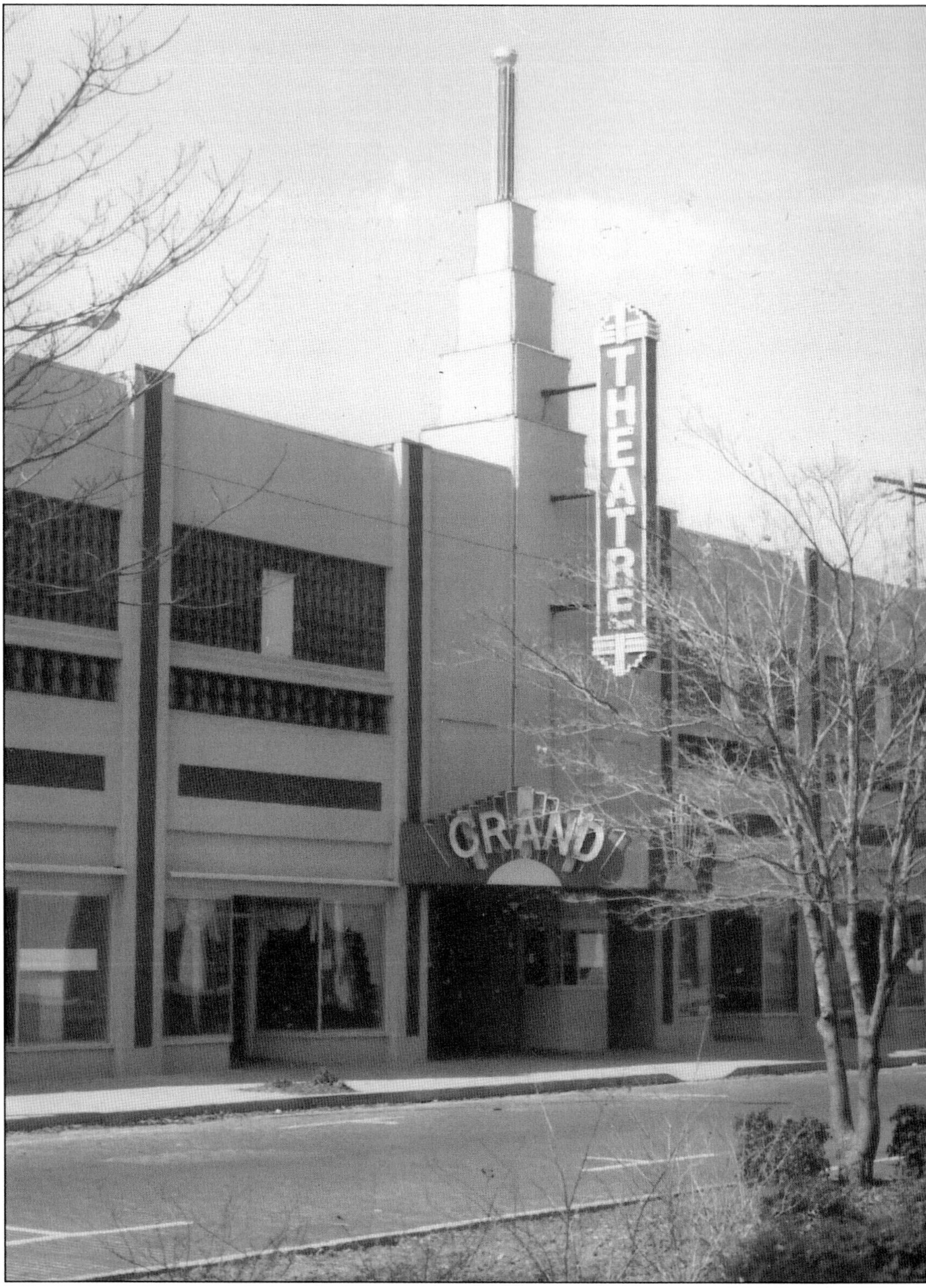

Grand Theatre on South Main Street. The theatre was restored to its former glory and the Fitzgerald Arts Council uses it for plays and musical performances. In the 1930s, admission was 9¢—this included a cowboy movie, a serial, and a short newsreel. The author sold many a bag of boiled peanuts out front.

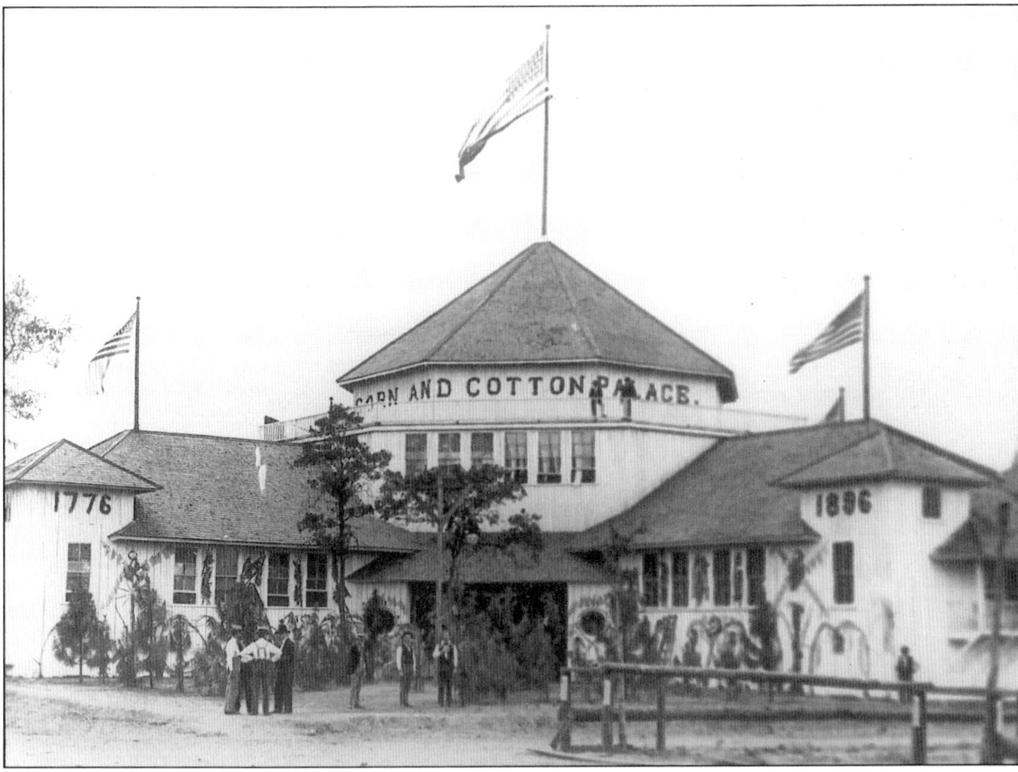

CORN AND COTTON PALACE, 1896. The palace was built at the corner of Main and Central but burned down shortly after. This view is from the northwest side.

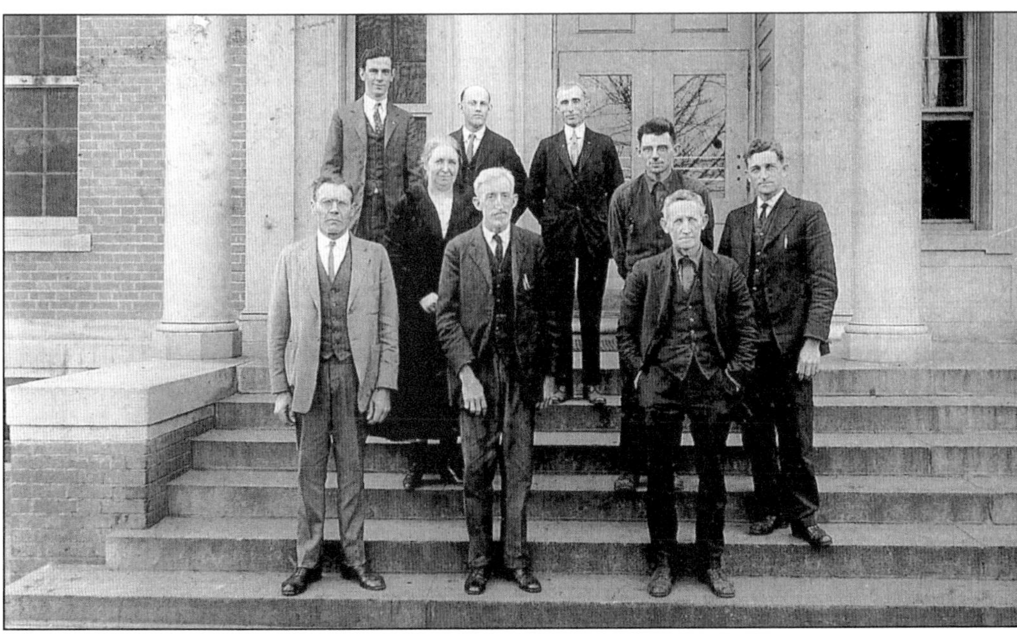

U.S. POST OFFICE STAFF, FITZGERALD. Included in this 1926 photograph are J.H. Burke (bottom row, first from left), and Milton Hopkins (top row, first from left).

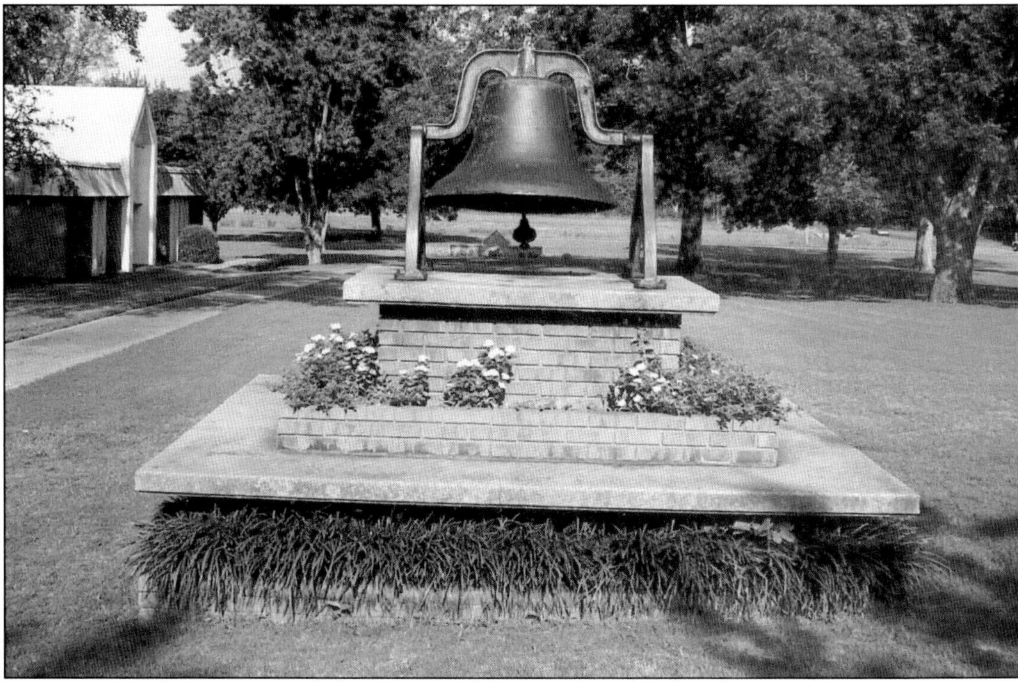

Governor's Gift. Gov. William J. Northern (1835–1913) gave this bell to the first church built in Fitzgerald in 1896–1897.

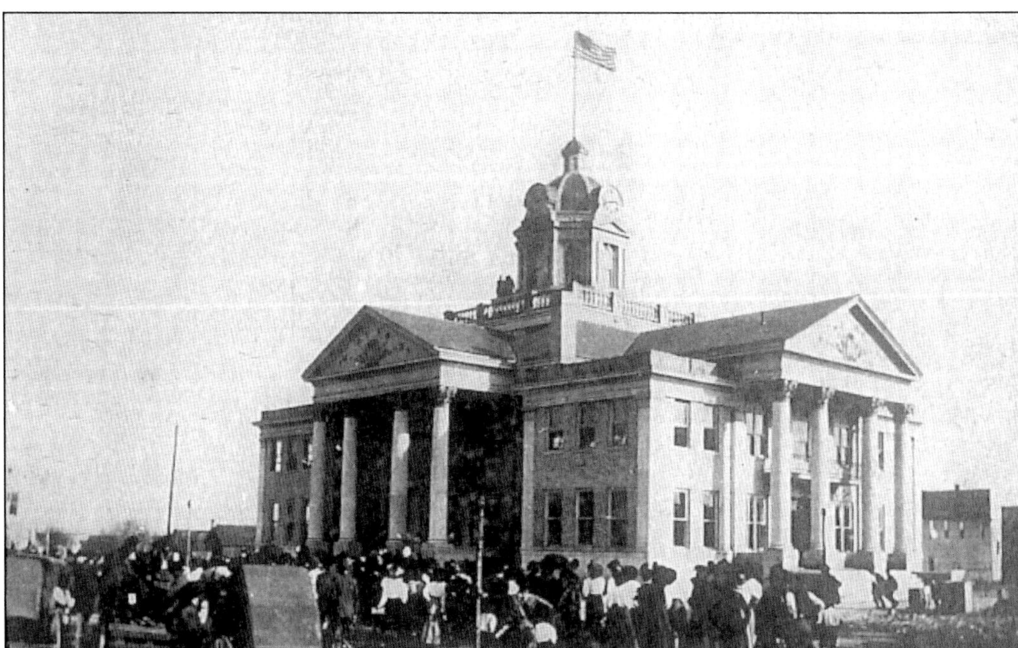

Ben Hill County Courthouse, Fitzgerald. This real-photo postcard depicts a dedication ceremony or some type of political gathering outside the courthouse. (Courtesy of Louis Harper.)

Bibliography

Doster, Gary L. ***From Abbeville to Zebulon, Early Postcard Views of Georgia***. Athens and London: The University of Georgia Press, 1991.

Doster, Gary L. ***Southwest Georgia in Vintage Postcards***. Charleston, South Carolina: Arcadia Publishing, 1998.

Doster, Gary L. ***Southeast Georgia in Vintage Postcards***. Charleston, South Carolina: Arcadia Publishing, 1998.

Chalker, Fussell M. "Fitzgerald: Place of Reconciliation." ***The Georgia Historical Quarterly***. Vol. LV, Fall 1971, Nov. 3.

Clements, James Bailey. ***History of Irwin County***. Atlanta: Foote and Davies, 1926.

Goolsby, Larry. ***The A. B. & C. Railroad***. Valrico, Florida: A.C.L. & Seaboard Airline Historical Society, Inc., 2000.

Scruggs, Carroll Proctor. ***Georgia Historical Markers***. Helen, Georgia: Bay Tree Grove, 1976.

Sullivan, Buddy. ***Images of America: Darien and McIntosh County***. Charleston, South Carolina: Arcadia Publishing, 2000.

Trowell, C.T. ***Moving to the Sunbelt A Century Ago: The Fitzgerald Experience***, ***1895-1896***. unpublished paper.

Yarbrough, Patricia Holt. A ***Historical Perspective on the Founding of Fitzgerald, Georgia***. Fitzgerald: Walker Printing Company, 1986.